"In this beautiful book, Joann
gift of trust. When your worl
control, she reminds us from Sc ... that we
have never actually been in control but that God always has and is."

Sheila Walsh, author of *Holding On When You Want to Let Go*

"Joanna Weaver has done it again—created a book that shares familiar Biblical truth in a new, life-changing way. Her words will encourage your heart, deepen your faith, and show you how to embrace God's best for you more than ever before."

Holley Gerth, bestselling author of *What Your Heart Needs for the Hard Days*

"If you have zero trouble loving God but find that always trusting him in the midst of your circumstances is much more difficult to do, this inspiring resource was written just for you! Joanna Weaver's *Embracing Trust* will beautifully and practically equip you to live a life of confident hope. You'll learn to calm your fears with faith as you replace your doubts with a determination to see God's hand in all of life. Highly recommended!"

Karen Ehman, *New York Times* bestselling author of *Trusting God in All the Things* and *Make Their Day*; Proverbs 31 Ministries speaker; wife and mother of five

"Joanna has personally championed me as a daughter of God and as a writer over the past fifteen years, so I am overjoyed that she has gifted us with this much-needed and anticipated offering! *Embracing Trust* is an invitation and a road map to living in the wholeness and freedom that comes from truly trusting God. May you read and discover his unrivaled peace as you learn to hold onto him in faith in every season and circumstance!"

Christy Nockels, worship leader, songwriter, author of *The Life You Long For*

"Trusting God is fundamental to faith, but so few of us embrace it with all its ramifications for our daily life. Joanna Weaver has given us a practical guide to help us embrace life-changing trust. I was convicted, challenged, and encouraged!"

Ruth Graham, author of *Transforming Loneliness*

"Joanna Weaver shares stories that soothe the soul and words that speak to matters of the heart. Kindly, gently, tenderly—she leads us to see the truth about God and to trust His love for us. If you're tired of striving for perfection, peace, and control, this book will guide you through letting go and embracing the gift of grace . . . as well as the God who freely gives it."

Rachel Marie Kang, author of *Let There Be Art*

"As with all her excellent books, Joanna Weaver writes from deep in her heart. Do you have a hiss of discontent striking your soul? Then this book is for you. Within these pages, you'll learn the beauty of trusting the One who designed our hearts. I sensed God's love within these pages. *Embracing Trust* goes beyond inspiration and enjoyment to transformation. It's perfect for sharing with a friend or a group!"

Tricia Goyer, bestselling author of over 80 books including *Heart Happy*

"If you've struggled with fear, uncertainty, disappointment, discouragement, or doubt, read this book. Joanna Weaver has written a masterpiece. Each chapter is a work of art that acknowledges our challenges and then provides faith-building action steps that can rebuild trust in our always-faithful God. Are you looking for a book to study with friends? This is it! Joanna's biblical depth, real-life stories, practical applications, and nuggets of truth will ignite fresh faith and a firm confidence in the One who never changes."

Carol Kent, Executive Director of Speak Up Ministries, author of *He Holds My Hand*

"Have you ever read a book that completely skewered yet somehow soothed your soul—each in the best possible way? I just finished reading *Embracing Trust: The Art of Letting Go and Holding*

On to a Forever-Faithful God by Joanna Weaver and I'll admit, I both ouched and aahed my way through its beautifully written, burgeoning-with-truth pages. In Joanna's moving personal stories (hers and others) and relatable metaphors, I recognized my own tendency to wander the maze of human mistrust towards God, especially when life scrapes away all hope and circumstances make absolutely zero sense. (Ouch.) But then my wise in-real-life friend, Joanna, weaves together solid Scriptural truths with fresh perspectives on why genuinely trusting God makes all the sense in the world—why it's both logical and liberating to those of us with wary, weary souls. (Ahhh.) This is a book sturdy enough to handle (and challenge) your doubts while fostering your exuberant embrace of trust in a forever-faithful God. Get ready to be skewered and soothed as you learn to let go and hold on. This is your next life-changing read."

Dr. Jodi Detrick, author of *The Jesus-Hearted Woman* and *The Settled Soul*

"Joanna dove deeply when she lovingly wrote this book. You'll dive deeply too, as you turn each page and find yourself growing in your trust and your love for God. Ideal for a group study."

Robin Jones Gunn, bestselling author of over 100 books including *Victim of Grace*

EMBRACING *Trust*

Books by Joanna Weaver

Having a Mary Heart in a Martha World
Having a Mary Spirit
Lazarus Awakening
At the Feet of Jesus
Embracing Trust

EMBRACING

The Art of Letting Go and Holding On
to a Forever-Faithful God

JOANNA
WEAVER

Revell
a division of Baker Publishing Group
Grand Rapids, Michigan

Published by Revell
a division of Baker Publishing Group
PO Box 6287, Grand Rapids, MI 49516-6287
www.revellbooks.com

Printed in the United States of America

Library of Congress Cataloging-in-Publication Data
Names: Weaver, Joanna, author.
Title: Embracing trust : the art of letting go and holding on to a forever-faithful God / Joanna Weaver.
Description: Grand Rapids : Revell, a division of Baker Publishing Group, 2022.
Identifiers: LCCN 2021059584 | ISBN 9780800736736 (paperback) | ISBN 9780800742003 (casebound) | ISBN 9781493423231 (ebook)
Subjects: LCSH: Christian women—Religious life. | Trust in God—Christianity. | Control (Psychology)—Religious Aspects—Christianity. | David, King of Israel.
Classification: LCC BV4527 .W379 2022 | DDC 248.8/43—dc23/eng/20220127
LC record available at https://lccn.loc.gov/2021059584

Baker Publishing Group publications use paper produced from sustainable forestry practices and post-consumer waste whenever possible.

22 23 24 25 26 27 28 7 6 5 4 3 2 1

To my husband, John
Thank you for your passionate love for Jesus.
Because He has first place in your life,
my heart rests secure in your love.
Because you trust God so completely,
I've learned to trust Him in a deeper measure.
For that and a thousand other reasons,
I'm so grateful to be your wife.

To my son, Josh
Oh, my sweet boy—my gift from heaven!
From the moment you were born,
you've taught me what trusting God looks like.
Thank you for allowing me to share your story.
Keep loving Jesus and sharing His love
with others—you do it incredibly well.
I'm so blessed to be your mother.

Contents

An Invitation

The book you hold in your hands is a book I've wanted to write for over twenty years.

From the moment I finished *Having a Mary Heart in a Martha World*, this was the message I felt certain God wanted me to write. Yet He kept asking me to lay it aside to work on other books. (Ironic when you consider my working title: *Letting Go and Trusting God.*)

When the Lord finally gave me the go-ahead, the topic had grown beyond surrender to include the importance of holding on in faith. With the message still big and strong in my heart, I was sure the "birth" of the book would be relatively easy. A few pushes and voilà! It would come out fully formed, dressed, and needing to shave. Instead, God took me on a four-year journey of trust that led to this book, but also radically changed my life.

Writing never comes easy to me, but the immensity of this message felt paralyzing. With deadlines looming and words still distant, the only thing that broke the fear was repeating, "I trust You, Lord. I trust You, I trust You, I trust You." Yet in the middle of the struggle to write, God graced me with so many personal breakthroughs that I almost felt guilty.

"We're getting a lot more done in my heart than we're getting words on the page," I told my mother as I tried to explain how simple truths from the Bible were exploding in my soul, stripping away lies that had kept me bound for years. In my desperate need of Jesus, I was experiencing Him in ways I'd never known before.

At the time, none of this seemed related to the book—hence, the guilt. But now, looking back, I'm convinced it was my utter dependence on God and the moment-by-moment choice to trust in Him that opened my heart to those life-changing revelations and led to the book you hold in your hands.

More than ever, I'm convinced that trusting God is the key to a victorious Christian life. Just as we trusted Jesus for our salvation, we need to trust Him for our transformation—and everything else in our lives!

I pray the Holy Spirit meets you in these pages and speaks between every line as He gives you personal revelations that come straight from the heart of God. As you let go in surrender, He'll enable you to hold on in faith so that you're no longer dominated by fear and doubt. For as we embrace trust, we embrace God—and it leaves us forever changed.

In the back of this book, you'll find a ten-week Bible study and a resource to help you grow close to God and strengthen your faith. Teaching videos are available for purchase at JoannaWeaverBooks.com.

Are you ready to build an unshakeable trust? I can't wait to begin!

Joanna

PART ONE

Trusting God

"Trust Me, My child," He says. "Trust Me with a fuller abandon than you ever have before. Trust Me, as minute succeeds minute, every day of your life, for as long as you live. And if you become conscious of anything hindering our relationship, do not hurt Me by turning away from Me. Draw all the closer to Me, come, run to Me. Allow Me to hide you, to protect you, even from yourself. Tell Me your deepest cares, your every trouble. Trust Me to keep My hand upon you. I will never leave you. I will shape you, mold you, and perfect you. Do not fear, O child of My love, do not fear. I love you."

Amy Carmichael[1]

One

The Journey to Trust

> Those who know your name trust in you,
> for you, Lord, have never forsaken those who seek you.
>
> Psalm 9:10

It's not surprising that we all come into life with some sort of trust issue. After all, birth itself is quite traumatic.

One moment we're safe and warm, floating in soft waves of amniotic fluid, cradled close inside our mother's womb. Every need met without our asking. Nothing to do except turn slow somersaults, suck our thumb, and kick Mama's ribs. Ah, what a life.

But then, suddenly, we're ejected into an unfamiliar world. Surrounded by bright lights, strange faces, and the slap of cold air against our skin, we begin screaming and kicking. Our arms flail. Our hands clench, then open—grasping, searching for something to tell us we're not alone. That we are not as helpless as we feel.

Somewhere a finger strokes our hand, and though it's foreign to us, we grasp it and refuse to let go. Finally. An anchor point.

Something bigger and more solid than we are. A source. Something or someone—we're not entirely sure which—that responds to our screams with food, touch, and, best of all, clean diapers. And for a moment we are satisfied—until the cycle repeats itself.

Until we finally grow up.

At least that's the way it's supposed to work. But I wonder. As an adult, I still find myself groping and grasping, reaching for something more. Longing for my needs to be met and my desires to be accounted for.

Unfortunately, when what I want and what I get don't coincide, I come to the unconscious conclusion: I'm all alone in the world and there's no one I can trust. At least that's how it feels.

Yet nothing could be further from the truth.

The Birth of Distrust

From the beginning of time, God has longed for a people to love and call His own. A people on whom He could lavish His provision and protection as well as His presence. Like Adam and Eve, you and I were intended to live as cherished children enjoying sweet communion with our Father. Walking together through life. Tenderly cared for and protected by His love. Every need met. Every longing satisfied.

But then sin happened, and everything changed.

Perhaps it started with a seed of doubt that had lurked in Eve's heart for a while. A distrust of God's goodness that led her to crave something more than she had. How else to explain Satan's ability to so easily tempt her with the forbidden and lead her astray?

After all, there were many, many trees in the Garden of Eden. Genesis 2:9 tells us, "The Lord God made all kinds of trees grow out of the ground—trees that were pleasing to the eye and good for food." Of all these trees, two were especially significant: the "tree of the knowledge of good and evil" and the "tree of life" (v. 9). And of these two, only one had been marked off-limits by God (v. 17).

Consider what that means. When God said no to one tree, He was saying yes to hundreds of others, including the very special Tree of Life. But then came a doubt-sowing snake, bringing a hiss of discontentment.

"God's withholding His best," the devil told Eve, attacking God's character. Eat this fruit and "your eyes will be opened, and you will be like God, knowing good and evil," he promised in Genesis 3:5.

With God's loving intentions called into question, Eve took the fruit, and both she and her husband ate it (v. 6). And with that act, Paradise was lost. Forced out of Eden because of disobedience, Adam and Eve found themselves on their own, consigned to a life outside the umbrella of God's protection and provision. Their rebellion would affect not only them, but those who followed—including you and me. All because our great-great-not-so-great grandparents chose to eat from the wrong tree.

It was the ultimate con job when you really think about it. Adam and Eve were tricked into trading the perfection of the Garden for something they already had. Made in the image of their Maker, they were already "like God." Surrounded by flawless beauty, the couple had firsthand knowledge of everything good. But the knowledge of evil was Satan's biggest deceit. Rather than giving Adam and Eve control over their lives, it left them powerless—tormented by fear, enslaved to temptation, and susceptible to suffering.

With the door opened to darkness, wickedness rushed in, leaving the couple terrified and unable to stop it. Just as we are when we try to live life apart from our trustworthy God.

The Struggle to Trust

It's interesting that Satan tempted Adam and Eve with the very thing that got him kicked out of heaven. Lucifer, as he was known, seemed to have been given a prominent role as heaven's worship leader (see Ezekiel 28:13 NKJV). But evidently, he grew tired of worshiping God and wanted to be worshiped instead.

Isaiah 14:13–14 records his prideful thoughts:

> I will ascend to the heavens;
> I will raise my throne
> above the stars of God; . . .
> I will make myself like the Most High.

Of course, the devil's attempt to take over heaven failed. Perhaps that's why he's so determined to take over the human heart. He sows suspicion and plants doubt in our minds by attacking God's character and trying to undermine our sense of His love:

Why would God forbid something that you need? He's just trying to control you.

If God was truly good, He wouldn't allow bad things to happen.

If He really loved you, He wouldn't allow you to feel such pain.

Living in a world marred by sin, we're especially vulnerable to his lies. For life is unpredictable and, at times, terribly hard. Every day we're given reasons to doubt, reasons to fear. And though I wish it weren't so, being a Christian doesn't exempt us from trouble. Tragedies happen. People let us down. No matter how much we exercise or how well we eat, our health will eventually fail. As it turns out, this life is fatal.

We shouldn't be surprised by any of that, for Jesus told us clearly, "In this world you will have trouble" (John 16:33). This isn't heaven, after all. But reconciling the promised blessings of being a Christian with the hardships we face in life can feel confusing at times. No wonder we all struggle to trust God when things are difficult.

Lysa TerKeurst talks about this in her book *Uninvited*. "I crave for life to make sense. I cringe when it doesn't," she writes, going on to explain:

> I want life to be as stable as a math problem. Two plus two always equals four. It will equal four today, tomorrow and into the tomorrows years from now. . . .
>
> [But] life doesn't add up. People don't add up. And in the rawest moments of honest hurting, God doesn't add up. All of which

> makes us hold our trust ever so close to our chests until it becomes more tied to our fears than to our faith.[1]

What is your trust tied to, I wonder? I like to think that I'm a woman of faith, but too often, I'm a woman of fear. People make choices that wound me. Hopes and dreams don't always come true. Sometimes the daily responsibilities and cares of life feel so overwhelming that I'm more likely to worry than take time to pray.

It helps me to remember a quote I heard years ago: "Christianity isn't the absence of problems. It's the promise of God's presence."[2] But to be honest, even that concept can be difficult to understand, especially for those of us with an Americanized view of Christianity.

Somehow we've come to expect continuous and tangible blessings as our spiritual birthright, forgetting to factor in the fallen world in which we live. When Adam and Eve rejected God's perfection, they left us with this mixed bag called *life*—some of it good, some of it not so good, some of it downright evil.

But here's the good news. Though Adam and Eve ate from the wrong tree, Jesus hung on another tree so that you and I could be reconciled to our heavenly Father. Through Christ's sacrifice, the Tree of Life is offered to us once more. Rather than wandering through life confused and alone, you and I are invited back to the intimacy of Eden and the beautiful security of belonging to the Lord.

"We proclaim to you what we have seen and heard," the apostle John writes in 1 John 1:3, "so that you also may have fellowship with us. And our fellowship is with the Father and with his Son, Jesus Christ." The man who enjoyed close friendship with Jesus as part of His inner circle, the one who leaned his head against the Savior's chest, welcomes us to intimacy with God as well.

But this sweet fellowship requires a choice. Will we surrender our lives and unreservedly follow Jesus, or will we retain control and follow from a distance? Will we eat from the tree that offers knowledge and self-reliance, or will we partake from the tree that gives us life?

10 SIGNS YOU MIGHT HAVE TRUST ISSUES

Trust doesn't come easily in this broken world. People have wounded us. Life has let us down. If we're not careful, we can project those trust issues onto God. Here are a few symptoms:

1. ***You keep God at a distance.*** It feels safer that way. You rarely spend time alone with Him or ask direct questions, for you're not sure you want to hear what He might say.

2. ***You remain in the driver's seat.*** When you say, "God is my copilot," you mean it. You can't imagine giving Him the wheel for fear of where He might take you.

3. ***Your prayer life tends to be lifeless—or nonexistent.*** You repeat prayers by rote if you pray at all. You say you don't want to bother God with your problems, but in reality, you don't want to be disappointed.

4. ***You limit God by your limitations.*** You may believe God can do anything, but you don't believe He can do it through you. Especially when the situation seems impossible.

5. ***You don't feel God's love.*** Though you believe Jesus died for your sins, you secretly think you must earn His favor. It seems impossible that He could fully accept and love you as you are.

6. ***You struggle to worship.*** The words feel flat on your tongue. While one part of you wants to express your love to God, the other part feels detached, empty, and dry.

7. ***You seldom connect with God's Word.*** You may read the Bible out of duty, but you struggle to identify with what you've read. The tender words of the Father rarely reach your heart.

8. ***You doubt God's goodness.*** Because life is hard, you struggle to believe that God is for you and is working on your behalf. When He blesses others, you sometimes resent the fact it isn't you.

9. ***You secretly believe God is mad at you.*** When something goes wrong, you assume God is punishing you. Even when you repent, you struggle to accept His forgiveness.

10. ***You feel stuck.*** Regret from the past, resentment in the present, and fear of the future keep you from fully trusting in God. You have a hard time imagining a different way of life.

If you find yourself in any of these descriptions, bring your trust issue to Jesus and work through it together. He wants to heal your heart and set you free from fear and unbelief.

> Don't be afraid, for I am *with* you. . . .
> I will *strengthen* you and *help* you.
>
> *Isaiah 41:10 NLT*

Choosing the right tree doesn't guarantee we'll escape the consequences of this fallen world. Following Jesus won't necessarily answer all our questions. But when we eat from the right tree, those questions won't feel so important. Instead of trying to understand the mysteries of life and why evil seems to win more often than good, we'll be able to rest our hearts in the Father's love. Trusting His character, His wisdom, and His power.

Experiencing the freedom that's made available when we give God control of our uncontrollable lives.

The Beautiful Logic of Trusting God

I don't know about you, but if I were God and Adam and Eve rejected me, I would have pushed the reset button and started over with creation. A new heaven and earth. A different man and woman. And not a snake to be found.

But instead of allowing sin to ruin His plan, God immediately began the process of redemption. In His mercy God covered the couple's nakedness. His love followed them out of the Garden and helped them navigate the cruel world. And His love and mercy still reach out to us today. Wooing us back to relationship with the One who knows us, yet loves us so much.

It's baffling to me that we so often reject our heavenly Father's advances and choose to do life on our own. For there's a beautiful logic in trusting God—along with multiple reasons that He deserves our faith:

- *God made us.* He formed us in our mother's womb and is intimately acquainted with all our ways (Psalm 139:3–13). It only makes sense that our Maker would know the best way for us to live.
- *God loves us.* No matter what we're going through, we can be confident that He's for us, not against us (Romans 8:31). God is always working on our behalf, and He wants to make His love real to our hearts.
- *God redeemed us.* He purchased our freedom through the death of His Son and restored us to right relationship with Him (Titus 2:13–14). He loves to redeem everything the enemy means for evil by turning it into something good.
- *God empowers us.* Because we are unable to live a godly life on our own, He gives us the Holy Spirit to guide and teach us, filling us with the power we need to become everything God wants us to be (2 Corinthians 3:18).

But there is another powerful reason for trusting the Lord that, in my mind, supersedes all other reasons. It's found in what our dependence means to the heart of our Father. Brennan Manning expresses it beautifully in his book *Ruthless Trust*:

> Why does our trust offer such immense pleasure to God? Because trust is the preeminent expression of love. Thus, it may mean more to Jesus when we say, "I trust you," than when we say, "I love you."[3]

In a very real sense, trust is God's love language. Nothing brings Him more joy than when we put our hope fully in Him. You and I aren't a cosmic experiment meant to keep heaven occupied. Humanity isn't part of a celestial science project tracking how eight billion mice interact in a lab called planet Earth. We are God's children, each of us uniquely loved and wanted. Intricately designed for a special place in the Father's heart.

But to speak God's love language and access the life we're meant to live, we must embrace trust—letting go in surrender and holding on in faith. For anything less affects every area of our lives.

- When we don't trust God, we're quick to worry and slow to pray.
- When we don't trust God, we struggle to forgive.
- When we don't trust God, we grumble and complain.
- When we don't trust God, we build walls of self-protection.
- When we don't trust God, we attempt to micromanage our world.
- When we don't trust God, we react poorly rather than respond wisely.
- When we don't trust God, we live as orphans rather than beloved children.
- When we don't trust God, we miss the joy and freedom of belonging to Him.

Instead, we walk around with a built-in label maker, defining life from our limited understanding—and all too often, getting it wrong.

Mislabeling Our Lives

Have you ever used one of those little handheld devices that crank out printed strips of adhesive to help you organize your life? With a few twists of the alphabetical dial or a few swipes at the built-in keyboard, you can label your sock drawer and find anything in your pantry with a single glance. But you have to be careful to put the right labels on the right items. Otherwise you might end up adding chili powder instead of cinnamon to your peach pie!

That's exactly what happens when we use the inner label maker installed at the fall. Eating from the Tree of Knowledge rather than the Tree of Life has skewed our perspective, causing us to mislabel things the way the world does, calling "evil good and good evil" (Isaiah 5:20). Because our human understanding is limited, it causes us to mark blessings "good" and trials "bad," not realizing that God is at work in both.

An often-told fable describes a farmer whose horse ran away. His neighbors came to express sympathy. "We're sorry to hear about your horse. That is most unfortunate," they said. But the farmer simply replied, "Maybe."

The next day the horse returned with seven wild horses. "This is so fortunate! Now you have eight horses," his neighbors said. But again, the farmer answered, "Maybe."

When the farmer's son tried to tame one of the horses, he fell and broke his leg. "Oh my, that's terrible," his neighbors said. But the old man just shrugged. "Maybe."

When soldiers came to the village to conscript fighters, they rejected the son because of his broken leg. "How lucky for you!" the neighbors cried out. But the farmer just smiled and said, "Maybe."[4]

There's a lot of wisdom in the farmer's response because only God knows what is truly good and what is evil. Eating from the wrong tree tends to make us believe that our wisdom is faultless and our perception of a situation is the last word, but only God knows the truth. He alone knows the *why* behind the situation and *how* it will all work out in the end. So doesn't it make sense to leave the labeling to Him?

For our great Redeemer specializes in redefining good and bad, repurposing the worst that hell dishes out so that it serves His eternal purposes. Just as He did in the life of a young shepherd boy named David.

A Better Perspective

Throughout this book, we're going to explore the life of David, for he's a great example of what trusting God looks like in every area of our lives. Thankfully, we have an abundance of material from which to learn. With sixty-six chapters dedicated to his story in the Old Testament and fifty-nine references to his life in the New Testament, more has been written about David than any other Bible character.[5]

Though he didn't always do it right, David tried to center his life around knowing and pleasing God. Throughout the Psalms, he continually calls us to *trust* God—using the word forty-nine times in the King James Version according to my count.

> Blessed is the one
> who trusts in the LORD. (40:4)
>
> Trust in him at all times, you people; . . .
> for God is our refuge. (62:8)
>
> Those who know your name trust in you,
> for you, LORD, have never forsaken those who seek you.
> (9:10)

This last verse is noteworthy, for in the Old Testament, each of God's names reveals an aspect of His character. Which is important, for we only trust the ones we know.[6]

From a young age, David sought to know the Lord intimately. It resulted in deep friendship and lifelong dependence on God that may have been cultivated during the lonely days and nights he spent caring for his father's sheep. Whatever the source, it was certainly present by the time he was a young man, when God singled him out to be king.

When Samuel was sent to anoint one of Jesse's sons to be the next ruler of Israel (1 Samuel 16:1–13), the prophet invited the entire family to a religious ceremony so he could discern the Lord's choice (v. 5). But for some reason—perhaps as the youngest he was needed to watch the family's sheep—David wasn't included in the lineup. After Samuel met David's older, more impressive brothers, God prompted the prophet to ask if there were any other sons. Jesse summoned David from the fields, and God confirmed that he was "the one" (v. 12).

As anointing oil rolled down the young man's face, his mind must have raced. Priests and kings received anointings—not insignificant, apparently forgotten-by-their-father shepherd boys. Though David wasn't publicly declared king at that moment, the first-century historian Josephus has said that Samuel whispered the anointing's symbolic meaning in the young boy's ear: "You will be the next king."[7]

Why me? David must have wondered. What set him apart from older, more capable men? In Acts 13:22, God reveals the reason: "I have found David son of Jesse, a man after my own heart; he will do everything I want him to do."

Oh, how I want God to be able to say that of me! I want to be known as a woman who knows God so intimately, she obeys Him implicitly—a woman after God's own heart. Don't you?

Having a heart like that requires that we lay down the label maker of our understanding and trust God to define and correct everything that touches our lives—including our view of Him. Because until we come to know the Lord intimately and view life through the lens of who He is, we won't have the proper perspective on what happens to us, nor will we fully comprehend the depth of His love.

I love the advice given by the sixth-century bishop Paternus:

> Think magnificently of God. Magnify His providence: adore His power; frequent His service; and pray to Him frequently and incessantly. Bear Him always in your mind; teach your thoughts to reverence Him in every place, for there is no place where He is not. . . . Fear and worship, and love God; first, and last, think magnificently of God.[8]

It's my prayer that as you read this book, you'll allow the Holy Spirit to expand your understanding of who God truly is: Your trustworthy Father. Your compassionate Savior. Your tender Comforter. Your faithful Friend. Don't let labels created by previous experiences or lack of experience minimize His work in your life. Let God out of the box of your small thinking—for our view of God determines our level of trust.

"If I have a low concept of God, my religion can only be a cheap, watery affair," A. W. Tozer writes. "But if my concept of God is worthy of God . . . it can be reverent, profound, beautiful."[9]

To help strengthen your understanding of God, I've included a list of His attributes in Appendix B. Choose one to meditate on this week and allow your concept of God to grow.

If we remain ignorant of God's character and purposes on earth, we'll constantly mislabel His work and question His motives. We'll live life looking through the wrong end of a telescope. God will appear tiny, and our problems will appear huge.

But when we "think magnificently" about God, the Holy Spirit flips the telescope so we see God correctly. Consequently, our problems shrink to their proper proportions. For in the light of His love, we view life—and ourselves—through the right lens.

Wholehearted Trust

Over the years, God has used Proverbs 3:5–6 to recalibrate my soul. It's become so precious to me that it's my life verse and the theme of this book:

> Trust in the Lord with all your heart
> And do not lean on your own understanding.
> In all your ways acknowledge Him,
> And He will make your paths straight. (NASB)

As we begin this journey together, I'd like to look closely at each line of this powerful Scripture. For it contains important clues as to how we can know God, trust God, and become people after His own heart.

"Trust in the Lord with all your heart."

Half-hearted trust won't cut it. We've got to bring everything to the table, including *all* that we are. We can't trust God with our whole being if we're making backup plans in case He doesn't come through. God is looking for wholehearted surrender and a continuous reliance on Him. Day by day. Minute by minute. As David writes in Psalm 62:5,

> I depend on God alone;
> I put my hope in him. (GNT)

"And do not lean on your own understanding."

Lingering residue from the Tree of Knowledge makes it hard to let go of our need to understand. Fix-it queens by nature, we think we should be able to figure out life on our own. But our human intellect will always be limited and often faulty. When we invite God into the equation, however, He promises to make us wiser. For as James 1:5 says, "If any of you lacks wisdom, you should ask God, who gives generously to all."

"In all your ways acknowledge Him."

So often, in the middle of trouble, I forget to consciously recognize that Jesus is with me, that nothing takes Him by surprise or is beyond His power to save. I've found that when I consciously "acknowledge" that He's present with me in *all* my ways—not just some of them—I don't default so easily to fear. Instead, I'm enabled to see God in the situation, which helps me "submit to him," as the NIV translates the last part of that phrase, so that God's will is accomplished instead of my own.

"And He will make your paths straight."

This part of the verse reminds me of the carpet runner in my grandma's apartment. The long strip of rug often buckled and created tripping hazards, to which I occasionally fell prey.

Though rumples in a rug are easy to smooth out, when they appear in my life, they often seem like impossible and impassable mountains. But in Isaiah 45:2, God tells us,

> I will go before you
> and will level the mountains.

For as verse 2 in the New King James Version promises, He specializes in making "crooked places straight."

Rather than giving in to fear when difficulties arise, I'm learning to declare my faith in Jesus out loud: "Lord, I trust You with all that I am and all that I face. I acknowledge that You are with me in this situation—I am not alone. Thank You for going before me and showing me the way to go."

Sometimes I have to repeat the declaration over and over as I step back from fear and unbelief. Though it may be imperceptible to me, as I wait on God, He begins to pull the edge of that runner toward Him. Rumple by rumple, ridge by ridge, He removes the obstacles and makes my path straight.

The classic hymn "'Tis So Sweet to Trust in Jesus" was written by Louisa M. R. Stead after her husband died trying to rescue a young boy from drowning. With little money and a four-year-old daughter to raise, the young widow faced a frightening future. But out of the crucible of her pain came these words:

> Jesus, Jesus, how I trust him!
> How I've proved him o'er and o'er!
> Jesus, Jesus, precious Jesus!
> O for grace to trust him more![10]

That's my prayer for this book. That fresh grace would be released in your heart and mine to trust Jesus more. For just as He's proven Himself faithful to countless generations, He wants to prove Himself trustworthy to us as well. When fear or doubt arise, we need to pray Louisa's prayer: "Lord, give me grace to trust You more."

For God's grace not only saves us, it also enables us to trust God in the middle of life's darkest and most desperate moments. Especially during those times when we can't see—and our hearts just don't understand.

Open Our Eyes, Lord

When my youngest son was five years old, he had to have his tonsils and adenoids out due to respiratory problems. The doctor warned me that post-op might be a little rocky, but I wasn't prepared for Josh's reaction coming out of the anesthesia.

"Mommy, mommy!" my normally even-keeled boy screamed as he woke up in the recovery room. Eyes wide open, he frantically clawed the air in an attempt to find me.

"I'm right here, honey . . . ," I tried to reassure him as I took him in my arms. "Mommy's right here."

But he pushed away from me and tried to reach for something beyond. Blinded to my presence and unable to absorb my love, he continued to call my name, unaware that I was standing in front of him. That I was waiting to comfort him if he'd only relax into my love.

I wonder how many times we do that to God. "Where are you, Lord?" we cry during difficult situations. "Don't you see my pain? Don't you hear my fear?"

I'm right here, my child, He whispers to our troubled hearts as He attempts to take us in His arms. *I've been with you the whole time.*

Perhaps you're going through a challenging time right now. Maybe you picked up this book because you know you need a deeper level of trust. Perhaps, like Josh, you're frantically searching for God in your situation. It's been a long time since you felt the Father's love. It's been years since you've experienced His presence.

Well, I have good news for you, my friend. Jesus is with you—right there in the middle of your circumstance. He loves you and wants to show Himself powerful. He wants to open your eyes to His presence and help you shake off the anesthesia of doubt, proving Himself faithful to the promise He declared through the prophet Jeremiah: "You will seek me and find me when you seek me with all your heart. I will be found by you" (Jeremiah 29:13–14).

Rather than groping and grasping, trying to live life on your own, reach out and receive the love that Jesus offers. As you relax into His love, you'll find everything you need—strength for the day, hope for tomorrow, and grace to trust Him more.

No matter what comes your way.

Two

Total Surrender

> In the same way, anyone who holds on to life just as it is destroys that life. But if you let it go, reckless in your love, you'll have it forever, real and eternal.
>
> John 12:25 MSG

I said I'd never do it. After all, who in their right mind jumps out of a perfectly good airplane?

But there I was, suiting up for my first skydive. My maiden plunge. As I buckled on the funny-looking helmet, I questioned the wisdom of it all. After all, I was terrified of heights. Growing up, my worst nightmares had always involved falling. Plummeting downward, arms flailing, mouth opened in a silent, endless scream. The fact that I always awakened before hitting the ground had never lessened the intensity of my fear.

Even the simple act of climbing a ladder put my heart in my throat. Skydiving? Well, that was the ultimate test of faith for me. Which is why, I suppose, God chose it.

I want you to trust Me, Joanna, the Lord had been whispering to my heart for months.* It wasn't just my fear of heights He was addressing. He was asking for an increased faith in every area of my life, including my kids. Apparently this challenge was part of helping me grow, so finally I said yes. John Michael and Jessica had always wanted to skydive. Now that both kids had graduated from high school, my husband and I decided it would be a good way to commemorate this chapter of life.

We'd given our children roots. Now it was time to give them wings.

On the way to the airfield that beautiful August morning, we decided that John would go up with Jessica and I would go up with John Michael in separate flights. That way if something happened, there would be someone left to parent our sweet four-year-old, Joshua, who later started crying as he watched us put on our gear. Apparently he, too, wanted to jump out of a perfectly good airplane.

Strapped uncomfortably to a rather large instructor in charge of the tandem jump, I found myself staring out the window of a small Cessna as it climbed into the sky. Excitement and sheer terror swirled in my stomach as I gazed at the receding landscape below.

Finally up to altitude and circling the landing field, tandem pairs began to jump from the plane. By that point, I'd almost convinced myself that this was fun. That if given a choice, I'd rather jump alone. After all, how hard could it be? They'd given us clear instructions before taking off, shown us how to use the rip cord, and explained how to land.

But then came our turn to leap, and all my resolve melted as we approached the plane's door. Grabbing the bar above our heads, the instructor leaned out, leaving me dangling in front of him. Ignoring my cries of "No, no, no!" he pushed off the plane's threshold, and we began to fall—down, down, down toward the earth below.

*To clarify, I've never heard the audible voice of God. Instead, I've learned to recognize His still, small voice speaking inside me through repeated promptings, gentle corrections, or thoughts that are far too wise to be my own.

When the parachute finally opened and slowed our descent, I stopped screaming and started to enjoy the journey. The view below was gorgeous, a patchwork of forests and meadows ringed by the majestic mountains of northwest Montana.

Strangely, even when free-falling, the plummeting feeling I'd experienced in my nightmares never came. Instead of the bottom-dropping-out sensation of a roller coaster, the air seemed to hold us up, cushioning our fall.

Though my jump lasted only minutes, the experience of skydiving has lasted a lifetime. Looking back at the sky from the safety of the ground, I wondered why I'd been so afraid. Why I'd resisted taking a leap of faith for so long. Not just in skydiving, but in other areas of my life as well.

Because, it turns out, when you're tandem jumping with Jesus, there's nothing you need to fear.

The Illusion of Control

Let's face it, we're all control freaks by nature.

Some of us are experts at keeping our controlling tendencies hidden. We tuck them behind benign smiles, saying, "Whatever you want," but then gently manipulate people into doing it our way.

Others of us are proud of the remote control we firmly grip in our hand. Convinced we know what's best for everyone, we wield our opinions like a magic wand. Like Lorelai from TV's *The Gilmore Girls*, we don't hesitate to proclaim: "As long as everything is exactly the way I want it, I'm totally flexible."[1]

Control isn't necessarily a bad thing. It's a type of survival instinct wired into the human DNA. Relinquishing control in the wrong situation can be dangerous—like when you're a recovering alcoholic considering a drink or a parent whose toddler is determined to run out into the street.

An appropriate amount of self-control, self-sufficiency, and self-care is healthy and important. Self-control is even listed in Galatians 5:23 as a fruit of the Spirit. But if we're not careful, our urge to control can cross the line and become delusional and damaging, not only hurting our relationships with people, but going so far as to sabotage our relationship with God. For the Lord of the universe will not be managed or manipulated, no matter how hard we try.

If we're going to be true followers of Jesus, we must be willing to be led. There can be only one leader in our relationship. Only one God. Only one King. Which means we must relinquish the magic wand and hand over the remote control, along with our passive-aggressive attempts to make God do things our way.

"You can have faith or you can have control," pastor Joel Schmidgall points out, "but you cannot have both."[2]

Jesus made that clear each time someone expressed an interest in being His disciple. Rather than offering incentives or a slick presentation of follower benefits, Jesus seemed to go out of His way to discourage followers by highlighting the cost. "Whoever wants to be my disciple," He said, "must deny themselves and take up their cross daily and follow me" (Luke 9:23).

Not the best lead, marketing experts would say. Nor the best metaphor, especially when crosses were used as instruments of torture by the Romans. Reserved for criminals, who were strung naked and bleeding for the whole world to see, crucifixion was considered the very worst way to die.

But rather than softening the image, Jesus went on to intensify it. "For whoever wants to save their life will lose it, but whoever loses their life for me will save it" (v. 24).

It isn't enough to carry your cross, Jesus was telling eager would-be followers. You've got to trust God enough to climb up on that cross and choose to die—for it's the only way to truly live. It's a theme Jesus repeats throughout His ministry. It appears five times in the Gospels[3] and another time in a discussion of end-time events in Luke 17:32–33, where Jesus warns, "Remember Lot's wife! Whoever tries to keep their life will lose it, and whoever loses their life will preserve it."

There's no way around it. As Christians, you and I are called to surrender. A total commitment of our lives that goes beyond a white flag weakly waved in God's direction or a shifty-eyed assent that agrees to follow Jesus but reserves the right to turn back if the going gets tough. Jesus requires total abandonment—a giving up and giving over of our lives to His rule. Anything less results in a watered-down Christianity, as Mark Batterson explains:

> [Sadly] people can go to church every week of their lives and never go all in with Jesus Christ. I'm afraid we've cheapened the gospel by allowing people to buy in without selling out. We've made it too convenient, too comfortable. We've given people just enough Jesus to be bored but not enough to feel the surge of holy adrenaline that courses through your veins when you decide to follow Him no matter what, no matter where, no matter when.[4]

Sometimes, in an eagerness to be "seeker sensitive," we can sidestep this issue of full surrender as ministry leaders, sugarcoating the gospel in hopes of making it more palatable. But the "holy adrenaline" all of us long for—the abundant life we need—is found only in trusting God with all our hearts. Going all in with Jesus so that He alone controls our lives.

Divided Loyalty

You'd think that being raised in a grace-filled home and a grace-filled church would have given me a leg up in Christianity. And in many ways it did. I'm eternally grateful for a godly heritage, and I wouldn't trade my parents, Cliff and Annette Gustafson, for anything in the world. They've consistently shown me "the shape of godliness"[5] as they've lived out their walk with God in tangible ways.

Because my mom and dad reflected Jesus so well, I feel like I came into this world knowing Him. Yet there came a time when I knew that being born into a godly family wasn't enough. I needed a Savior. So somewhere around the age of four or five, I accepted Jesus into my heart. My love for Him was genuine, and I wanted to serve Him always.

ACCEPTING JESUS AS SAVIOR

Before we can make Jesus our Lord, we must receive Him as Savior. If you haven't yet made that all-important decision, you can do it today. Pastor and evangelist Greg Laurie outlines the following steps:

Realize that you are a sinner. No matter how good a life we try to live, we still fall miserably short of being a good person. That is because we are all sinners. The Bible says, "No one is good—not even one" [Romans 3:10, paraphrased]. We cannot become who we are supposed to be without Jesus Christ.

Recognize that Jesus Christ died on the cross for you. The Bible tells us that "God showed his great love for us by sending Christ to die for us while we were still sinners" [Romans 5:8 TLB]. This is the Good News, that God loves us so much that He sent His only Son to die in our place when we least deserved it.

Repent of your sin. The Bible tells us, "Repent of your sins and turn to God, so that your sins may be wiped away" [Acts 3:19 NLT]. The word repent means to change our direction in life. Instead of running from God, we can run toward Him.

Receive Jesus Christ into your life. Becoming a Christian is not merely believing some creed or going to church. It is having Christ Himself take residence in your life and heart. Jesus said, "Behold, I stand at the door and knock. If anyone hears my voice and opens the door, I will come in . . ." [Revelation 3:20 ESV].

If you would like to have a relationship with Jesus, simply pray this prayer and mean it in your heart: "Dear Lord Jesus, I know I am a sinner. I believe You died for my sins. Right now, I turn from my sins and open the door of my heart and life. I confess You as my personal Lord and Savior. Thank You for saving me. Amen."[6]

For this is how God *loved* the world:
He gave his one and only Son,
so that *everyone* who believes in him
will not perish but have *eternal life*.

John 3:16 NLT

Midway through middle school, however, I began compartmentalizing our relationship. Though I'd given my heart to Jesus, as someone once put it, "the rest of me kept going out with other guys." Desperate for people's approval, I did a lot of silly things looking for acceptance. Nothing dark or sordid—I was too much of a Goody Two-shoes for that! But my heart was definitely more interested in the opinions of others than in prioritizing the opinion of God.

Though I didn't realize it, a dichotomy had developed in my soul. An invisible line divided my life down the middle, with one part of me loving God and the other part admiring the world. Jesus was my Savior, but I hadn't made Him my Lord. Sitting on the throne of my life, I kept on calling the shots—because deep down I wasn't sure I could trust God. What if He asked me to do something I didn't want to do? What if abdicating the throne of my heart meant I had to surrender my hopes and dreams as well?

Complicating matters was something Paul refers to over and over in Romans as the "flesh" (7:18 NKJV)—also translated as "sinful nature" (NIV). Though as Christians we've been reconciled to God, Paul reminds us that there's an ongoing battle still raging within us, a type of civil war between our redeemed selves and our sin-marred nature (7:15–25). I've come to think of these struggling rivals as Flesh Woman and Spirit Woman.

I write extensively about this inner conflict in my book *Having a Mary Spirit: Allowing God to Change Us from the Inside Out*.[7] Deciding who wins the battle each day—flesh or spirit—is crucial to lasting positive change in our lives. But it's also important when it comes to trusting God, for it explains why so many of us struggle to surrender and why we sometimes sense a vicious tug-of-war inside our hearts and minds.

My Spirit Woman is that part of me that was made alive at salvation (Ephesians 2:4–5), the part that is completely submitted to God. My Flesh Woman, however—well, she's a different story. Though happy to do the Christian thing as long as it serves her, my Flesh Woman is actually a 683-pound sumo-wrestler control freak determined to have her own way. Telling God one thing, yet doing the other, she's a double agent dedicated to undermining His rule in my heart. For as Romans 8:7 tells us, the flesh is "hostile to God."

Until Flesh Woman is dethroned and defeated, we'll never get around to enthroning Jesus as Lord over our lives. Instead, we'll be double-minded people living double-minded lives, wanting God with one part of our heart yet distrusting Him with the rest.

It's the dichotomy—the battle—I felt as a teenager. I was pretty sure that if I gave my life entirely to Jesus, He'd ask me to do something I didn't want to do. Like give away all my possessions to feed the poor. Or any one of the myriad of things Flesh Woman told me He might do. So I kept on living a double life.

But the Lord, in His mercy, wouldn't settle for part of my heart. He wanted all of me. Just as He wants all of you.

Who's on the Throne?

Saul had the markings of greatness. Standing head and shoulders above other Israelites, he was handsome and impressive. But when God chose him to be the first king of Israel, Saul was resistant (1 Samuel 9:17–21), to the point he even hid in the baggage at his own coronation (10:20–22). Eventually the role grew on him, however. After all, being the king of Israel had its perks—power, prestige, servants, and riches.

According to scholars, Saul was thirty years old when he became king, and he held the position for forty-two years (1 Samuel 13:1). But while the man was impressive on the outside, an inner instability showed up periodically throughout his reign—a foolish insecurity that looked to people for approval and a dark jealousy that erupted when that approval was given to someone else. These unresolved flaws eventually caused God to disqualify Saul as ruler. But it didn't have to be that way.

From the beginning, God had promised to equip Saul for the position. "The Spirit of the Lord will come powerfully upon you . . . ," the prophet Samuel told him, "and you will be changed into a different person. Once these signs are fulfilled, do whatever your hand finds to do, for God is with you" (1 Samuel 10:6–7).

According to verse 9, everything happened as Samuel predicted. "God changed Saul's heart, and all these signs were fulfilled that day." Unfortunately, as time went by, Saul stopped depending on God and started depending on himself.

His self-reliance first showed up at a place called Gilgal (1 Samuel 13:7–9). Samuel was supposed to offer sacrifices to God before a looming battle with the Philistines. But when the prophet was delayed, Saul's army began to scatter. So the anxious king offered his own sacrifices rather than waiting for Samuel to arrive.

Sadly, this impatient and impulsive pattern only continued. Even when it became clear God had chosen a different king (1 Samuel 15:22–26), Saul refused to acknowledge his replacement and instead spent most of the next decade trying to hunt down and kill David.

Though we might not go to such extremes, I think we all have an inner Saul. It shows up when we try to control people and situations to benefit or protect ourselves. If we continually give in to it, we may hear a variant of what God told Saul in 1 Samuel 15:23:

> Because you have rejected the word of the Lord,
> he has rejected you as king.

I'm grateful that we live under the new covenant and can experience the Lord's forgiveness when we humbly repent. But I must warn you: God is impossible to fool. He knows whether we're truly living for Him or going through religious motions to get what we want.

"No one can serve two masters," Jesus warns in Matthew 6:24. "Either you will hate the one and love the other, or you will be devoted to the one and despise the other."

No wonder so many Christians suffer from a self-induced identity crisis. We want to know who we are in Christ, but we don't want His lordship. We want the blessings of being His people but without the guidelines of His Word. Like the prodigal son (Luke

15:11–32), we want our inheritance now—and the freedom to spend it any way we like. Caught between two loyalties, we live as citizens of two kingdoms, yet feel like strangers in both—not at home in the world, but not fully at home in God.

For until Jesus is Lord *of all*, He isn't Lord *at all*.

Going All In

When God put His finger on my divided teenage heart, I spent months in weary wrestling between faith and fear. I knew that total surrender was the only answer, but my Flesh Woman didn't want to relinquish her power base, for she knew it would involve abdicating control of my life forever.

I'll never forget what that time felt like. It was as though I stood on the edge of a thirty-foot diving platform. Peering down into the darkness, I sensed the Lord saying, *I want all of you, Joanna. I'm not making any promises. I'm not offering any rewards. I'm asking you to choose Me. Unconditional surrender.*

The fear was tangible as I stood shivering on the edge of submission. Every part of my being screamed for me to step back from the edge and remain in control. I was so afraid of what I might lose if I were to give in.

Yet I really didn't have a choice. I'd tasted God's love and presence in my life even as a young teenager. How could I turn down His request?

Jesus's call came cloaked in so much love and longing, it nearly overwhelmed me. Though insistent and firm, it romanced the deepest part of me. Behind His voice I could sense Flesh Woman shouting her objections. But ignoring her shrill rantings, I pushed past the fear and leaped into the dark unknown.

With nothing held back, I committed my life entirely to Jesus. And in that moment everything changed. Truly changed. So much so that even decades later my eyes fill with tears at the memory of what happened that night.

Instead of the nightmare plunge I anticipated and the unending fall I feared, there immediately came beneath me a sense of my heavenly Father's "everlasting arms" (Deuteronomy 33:27). Catching me, then holding me. Steadying me, then cradling me. Drawing me closer and even closer to His heart than I'd ever felt before.

It's interesting that I write these words just yards from the spot where I made that life-changing decision. The altar at Glacier Bible Camp has been my own personal Bethel.[8] It's here that I've met God time and time again in powerful, life-changing ways. But none of those encounters have been as important as the moment I just described. For in my teenage transaction with God, a decisive battle was settled, and the war for my soul was essentially won.

Oh, there have been skirmishes since then. Encounters with the enemy that have made me tremble with fear. Unholy coups staged by my flesh and subtle temptations designed to woo me from my first love. But none of these have affected the most important questions, for they've already been settled:

- I am not my own. I've been bought with a price.
- God can do whatever He wants with me (or not—it's up to Him).
- I withhold nothing from the Lord.

That last point is important, for until we fully surrender, we will never fully trust. In trying to manage the parts we've held back, we'll miss the joy and freedom that come when we give all that we are and all that we have to the One who made us.

Though it's taken a lifetime of countless surrenders—both big and small—I think I've come to a place where I can honestly say God can have my children, my husband, my health, my ministry. None of it belongs to me. It all belongs to God.

While I have to reaffirm my submission at times, that initial soul surrender has brought with it a beautiful security that has created a steadfast certainty. I don't always live from it as I should, but being sold out to Jesus has cultivated a faith that is able to supersede my fears.

Like everyone, life continues to be hard at times. Bad things happen to me and those I love. It's important to understand that being fully devoted to Jesus doesn't guarantee that everything will go our way. But that realization doesn't shake me the way it used to, and I pray you'll find that firm foundation under your spiritual feet as well. Though your Flesh Woman may pull back at the idea of letting go and trusting God, I hope you'll work through the resistance until you can. For there is so much freedom on the other side of surrender:

- *Freedom from fear.* I don't have to be afraid of tomorrow because God is working on my behalf. No matter what happens, He'll take care of me (Matthew 6:25–27).
- *Freedom from regret.* God can redeem my worst mistakes and turn my life into a display of His amazing grace (Ephesians 1:7).
- *Freedom from resentment.* I can forgive others (even myself) because nothing and no one thwarts God's purposes in my life (Isaiah 54:17).

As I've relinquished control and placed myself completely in God's hands, I've found that Romans 8:28 is true. Even the most painful trial is working *for* me, not *against* me. Because my heavenly Father "causes all things to work together for [my] good" (NASB).

Free-Flying with Jesus

During the last year of his life, the Dutch priest and theologian Henri Nouwen became fascinated with a trapeze act called the Flying Rodleighs. Henri was invited to practice sessions and spent a lot of time talking to the leader of the troupe about how it all worked. Nouwen describes the encounter like this:

> One day, I was sitting with Rodleigh, the leader of the troupe, in his caravan, talking about flying. He said, "As a flyer, I must have complete trust in my catcher. The public might think that I am the

> great star of the trapeze, but the real star is Joe, my catcher. He has to be there for me with split-second precision and grab me out of the air as I come to him in the long jump." "How does it work?" I asked. "The secret," Rodleigh said, "is that the flyer does nothing and the catcher does everything. When I fly to Joe, I have simply to stretch out my arms and hands and wait for him to catch me." . . .
>
> "You do nothing!" I said, surprised. "Nothing," Rodleigh repeated. "The worst thing the flyer can do is to try to catch the catcher. . . . It's Joe's task to catch me. If I grabbed Joe's wrists, I might break them, or he might break mine, and that would be the end for both of us. A flyer must fly, and a catcher must catch, and the flyer must trust, with outstretched arms, that his catcher will be there for him."[9]

You and I were made to go free-flying with Jesus! But we must let go in surrender before He can take hold of us with His capable hands.

When a frightened young Joshua took Moses's place as leader of the Israelites, God gave him a promise filled with encouragement: "I will be with you as I was with Moses. I will not fail you or abandon you. Be strong and courageous" (Joshua 1:5–6 NLT).

Interestingly, the Hebrew word for *fail* in this verse means "to become slack, to relax . . . to let drop,"[10] while the word for *strong* can mean to "be firm, be caught fast, be secure."[11] As we let go of self-reliance and choose God-reliance instead, Jesus will not only catch us and hold us, He promises to never let us go.

After all, the Lord has spent eternity waiting to be everything that He's promised to be in His Word. So don't be afraid to let go and trust your forever-faithful Father.

He wants to make you strong and courageous so that together you can fly.

Three

Unshakeable Faith

Continue in your faith, established and firm.

Colossians 1:23

The dream was so strange, I couldn't get it out of my mind.

For some reason I stood in a gymnasium that was being refurbished by our church. The outside had been painted and the parking lot cleaned. Inside, fresh paint and polished wood floors made the place feel almost new. However, there was a problem: a gaping hole in the middle of the gymnasium floor.

A young girl stood next to me, pointing at the opening. As I bent down to look, I could see large boulders lit by a flickering red glow. Troubling gaps honeycombed the bedrock beneath the concrete pad that held up the floor.

"Shouldn't we do something about the hole before fixing this place up?" the girl asked, her eyes confused and slightly perturbed.

Indeed, we should, I thought midway between dream and waking. *But it would be so much work.*

To deal with the faulty foundation, we might have to demolish the building entirely. We'd lose all the money we'd spent, not to mention our time.

Perhaps it's okay to cover up the hole and continue with the remodel, I thought unreasonably. *Perhaps it's okay to pretend I haven't seen what lies beneath*.

Holes in Our Faith

For months after the dream, I struggled to understand its significance. But then I started working on this chapter, and the meaning became clear. Our faith can look good on the outside yet still be riddled with holes. Which leads to an important question: What's the condition of your spiritual foundation?

Sadly, few of us take time to examine what lies below the surface of our faith. Even when presented with fault lines in our thinking or gaping holes in our theology, most of us prefer to ignore the information. Instead, we do our best to patch up the inconsistencies with good intentions and several yards of duct tape.

To go back and repair the foundations of our faith seems too daunting, too costly. We fear it would require too much time and effort, perhaps the absolute dismantling of our lives. So we ignore our true condition and go through the motions of Christianity instead. Sprucing up the outside. Trying to be good people. Trying to love God. All of which might seem to solve the issue temporarily.

But then trouble hits. A business fails. A marriage shatters. An unexpected diagnosis slams into the life of someone we love. And suddenly the gaps in our faith are exposed.

But how do we fix the holes? Where do we find more faith?

Strangely, it's often in the things that shake us emotionally and threaten to dismantle our trust that we find the material needed to build it. For there's nothing more effective than trouble to make us run to God—coming "boldly to the throne of grace, that we may obtain mercy and find grace to help in time of need" (Hebrews 4:16 NKJV).

The Greek word for "faith"—*pistis*—is used 243 times in the New Testament. It can be translated "trust" as well as "belief."[1] I find that helpful to remember, because the word *faith* has always felt a little ethereal to me, a bit hard to grasp. Oh, I know I've been raised *in* the faith, and I know I've been saved *by* faith. And I know I need to *live out* my faith by being obedient to God's Word. But how to *activate* my faith so I rely solely on Jesus? Well, that's where I sometimes struggle.

It helps me to think about it like this: Faith is a noun, but trust is a verb. Faith is something I *have*, but trust is something I *do*. It's a choice, an active decision.[2] I know when I'm trusting God and I know when I'm not. My trust (or lack of it) shows up in the sources I go to for wisdom. The places I run to when I'm afraid. Even the emotional responses I give in to when everything seems to go wrong.

My beautiful friend Jodi Detrick, author of *The Jesus-Hearted Woman*, has been struggling with a virulent eye infection for more than nine months. Currently the battle has left her mostly blind in one eye. "But I'm choosing to trust Jesus," she told me the other day. "And when my faith starts to waver, I'm choosing to *retrust* Him again and again."

It will take another surgery and several more months to know whether she'll regain sight in that eye. But Jodi's trust in the Lord is beautiful to behold. Though she's had to do her part to "contend for the faith" (Jude 3), Jesus is meeting her in the long struggle, strengthening her soul as her faith grows in the dark.[3]

"For you know that when your faith is tested, your endurance has a chance to grow," James 1:3–4 tells us. "So let it grow, for when your endurance is fully developed, you will be perfect and complete, needing nothing" (NLT).

Though none of us enjoy trials, they often contain a precious blessing. God uses times of shaking to fill up holes in our spiritual foundation so that we're "mature and complete, not lacking anything" (v. 4). As we hold onto Him, we become God-centered believers who know how to endure hardship—impervious to floods of trouble, the rot of doubt, and the decay of time.

10 FAITH-BUILDING EXERCISES

According to the Bible, we can't work up the faith we need on our own. It is a gift of God (Ephesians 2:8–9). But if we'll invest the "measure of faith" we've been given (Romans 12:3 NKJV), it will grow and fill the gaps in our soul. Here are some ways to do that:

1. ***Ask God to increase your faith.*** That's what the disciples did in Luke 17:5, and we can do the same. Without God's help, our faith remains small. So we echo the father's prayer in Mark 9:24: "I do believe; help me overcome my unbelief!"

2. ***Practice trusting God in little things.*** As we trust God in small things—even things we might not think He cares about—we see Him work and our "mustard seed" faith grows. As a result, we learn to believe Him for bigger things (see Mark 4:30–32).

3. ***Remember what God has done for you.*** We often lack faith in the present because we don't remember what God has done for us in the past. Recalling His goodness and sharing it with others not only strengthens our faith, it blesses God (Psalm 103:2–5).

4. ***Practice gratitude for your blessings.*** When we regularly express thanks to God, our heart enlarges along with our faith (Colossians 2:7). We see connections we didn't see before as we recognize God's work in our lives—both in the past as well as in the present.

5. ***Spend time in God's Word.*** Don't just *read* the Bible—allow it to dwell in you richly (Colossians 3:16). Memorize verses, meditate on passages, and allow the Holy Spirit to use Scripture to rewire your soul.

6. ***Invite Jesus into your daily life.*** Consciously place Him on the throne of your heart each morning. Ask the Holy Spirit to lead and guide you throughout the day (Psalm 32:8). Practice being interruptible and ready for random God assignments.

7. ***Ask the Holy Spirit to help you pray.*** As we allow the Spirit to shape our prayers to match God's concerns (see Romans 8:26–27), we not only pray according to God's will—our Spirit-led intercession opens the door for God's intervention.

8. ***Spend time with other believers.*** God promises to be with us when we worship together, encouraging our hearts with His presence. As we share what God is teaching us and learn to work together, everyone's faith grows (1 Thessalonians 5:11).

9. ***Seek out faith-building resources***. Listen to sermon podcasts. Read Christian books and biographies. Attend Bible studies and be faithful in church attendance. As we "listen to [Christ's] teaching, more understanding will be given" (Matthew 13:12 NLT).

10. ***Share your faith***. You don't have to have it all together or know a lot of theology, just share the story of what Jesus has done for you (Psalm 9:1). But allow God to write multiple testimonies in your life—for the fresher the bread, the more you want to share it!

Let your *roots* grow down into him,
and let your lives be built on him.
Then your *faith* will grow strong
in the truth you were taught,
and you will overflow with *thankfulness*.

Colossians 2:7 NLT

What Are You Building On?

If you grew up attending Sunday school like me, you've probably heard the story of the wise man and the foolish man who were both building a house. Jesus told the parable in Matthew 7:24–27 and Luke 6:46–49. The first man built his life on Jesus's words by putting them into practice. The second man heard Jesus's words but preferred to do his own thing.

The foolish man was so eager to finish his dwelling, he didn't think he needed a foundation. So he built directly "on sand" (Matthew 7:26). But sand is fickle. It shifts and moves. It's here today and gone tomorrow, especially when the wind and waves hit it just right.

The wise man, on the other hand, "dug down deep and laid the foundation on rock" (Luke 6:48). Proven and tested by time, rock is relatively permanent—stable and not easily moved. Important qualities to have when building a home, they are absolutely necessary when building a life.

Both men were able to build their structures. Both men appeared to create successful lives. But then the storms came—just as they do to every life—and revealed the true condition of each man's work.

While the house on the rock stood firm, the house on the sand didn't fare nearly as well. "The moment the torrent struck that house," Luke 6:49 tells us, "it collapsed and its destruction was complete."

So how can you and I know which type of foundation we're building on? I think it comes down to our response to storms.

Shallow faith rests on the shifting sand of circumstance. As a result, it's easily moved. When life is good, fair-weather Christians don't struggle to trust God. In fact, many are quick to express thanks for all His blessings. But when things go wrong—and especially when they stay wrong—that's when fault lines in their faith appear.

Deep faith, on the other hand, is anchored to the Rock, Jesus Christ. Because it isn't dependent on blessings, this kind of faith isn't shaken by storms. All-weather Christians aren't surprised by the difficulties of life, for they understand "the good man does not escape all troubles—he has them too. But the Lord helps him in each and every one" (Psalm 34:19 TLB).

I fear that most twenty-first-century believers, myself included, tend to be fair-weather Christians. Somewhere in the prosperity of the last fifty years, we've developed an entitlement mentality. We not only *want* life to be easy, we *expect* it. We not only *desire*

God's blessings, we subconsciously believe we *deserve* them. So when life goes sideways and God doesn't intervene, that's when many of us get our feelings hurt. We may even find ourselves blaming God for our problems or giving up on Him entirely as our trust erodes into distrust.

"I still believe in God," one woman told me, "but I don't believe He's a good Father anymore. My life has been one heartache after another, and none of my prayers have been answered."

My heart breaks for this woman. Her life has been terribly hard. But rather than allowing the struggle to push her closer to God, she's allowed it to push her away to the point of unbelief. And to me, that's the real tragedy. For in allowing the pain to become a wedge between her heart and God, she's not only cutting herself off from the love she needs but she's also shutting out the only One who can help her navigate the questions and disappointments of life.

The Problem of Evil

When our prayers go unanswered and our situations remain unchanged, we all tend to convict God on circumstantial evidence. If we don't consciously remember all the ways the Lord has helped us in the past, frustration over His apparent failure to act in the present can harden our doubt into unbelief.

Living in a world filled with evil and suffering only intensifies the struggle. The problem of evil has sparked debate and speculation (as well as anguished questions) ever since Adam and Eve left the Garden. Atheists and faith critics have made it the cornerstone of their arguments against God's existence. But even those who love Jesus can struggle with questions when they take an honest look at all the pain in the world. The circumstantial evidence can certainly seem damning.

While I don't pretend to have all the answers to this huge question, it's helped me to consider the following facts.

1. *We live in a fallen world.* When Adam and Eve chose to rebel against God, sin entered the world, leaving it

damaged and flawed. The results were sickness and death and every kind of evil.

2. *We have an enemy.* Because Satan hates God, he does everything possible to destroy the Father's relationship with His children. Like a slick, ambulance-chasing lawyer, Satan maligns both God and us to turn us against each other—for his name literally means "accuser."[4]
3. *We have a free will.* Because love requires an unforced response, God allows us to choose whether we'll follow Him. Unfortunately, free will also gives us the opportunity to sin—against ourselves, against each other, even against God. The devastating consequences can be seen all around us.
4. *God is sovereign.* While sin and free will are powerful forces, God rules above it all. John Piper defines God's sovereignty as His "right and power to do all that he decides to do."[5] Though He never causes evil, at times God allows it to accomplish His purposes.
5. *God is our Redeemer.* Though He might not interrupt or intervene, God promises to always redeem. He takes everything the enemy intends for evil—abuse, tragedy, even our own mistakes—and works it for our good and His glory.

When I consider all these factors, I believe the problem of evil and suffering actually vindicates God instead of vilifying Him. Of all the world's religions, only Judaism and Christianity seem to offer an adequate explanation for why evil exists (Genesis 3). And of those two, only Christianity offers a remedy.

Jesus.

God, in His infinite wisdom, chose instruments crafted by the devil to play key roles in the salvation of the world.

When "wicked men" put Jesus "to death by nailing him to the cross" (Acts 2:23), it appeared that *evil* had conquered.

When He was brutally beaten and disfigured to the point that "one would scarcely know he was a man" (Isaiah 52:14 NLT), it appeared that *suffering* had won.

But God turned the problem of evil and suffering upside down by allowing His Son to pour out His life for us. Bringing us back to right relationship with the Father and giving us the privilege of sharing "in [Christ's] sufferings in order that we may also share in his glory" (Romans 8:17).

Assuring once and for all that nothing we face is beyond the power of our great Redeemer God.

Trusting God When Life Disappoints

When God called me to full-time ministry at sixteen, He used a unique method to do it. Two years after the all-in surrender I describe in chapter 2, God asked my teenage heart to lay down any desire for a boyfriend. With His request came the grace to do it. I was able to attend youth camp that summer completely undistracted, with my heart and mind fully fixed on the Lord.

But one evening while praying at the altar, in my mind I saw one of the camp counselors preaching at a pulpit. I had always admired John Weaver's heart for Jesus, and I knew he was studying for the ministry. But I quickly dismissed the image—only to have it followed by a thought: *I wonder what it would be like to be a pastor's wife?*

Well, of course I immediately rebuked Satan and tried to get back to prayer. But the thought and the image kept pressing forward in my mind. Finally I had to tell the Lord, "If this is from You, I accept it. But if it isn't, please take it away."

The next evening after the service, God confirmed His call on my life by prompting John to tell me he thought I'd make a great missionary or pastor's wife. It all felt so surreal, especially when John and I started corresponding. And more so when he invited me to visit during Christmas break and took me out for a romantic dinner the final night.

In the flicker of candlelight, he handed me a small plaque. "I'd like this to be our verse," he said, reading the words of Romans 8:28: "And we know that God causes all things to work together for good to those who love God, to those who are called according to His purpose" (NASB).

I had no idea how much I would need that promise—or how soon. Four months later the man I thought I would marry told me he was dating another girl.

As it turned out, God hadn't given John a vision about me.

While I understand that my romantic disappointment may not measure up to some of the suffering other people have faced, it was certainly devastating to me at the time. After all, what do you do when life doesn't turn out the way you planned? When the hopes and dreams you've longed for come up empty? When the promises you thought were from God don't come to pass?

David must have wrestled with similar questions, especially when his dream job turned into a nightmare.

Asked to play harp for King Saul in 1 Samuel 16:15–19, young David must have leaped at the opportunity to see the monarchy at work. When the king's son Jonathan made a lifelong covenant of friendship by giving his robe to David, then added his "tunic, and even his sword, his bow and his belt" (18:1–4), the former shepherd must have marveled at the unfolding of God's plan—especially since, as one commentary points out, Jonathan's gifts may have signified his "recognition that David was to assume his place as successor to Saul."[6] His position in the palace must have seemed solidified when King Saul gave his daughter Michal to be David's wife (v. 27).

But everything quickly unraveled as the insecure king's jealousy emerged and grew to a murderous rage. "My father Saul is looking for a chance to kill you," Jonathan told David in 1 Samuel 19:2, and David's wife Michal had to warn him as well. "If you don't run for your life tonight, tomorrow you'll be killed" (v. 11).

It certainly wasn't the peaceful succession David had hoped for. Satan must have chortled at the chaos he'd caused. But God just smiled and continued to leverage the "testing of [David's] faith" (James 1:3). For He was using David's trials to build a man after His own heart.

A king that God could trust.

The Secret of Unshakeable Faith

When it comes down to it, unshakeable faith can't be fully formed unless it is shaken. Absolute trust in God appears only when everything else has been stripped away. Until we come to the end of ourselves, I don't think we can fully understand what it means to "have faith in God" (Mark 11:22).

It happened in David's life and the lives of all our Bible heroes. But it also happened to great Christians from the past.

As leader of the China Inland Mission in the late 1800s, J. Hudson Taylor carried a great burden for the mission and the Chinese people they served. During a particularly difficult period, he grieved the lack of power in their ministry, but it was his own sense of sin and failure that nearly crushed him.

Taylor dedicated himself to prayer and fasting, making resolutions to read the Word more diligently. But it wasn't until he received a letter from a friend that everything changed. Hudson's friend wrote of the fullness of life that is ours in Christ, and what it means to abide in the Vine (John 15:1–8). Hudson's spirit quickened as he read the letter, but he still felt too weak, too faithless to receive the message.

Then he read these words: "How to get faith strengthened? Not by striving after faith, but by resting on the Faithful One."[7] Immediately something opened up inside his heart, as Taylor remembered the promise of 2 Timothy 2:13: "If we believe not, yet he abideth faithful" (KJV).

It was such a relief! In relinquishing his striving, Hudson learned the secret of abiding. Surrendering his life completely so that the life of Jesus could be his.

Later, as he studied Mark 11:22, "Have faith in God," he discovered that the original Greek, *ekete pistin Theou,* meant to "have (or hold) the faithfulness of God."[8] Rather than trying to work up faith on his own, he simply needed to hold on to God's faithfulness.

Hudson Taylor was never the same after that day. Previously anxious and driven, he became "an object lesson in quietness. . . .

Whatever did not agitate the Savior, or ruffle His spirit was not to agitate him."[9]

What that weary missionary came to understand can change our lives as well. It isn't the amount of faith we work up that brings us peace, but trusting in the finished work of our faithful Savior. As we rely on the steadfast faithfulness of God, you and I acquire the unshakeable faith we need.

Prepared for Testing

I wrote much of this book during 2020 and 2021, while the world was reeling from a global pandemic. As of October 2021, the *New York Times* reported that more than 236.5 million people had been infected worldwide and that more than 4.8 million had died.[10] That first year, schools shut down, businesses shuttered, and many churches had to hold services online. With a contentious presidential election and all kinds of civil unrest, it's not an exaggeration to say that our nation, as well as the world, was in chaos. And then, just as we thought the crisis was ending, new variants of the virus brought a fresh wave of challenges.

By the time you hold this book, the pandemic may have ended and much of the strife settled down. I hope so! It's what we've been praying for during this frightening time. But if we come out of the crisis the same people as when we went in, I believe we will have missed a crucial chance to reinforce our foundations to match the "end-times" specifications given in God's Word.

"In the last days perilous times will come," Paul warns in 2 Timothy 3:1 (NKJV). It's an echo of Jesus's words in Mark 13:7–8:

> When you hear of wars and rumors of wars, do not be alarmed. Such things must happen, but the end is still to come. Nation will rise against nation, and kingdom against kingdom. There will be earthquakes in various places, and famines. These are the beginning of birth pains.

Though these somber warnings could cause more anxiety, we as God's people don't need to be afraid. We do, however, need to be prepared. With everything going on in the world, the second coming of Christ could be just around the corner. But even if it's not, we need to be ready, for none of us is promised tomorrow. Because we are all mortal, each of us is living in what could be called our "last days."

All of which makes this question of faith especially vital. In Luke 18:8, Jesus says something that has haunted me for years, especially during the writing of this book. "When the Son of Man returns, how many will he find on the earth who have faith?" (NLT).

Oh, how I want all of us to be counted among those faith-filled followers should we be living on earth when Christ returns. But that kind of faith requires a deep-rooted trust in God and an unwillingness to compromise if we're going to be like the extraordinary believers described in Hebrews 10:32–34:

> Remember those earlier days after you had received the light, when you endured in a great conflict full of suffering. Sometimes you were publicly exposed to insult and persecution; at other times you stood side by side with those who were so treated. You suffered along with those in prison and joyfully accepted the confiscation of your property, because you knew that you yourselves had better and lasting possessions.

Rather than giving in to fear and questioning God's goodness when persecution hit, these all-weather Christians refused to deny Christ. Though their faith literally cost them everything, they were unwilling to forfeit forever joy to gain a few years of earthly peace.

The Lord wants to help us forge this unapologetic and selfless kind of faith, but it doesn't happen overnight. It's shaped in the quiet moments we spend alone with Jesus. It's formed as the Holy Spirit speaks to us through God's Word. It's honed as we worship God and walk in fellowship with other believers. But its purity and strength are most fully developed when we choose to trust God during times of severe testing.

For God allows our lives to be shaken, according to Hebrews 12:27, so that "only unshakable things will remain" (NLT).

This global pandemic has shown us how little of life is actually under our control. When we embrace that uncomfortable truth, we discover a blessing: for at the end of ourselves, we find the all-sufficient power and grace of our God.

Trusting God No Matter What

The Lord definitely used my teenage breakup with John to build a deeper, more solid faith within me. But I have to confess, it was a confusing and painful time. Both Flesh Woman and Satan tried to insist that God was to blame for the situation. After all, He was the One who'd given me the vision and what felt like a promise that John and I would be in ministry together.

But in my spirit I knew that John had a free will. God wouldn't force him to marry me if he didn't want to. And if he chose someone else, it didn't mean I'd be disqualified for God's best.

Two weeks into the heartbreak, I knew I had to let go of the relationship. I wasn't giving up on the promise, but I needed to give it over to God. Clinging to the dream would make it difficult to fully live in the present. Worse, it would affect my relationship with Jesus.

"If it's Your will that we be together, Lord, it's up to You to make it happen," I prayed. "Please take this love I feel and help me see John as a friend."

As I surrendered my broken heart to Jesus, He enabled me to forgive John so completely that I found myself praying for him and his new girlfriend. It was a miracle like nothing I'd ever experienced before. God so radically changed my heart that I honestly wanted God's best for John—even if it meant we'd never be together.

I still marvel at God's work in my life during that time. The peace I felt was nothing short of supernatural. In some ways it exceeded the miracle that followed eighteen months later, when John finally came to his senses (smile) and realized I was the girl for him.

Fourteen months later, we were married.

But in case you think I've received all the things I've hoped for since then, rest assured that isn't true. There have been plenty of other heartbreaks in my life that didn't end so well. But as I've learned to let go and trust God, He's used every disappointment to wean me away from magic wands and easy answers so that together we could forge an increasingly unshakeable faith.

An Anchor for the Heart

Though I don't know what you've gone through, my friend, I do know it's impossible to live in this broken world without being sliced by its edges. It may be a daily battle for you to trust that God cares about your life. The foundation of your faith may seem so riddled with holes, you're not sure what you believe anymore.

But remember, faith isn't a feeling. It's an active decision to trust and retrust God, even when it feels like your world has been turned upside down. Rather than giving in to fear, you anchor your heart to the bedrock of His unfailing love and unchanging character. So that when the rains come down and the floods rise up, your life is grounded in four unshakeable truths.

1. *God is good.* His heart toward you is unchanging and perfect. Our good and all-wise Father loves to give "good and perfect gift[s]" (James 1:17). Which means you can trust Him to provide everything you need—at the right time and in the right way.
2. *God loves you.* His love is so vast, it "surpasses knowledge" (Ephesians 3:19). But don't let that keep you from receiving and believing it. For as you get "rooted and established in love" (v. 17), you will be "filled to the measure of all the fullness of God" (v. 19).
3. *You belong to Him.* You've been reconciled to the Father by the precious blood of Jesus (Colossians 1:20). You don't have to earn His favor; it's already been given to you.

As His beloved child, nothing can touch your life without His permission.

4. *God takes care of His own.* You can rely on God's provision, protection, and power. Though the "earth give way" and the "mountains fall into the heart of the sea," you don't have to worry—for God will be your "ever-present help in trouble" (Psalm 46:1–2).

So on those not-so-great days when your faith wavers and fear knocks at the door, take a moment and whisper these truths to your soul. *God is good. He loves me. I belong to Him, and He takes care of His own.*

Allow God's unchanging love and ever-present kindness to flow over your heart and fill in every hole. Hold tight to Jesus's hand and let Him strengthen and lead you. Declare "I trust You, Lord!" over your situation. Say it over and over until worry gives way to peace.

Though Satan may huff and puff and try to blow your faith down, remember who you belong to and refuse to be afraid.

For your house is built on the Rock of Ages. A firm and steady foundation that will never give way.

PART TWO

Letting Go

Father, I want to know Thee, but my cowardly heart fears to give up its toys. I cannot part with them without inward bleeding, and I do not try to hide from Thee the terror of the parting. I come trembling, but I do come. Please root from my heart all those things which I have cherished so long and which have become a very part of my living self, so that Thou mayest enter and dwell there without a rival. Then shalt Thou make the place of Thy feet glorious. Then shall my heart have no need of the sun to shine in it, for Thyself wilt be the light of it, and there shall be no night there. In Jesus' name. Amen.

A. W. Tozer[1]

Four

Laying Down Fig Leaves

They realized they were naked; so they sewed fig leaves together and made coverings for themselves.

Genesis 3:7

"Good morning, good morning, the little bird said!" That's the greeting my best friend, Christie Chaussee, used to wake me up with early each weekday to make sure I made it to drill-team practice on time.

Never a morning person, I resented the little bird but appreciated Christie's support. Though I wasn't as flexible or coordinated as she was, Christie stuck by me our entire sophomore year. Teaching me routines but also helping me stretch out each day with the goal of doing the all-important splits required by the elite squad.

My pom-pom skills were good, and I could match high kicks with the other Rockette wannabees. But for the life of me, I couldn't do the splits.

I tried. I really did. Practice makes perfect, they say. But it didn't in my case. Despite six months of regular stretching, the closest my legs came to the floor was five inches. Five stinking inches that refused to shrink no matter how hard I tried.

Ever the optimist, Christie would encourage me as she pressed down on my split each morning, adding her weight to my stretch. "You can do this, Joanna! I believe in you!" Finally, when I could bear it no more, she'd release her hold and invite me to help *her* stretch.

Standing against the gym wall, she'd extend her beautiful Barbie-doll leg high in the air and ask me to push it upward. "Higher," she'd say as I pushed her leg to her shoulder. "Higher, Joanna, higher," her chipper little-bird voice would demand as her leg went past her ear. Leaning forward to extend her already amazing stretch, she looked like a set of inverted scissor blades.

Have I mentioned that life isn't fair?

Gratefully, the coach didn't kick me off the squad. It's hard to discriminate against flexibility-impaired girls who work so hard. Plus, I'd discovered a way to hide my deficiency. At the end of each performance, when splits were required, I'd drop to the floor with the rest of the girls. Nestling huge, fluffy balls of plastic streamers against my hips to cover the gap, I'd smile really big and enjoy the applause. Weekend after weekend, game after game, all through my short-lived drill-team career, no one seemed the wiser.

To which I must say . . . thank God for pom-poms.

Naked and Afraid

We humans have become experts at covering our inadequacies. No wonder the beauty industry is a multibillion-dollar-a-year enterprise and Spanx are a girl's best friend. With help from a photo app, we can alter reality nearly any way we want—whiten our teeth, erase wrinkles, even shave off a few pounds. The results can be so good that experts have trouble knowing what's real and what's not.

This kind of subterfuge comes naturally, I suppose. From the moment sin entered the world, Adam and Eve tried to hide the fact that they'd messed up. Though they'd lived naked and unashamed before God and each other (Genesis 2:25), fully themselves without any pretense or fear, the moment they ate the forbidden fruit, everything changed. Their eyes were opened to their new reality apart from God, and it was terrifying.

Stripped bare by sin and overwhelmed with shame, Adam and Eve rushed to remedy the situation. "They sewed fig leaves together," Genesis 3:7 tells us, "and made coverings for themselves."

But covering their nakedness from each other wasn't enough to hide their condition from God. That evening the Father came calling, inviting the couple to walk with Him in the cool of the day. But instead of running toward His love, Adam and Eve ran away. They covered themselves with leaves and hid behind trees, hoping that the camouflage would keep God from finding out what they'd done (v. 8).

We all attempt similar cover-ups now and then. Rather than running to our Savior and confessing what we've done, we rush to sew together fig leaves. But to no avail, for despite our best effort our "sin is always before [us]" (Psalm 51:3).

Overwhelmed by shame, many of us settle for a kind of halfway life. Not fully trusting that God will forgive us—not fully believing, by His power, we can change—we step back from the One who can truly save us. Hiding in the shadows, we settle for a "form of godliness," yet never experience "the power thereof" (2 Timothy 3:5 KJV). Though we have hope of heaven one day, we're not confident there's help for us on earth.

Others of us shift into overdrive, defaulting to works and self-improvement plans. "This is fixable," we tell ourselves, hoping to piece together enough good behavior to cover our inadequacy. But no matter how hard we try to manufacture holiness, it takes only a single sin to shred our flimsy robes of self-made righteousness. Leaving us just as fearful, just as ashamed as we were in the first place.

Still others default to the blame game like Adam and Eve did. Rather than repenting and admitting our sin when God points it out, we race to defend ourselves. Attempting to deflect responsibility, we point the finger at someone else.

Like Eve, who blamed the serpent who tempted her (Genesis 3:13): *The devil made me do it!*

Or like Adam, who not only blamed his wife for the forbidden snack but accused God as well (v. 12): *It was the woman You gave me!*

Fig leaves. That's what all of these responses are—crude attempts to deflect blame and hide shame. Sadly, we often do anything but actually confess what we've done to the Lord. Which is heartbreaking when you think about it.

Though they'd spent so much time with God in the Garden, Adam and Eve didn't really know Him. Despite His lavish provision and the sweet communion they'd shared, they didn't understand the depth of God's love. As a result, they didn't trust Him. That distrust not only led to sin, it also caused them to miss the matchless grace that flows to everyone who humbles themselves before God and truly repents.

> Who is a God like you,
> who pardons sin and forgives the transgression
> of the remnant of his inheritance?
> You do not stay angry forever
> but delight to show mercy.
> You will again have compassion on us;
> you will tread our sins underfoot
> and hurl all our iniquities into the depths of the sea.
> (Micah 7:18–19)

As we confess our sins, 1 John 1:9 tells us that God will not only "forgive us our sins" but will also "cleanse us from all unrighteousness" (ESV). Rather than hiding in the shadows or behind flimsy facades, we'll be able to live in the light "as he is in the light" (v. 7).

Fully known and fully loved.

With nothing to prove and nothing to hide.

When Insecurity Meets Ministry

When God called me to ministry at sixteen, I wanted to be used by Jesus. But the call of God can be fancy food for the flesh. Without realizing it, a desire for significance can grow up around a pure desire to serve Him, choking out the life and ministry God intends us to have.

While the Flesh Woman in some people might lean toward darker things, my flesh has always craved people's approval. My constant need for affirmation often led to an unhealthy "fear of man" (Proverbs 29:25) that eclipsed my fear of God.

It was as though I walked around with an empty picture frame, holding it up to faces I longed to impress. Treating the frame like a mirror, I'd look into their eyes to find my identity. If they smiled and received me, I was okay—even great. But if they seemed detached or disinterested, it wasn't because they had a bad day. It was because I was deficient, unworthy of their attention or love. So I'd work harder and serve longer, trying to do whatever it took to change their opinion of me.

Shape-shifting to meet the situation, my ego sewed fig leaves and donned costumes—anything to gain acceptance and fit in. It wasn't a conscious hypocrisy, but a deep-rooted insecurity that drove me to gain approval no matter the cost.

That tendency followed me into ministry. Though there was a purity to my passion, it was tinged with a need to do something impressive for God. After all, that's what youth camp speakers told us would happen if we gave our lives fully to Jesus. "*God has incredible plans for your life. He wants to use you to change the world!*"

It was inspiring stuff for a Jesus-hearted girl like me. But deadly and dangerous for my flesh-driven soul.

When I met and married John, I was certain that together we would do big things for Jesus—really, really big things! We'd have a thousand kids in the youth group at our little church. Never mind the high school in our small town only had 250 teenagers—we'd bus them in!

Each Wednesday night I'd set up thirty or forty chairs in preparation for the influx of souls. But when it came time to start, it wasn't unusual to have twenty-five or thirty empty ones. I'll never forget the night we showed up for youth service to find three people in attendance—John, myself, and the pastor's kid. And from the look on his face, you could tell he didn't want to be there.

Looking back, I'm glad that God didn't give my Flesh Woman what she so desperately craved. For in confounding my need for success and refusing to reward my drivenness, God took the faulty mirror I'd been looking to for identity and the fig leaves I'd clumsily crafted to prop up my worth. With a loving yet firm hand, He removed them so I could focus my heart only on Him.

I wish I could say that I've lived facade-free ever since, but that wouldn't be true. I still find myself turning to fig-leaf coping mechanisms at times. However, I'm learning to recognize them quickly. Rather than trying to cover my inadequacies, I'm learning to take them to Jesus. For His love "covers a multitude of sins" (1 Peter 4:8 ESV).

Clothed in the Lord's Strength

For over a month, the army of Israel had been frozen in terror by the taunts of a single Philistine warrior named Goliath. Standing over nine feet tall, the massive mountain of a man had spewed abuse for forty days (see 1 Samuel 17:1–16).

"Choose a man and have him come down to me," the giant bellowed, sparking terror in the hearts of Israel's mighty men. "If he is able to fight and kill me, we will become your subjects; but if I overcome him and kill him, you will become our subjects" (vv. 8–9).

King Saul's offer of great wealth and his daughter's hand in marriage hadn't been enough to persuade Israel's finest to go down and fight the giant. Not even the promise of lifetime tax exemption could persuade them to volunteer (v. 25).

So when a young shepherd boy came along offering to fight Goliath, it must have been downright embarrassing. Perhaps that's why David's oldest brother lashed out with contempt. "Why have you come down here?" Eliab asked with a sneer. "And with whom did you leave those few sheep in the desert?" Adding accusation to insult, he told David, "I know how conceited you are and how

IDENTIFYING FIG LEAVES

What do you turn to when you're feeling undone and uncertain, a bit naked and ashamed? Fig leaves can take a lot of forms. Here are a few I've identified in my life and seen in the lives of others:

- *Props*. We use crutches like talents or possessions (or a really handsome husband like mine!) to build ourselves up so that we feel important and unique.
- *Posturing*. We adopt certain behaviors, such as dropping names or seeking the favor of people with more clout than us, hoping to impress others and increase our worth.
- *Control*. Attempting to shape reality to our liking, we secretly believe that if people do what we want them to do, everything will be all right.
- *Self-protection*. Constantly on guard, we build walls around our hearts to keep from being hurt and erect invisible force fields to keep people out.
- *Projecting*. Looking for approval, we project a certain image, hoping to draw people to our glow. But in all the shape-shifting, we forget who we are.
- *Invisibility*. Our natural reserve morphs into timidity and a deep fear of being noticed, so we live in the shadows rather than the full light of day.
- *Escapism*. To avoid reality, we turn to mindless entertainment, numbing substances, even mental fantasies. But habitual hiding places can turn into life-controlling behaviors.
- *Anger*. When we feel defensive, we go on the offensive. Quick to justify ourselves, we point out the deficiencies of others in hopes of concealing our own.
- *Victimhood*. Allowing pain from the past to dictate our present, we hide behind the wrongs we've suffered rather than doing the work required to live a different life.
- *Ego-building*. Believing that self-esteem will fill the emptiness in our souls, we focus on self-love and self-care, only to find ourselves even more needy.

Cursed is the man who trusts in man
And makes flesh his *strength*.

Jeremiah 17:5 NKJV

wicked your heart is; you came down only to watch the battle" (v. 28).

Ridicule and cynicism. Another set of fig leaves humans try to hide behind when they feel threatened or inadequate. Especially when someone else's faith is bigger than their own.

When Eliab and the army of Israel looked at Goliath, they saw a giant too big to hit. David, on the other hand, saw a giant too big to miss.[1] For he knew he would not fight alone—God would be with him.

Hearing that David was willing to fight Goliath, King Saul put his custom-made armor on the young man (v. 38). But the armor didn't fit. To David it felt clunky and cumbersome.

"I cannot go in these," he told the king in 1 Samuel 17:39, but David was still determined to fight. He'd experienced the enabling power of God to kill a bear and a lion when they attacked his father's sheep (v. 37). Surely this "uncircumcised Philistine" (v. 36) wouldn't be an obstacle. With God-confidence in his heart and five smooth stones in his pocket, David picked up his sling and headed for the battlefield (v. 40).

When Goliath saw the boy coming toward him to fight, he was furious and roared curses (v. 43). But David wasn't intimidated, and he didn't back down. Because he trusted God was with him, the boy ran to the giant with a roar of his own.

"The battle is the Lord's, and he will give all of you into our hands," David shouted as he readied his sling (v. 47).

Imagine the next few moments with me.

Goliath lumbering toward David, spitting and frothing and hurling abuse.

David striding toward Goliath, calm and collected and hurling a stone.

Shock and disbelief must have marked both men's faces as the rock connected with Goliath's head and he started to fall (v. 49). But David quickly regained his composure and ran toward the comatose giant, removing his head with Goliath's own sword.

Seeing that "their hero was dead" (v. 51), the Philistines began a frantic retreat. Emboldened by David's courage, the Israelite army gave chase (v. 52), and the enemy of God was completely defeated. Put to flight by a young man who refused to wear armored fig leaves and trusted in the power of God instead.

The Problem with Fig Leaves

Online sources say there are more than seven hundred named varieties of fig trees in the world.[2] Figuratively speaking, there must be far more types of fig leaves. For even the good things of life can be used to cover our inadequacies or prop up our worth. Not trusting our acceptance in Christ, many of us clutch at *anything* we think might provide a camouflage and keep us from being fully known or seen—even by ourselves.

The problem with fig leaves, as Adam and Eve found out, is that they make lousy coverings. Researching, I discovered interesting facts about certain fig species:

- *Fig leaves are uncomfortable.* Rather than the smooth surface you find on most leaves, a fig leaf is rough and hairy.[3]
- *Fig leaves can be poisonous.* Fig sap contains chemicals that can cause a blistering rash in some people.[4]
- *Fig leaves are unreliable.* Like most leaves, they are dependent on the tree for moisture, so they wither and die when separated from it.[5]

None of these are great qualities when you need something to cover your nakedness. And the same thing applies to the spiritual fig leaves we often use to disguise our sin.

Just ask our giant slayer. Though David started out well—wanting only what God wanted and willing to wait until God gave it—once he got older and more powerful, David took matters into his own hands. After partaking of the forbidden and having sex with another man's wife, he went so far as to use murder to cover his indiscretion.

We'll look at that episode in a later chapter. But for now let's just say it was a miserable time as the poison of sin began to eat at David's soul. Here's how he describes it in Psalm 32:3–4 (NLT):

> When I refused to confess my sin,
> my body wasted away,
> and I groaned all day long.
> Day and night your hand of discipline was heavy on me.

It wasn't until David got honest with God that he was able to experience relief. In verse 5, he writes,

> Finally, I confessed all my sins to you
> and stopped trying to hide my guilt.
> I said to myself, "I will confess my rebellion to the LORD."
> And you forgave me! All my guilt is gone. (NLT)

Laid bare by repentance, David was washed clean by love. Healed by the balm of God's mercy.

The same freedom can be ours as well. When the Lord's "hand of discipline" comes upon you, don't resist it. When God points out sin in your life, don't ignore your iniquity or try to deflect blame. Instead, agree with the diagnosis—confess and repent. Then trust your loving Savior to bring the cure.

For God only reveals so He can heal.

Getting Real before God

The world is so noisy right now, filled with voices telling us what we should do, who we should be, and how we should live. If you're looking for fig leaves to make you feel significant, you can find them just about anywhere.

But rather than making us feel better about ourselves, the abundance of options only seems to intensify our lack. With an estimated 87,000-plus drink combinations available at Starbucks and more than 2.2 million iPhone apps to keep us entertained,[6] you'd think that Americans would be the happiest people on earth. But we're not.

According to the 2019 World Happiness Report, the United States dropped in the happiness ranking of countries to the nineteenth spot. As online usage soared, the study showed that markers of well-being such as personal relationships, adequate sleep, and happiness had plummeted.[7] As Barry Schwartz puts it, "We get what we say we want, only to discover that what we want doesn't satisfy us to the degree that we expect."[8] Because more isn't necessarily more. Especially when it comes to fig leaves.

Do you remember Hans Christian Andersen's fable "The Emperor's New Clothes"? The story has been around nearly two hundred years, but it seems especially relevant in today's culture of excess and the crazy things people do in search of meaning and worth:

> Many years ago there was an Emperor so exceedingly fond of new clothes that he spent all his money on being well dressed. . . .
>
> Every day many strangers came to town, and among them one day came two swindlers. They let it be known they were weavers, and they said they could weave the most magnificent fabrics imaginable. Not only were their colors and patterns uncommonly fine, but clothes made of this cloth had a wonderful way of becoming invisible to anyone who was unfit for his office, or who was unusually stupid.
>
> "Those would be just the clothes for me," thought the Emperor. "If I wore them I would be able to discover which men in my empire are unfit for their posts. And I could tell the wise men from the fools. Yes, I certainly must get some of the stuff woven for me right away." He paid the two swindlers a large sum of money to start work at once.[9]

For several weeks, the two strangers pretended to weave furiously. But instead of using the fine silk and golden thread that had been supplied, they tucked the expensive items into their traveling bags. When the emperor sent his advisers to check on how the work was progressing, none would admit they couldn't see anything on the looms. Afraid of losing their positions, they took back glowing reports of the fabric's beauty, repeating details they'd been told by the swindlers.

With the new suit finished in time for a grand procession through town, the emperor eagerly disrobed so that the so-called tailors could put the beautiful garments on him. He was momentarily unsettled when he realized he couldn't see his new clothes, but pushing away his concern, he proudly walked out to meet the waiting crowd. Everyone oohed and aahed admiringly, for no one wanted to admit they couldn't see their leader's fine clothing and be considered a fool.

The new costume seemed an overwhelming success. But then, from the back of the crowd, came the voice of a child: "But he hasn't got anything on." The boy's father tried to hush him, but his words spread through the crowd until they were voiced by all: "But he hasn't got anything on!"[10]

What kind of fig leaves have you been wearing? If you're trusting in anything less than the righteousness supplied by Jesus and the deep-rooted identity that the love of God provides, you're not only being swindled, you're leaving yourself terribly exposed.

Clothed in Christ

Laodicea was a thriving metropolis in New Testament times. Known as a banking center,[11] it was famous for its garment industry and medical resources.[12] The city was so rich that when it was hit by a major earthquake in AD 60, city leaders turned down Rome's offer of help and reconstructed the city themselves.[13] Inscriptions on many of the rebuilt structures read, "Out of our own resources."[14]

The Laodiceans were a self-sufficient people and proud of it. So much so, Jesus had to rebuke the local church in Revelation 3:17–18, exposing the sin and pride which hid beneath their healthy appearance:

> You say, "I am rich; I have acquired wealth and do not need a thing." But you do not realize that you are wretched, pitiful, poor, blind and naked. I counsel you to buy from me gold refined in the fire, so you can become rich; and white clothes to wear, so you can cover your shameful nakedness; and salve to put on your eyes, so you can see.

Most of us have heard sermons about the Laodicean church and their "lukewarm" condition (vv. 15–16). Without a water source of its own, according to Warren Wiersbe's commentary, the city may have piped hot water from nearby Hierapolis and cold water from Sardis, creating the tepid water Jesus threatened to spit out of His mouth (v. 16).[15] But there's more fascinating symbolism in this passage of Scripture.

Though the Laodiceans gloried in their position, saying, "I am rich . . . and do not need a thing," Jesus diagnosed their true condition as "wretched, pitiful, poor, blind and naked" (v. 17).

To a city of merchants known for their premier banking system, Jesus said, "Buy from me gold refined in the fire, so you can become rich" (v. 18).

Though they lived in a region known for producing garments of the finest black wool,[16] He instructed them to buy "white clothes to wear, so you can cover your shameful nakedness" (v. 18).

To innovators who'd created an eye ointment used around the known world, He counseled, "Buy from me . . . salve to put on your eyes, so you can see" (v. 18).

Everything the Laodiceans had put their trust in was actually harming them, Jesus pointed out. Worse, their pride was making them spiritually blind.

You're naked, My children, He told them. *You're trusting in the see-through robes of your own righteousness. Blinded by your blessings, you're being led astray by the world.*

But there was a healing purpose behind the harshness of Christ's rebuke—just as there is when He points out sin in our lives. For trusting in the fig leaves of our righteousness won't bring us closer to Jesus. Instead, it will stand in the way.

The words that follow Jesus's warning to the Laodicean church hold such love and longing, I believe He wants to speak them to His people today. "Behold, I stand at the door and knock," Jesus says in Revelation 3:20. "If anyone hears my voice and opens the door, I will come in to him and eat with him, and he with me" (ESV).

Do you hear that? Though you and I may have strayed from our first love, lured away by the glittering things of this world, we are invited back to intimate fellowship with our Savior and a life lived in the beauty of His presence.

If we'll respond to the invitation of Jesus—laying down our fig leaves and trusting Him for everything we need—He promises to clothe us in "garments of salvation" and give us a beautiful "robe of his righteousness" to wear (Isaiah 61:10).

Wrapped in Christ's love and cloaked in His likeness, together with Him we'll walk unashamed in this world. Filled with the joy and peace that comes from living in His presence.

No longer hiding behind fig leaves.

No longer naked, wretched, and cold.

Five

Not-So-Great Expectations

> My soul, wait silently for God alone,
> For my expectation is from Him.
> Psalm 62:5 NKJV

The Oregon night lay thick above me, studded with diamonds dancing amid the dark pines. Though I stood at a distance, I could feel the bonfire's heat as orange-red flames sent sparks upward. Shadowy shapes moved around me, drifting slowly toward the fire then back again, but I barely noticed. All my attention centered on one thing. The crumpled piece of paper I held in my hand.

Victory Circle—that's what they'd called the event during morning announcements. A unique and memorable way to end a week of kids' camp, they'd said. A way to nail down what God had been speaking to young hearts. "Get a piece of paper and write down something you need to commit to the Lord, then toss it in the fire at Victory Circle after the service tonight," they'd told the campers, inviting those of us who served as counselors to participate as well.

My cheeks flushed with the fire's heat but also with the memory of the one-sided conversation I'd had with the Lord that morning as I walked back to the cabin after worship.

"Oh, Jesus, it's so wonderful to be in right relationship with you," I'd whispered. "I can't think of anything I need to surrender tonight. But if there is, please let me know."

It was a dangerous but glorious prayer. For out of that invitation to examine my heart would come an encounter with God that would transform my life—and my marriage—forever.

As I opened my Bible for quiet time later that afternoon, I was shocked to find a piece of paper listing all the ways my husband needed to change. All the reasons our ministry wasn't thriving. All the ways he'd let me down. Though I remembered writing the list, I was certain I'd thrown it away.

Give it to Me, Joanna. The words came soft and low to my spirit as I stood by the fire that night. But objections flooded my mind as my eyes filled with tears. How could I let go of what felt like legitimate concerns? What if John never changed?

I had a decision to make. Would I hold on to my expectations? Or would I entrust my husband—and myself—to God alone?

Dangerous Expectations

In some ways, expectations are a necessary part of life. As students we need to know what the teacher requires to get a good grade. As drivers we need to know the traffic rules to keep ourselves and others safe. As employees we need to know what time to show up for our job and how to do the work. Healthy expectations form the basis of society and give shape to useful and happy lives.

But less healthy types of expectations often lay below the surface of our hearts, causing us to act and overreact when people don't do things our way. Formed by our past experiences, temperament, family of origin, and the culture we live in, expectations can be so ingrained that we rarely recognize them. Instead we assume that everyone sees life the way we do. That they think like us, share our priorities, and navigate life's difficulties as we do.

It's a rude awakening when we discover they don't.

"We all carry around expectations about how the world should work, whether we realize it or not," author Melissa Camara Wilkins writes. "When reality smacks our expectations upside the head, we have to deal with not just the annoying reality, but also with our unmet expectations."[1]

In a sense, Wilkins concludes, "Expectations mean we suffer twice."[2]

Preach, sister. Preach.

When I entered marriage and ministry at nineteen, I arrived with a boatload of expectations. Because John and I shared the same values and had so much in common, I was certain we were bound for marital bliss. Because we both loved Jesus and had natural giftings, I expected our ministry to be a wild success. Filled with affirmation. Approval. Applause. Everything my Flesh Woman so desperately craved.

When those expectations weren't fulfilled, naturally I set out to change my husband.

If he would just do this . . .

If he would stop doing that . . .

If he would be more like that person, then we could have that kind of success . . .

But instead of appreciating my help, God clearly told me, *Get your hands off My man, Joanna. Changing John isn't your job. It's Mine.*

Looking back, I can see that God frustrated my expectations for the simple reason that He wanted to get His hands on me. For it turns out that God's more interested in building His kingdom *in us* than He is in building His kingdom *through us.*

That night beside the fire, the Holy Spirit whispered to my heart: *Stop praying, "Lord change my husband," and start praying, "Lord, change me."*

It remains one of the most important instructions that I've ever received. I tremble to think of the beautiful marriage—the beautiful life—I almost missed.

Had God not demanded my list of grievances and had I not surrendered it to Him, John and I would have ended up as married singles. Appearing united on the outside, but, on the inside, living as far apart as two people could be.

I'm so grateful God didn't let us settle for that.

As I began to let go of my expectations, God began to heal my marriage. But He did a deep work in my heart as well, giving me a revelation of His grace and love that shattered several false beliefs that had always kept me bound.

The belief that I had to be successful in order to be valuable.

The belief that God required perfection, so I'd better not mess it up.

And most damaging of all, the unconscious yet ever-present belief that I had to earn God's favor to experience His love.

The Yardstick of Expectations

Remember the wooden yardsticks they used to hand out at hardware stores and state fairs to advertise businesses? People don't use them much anymore, except maybe to measure fabric or to cut a straight line.

In olden days, teachers often used them to keep order in the classroom. Useful for pointing out important facts on a chalkboard, they also came in handy when students whispered during class. One sharp rap on the edge of a desk would bring everyone to attention. A big infraction like cheating might involve a visit to the principal's office and—whack!—a stinging reminder that lingered the rest of the day.

In my life, the yardstick has been a constant reminder of my inadequacy and failure to measure up. Rather than waiting for a teacher or principal to administer punishment, I'm quite adept at doing it myself.

"Bad me, bad me, terrible me," I cry, whacking myself with my own expectations. I know what I ought to be, and I'm fully aware of what I'm not.

In the past, I used to project the resulting self-hatred onto God, assuming He was as disappointed in me as I was. Rather than viewing Him as a loving Father, I saw Him as a distant taskmaster, patrolling the classroom of my life. Waiting for me to break a rule or fail a test—then whack! Down would come the yardstick of His displeasure.

I lived by a distorted version of Philippians 2:12, which says to "work out your salvation with fear and trembling." But basing my salvation on performance rather than on the sufficiency of Christ's work meant that I missed the best part of the gospel. For the call to "work out your salvation" wasn't meant to be done alone. In the very next verse we're told, "For it is God who works in you to will and to act in order to fulfill his good purpose" (v. 13).

God works it *in*, and we work it *out*. Now that's what I call good news!

But I nearly missed it. I was so busy rating and berating my performance that I never trusted God to do His transforming work in me. Like the foolish Galatians I tried to finish "by [my] own human effort," what had started by the Spirit (Galatians 3:3 NLT). Which of course, was an exercise in frustration.

My Flesh Woman not only used the yardstick to punish my infractions. She also used it to see how well I measured up against others: who was the smartest, the prettiest, the most talented, the most godly, the most successful.

But that comparison turned out to be a double-edged sword. When measuring myself against others, I'd feel either inordinately proud or paralyzingly inept. Either way, I'd end up on the wrong end of the yardstick—punishing myself for my failures or, if I happened to excel, punishing myself for my pride.

Perhaps it was this kind of inner torment that sent a well-meaning man running to Jesus in Mark 10:17–22. Ironically, he's commonly known as the rich young "ruler."

"Good teacher . . . what must I do to inherit eternal life?" the man said as he fell at Jesus's feet (v. 17). Unlike other religious people who pretended to be interested in Jesus but secretly wanted to trap Him in His words, this man sincerely wanted to be right with God. Though he'd lived by the yardstick all his life, trying to keep all the commandments that had been drilled into him since childhood (vv. 19–20), he instinctively knew his good works weren't enough.

So he came to Jesus. And, the Bible tells us, "Jesus looked at him and loved him" (v. 21).

I don't know about you, but that blesses me. It's a comfort to know that Jesus looks beyond our messy motives and sees the intention of our hearts. He understands that we're a "bundle of paradoxes" as Brennan Manning puts it,[3] wanting God one minute but ignoring Him the next. Jesus was "tempted in every way, just as we are," Hebrews 4:15 reminds us. He understands the weary wrestling we endure in our flesh.

But because Jesus loves us, He refuses to coddle us. Rather than applauding the young man's devotion, giving him a high five and a bunch of gold stars, Jesus pointed to the one thing the young man loved more than he loved God: his wealth and possessions. "One thing you lack," Jesus told him in Mark 10:21. "Go, sell everything you have and give to the poor. . . . Then come, follow me."

"At this the man's face fell," verse 22 says. "He went away sad, because he had great wealth."

And surprisingly, Jesus let him go. He didn't call after him or send His disciples to negotiate a compromise. Instead, He allowed this very influential person to walk away.

Why? Because Jesus knows that trusting in our own righteousness will never bring us closer to Him. I think that's why Jesus's teaching often ups the ante on biblical requirements, increasing His demands on our lives in order to bring us to surrender and the point of trusting only in Him (Matthew 5:27–48).

Not just for our salvation—but for our transformation as well.

Life by the Yardstick

It started early in our ministry. I would wake up with a cloud of impending doom hanging over my head. Sometimes the heaviness was clearly linked to a mistake I'd made or a responsibility I'd allowed to slip through the cracks. But most of the time I couldn't pinpoint the source. Instead, the emotional cloud just hung there, thick with foreboding, issuing a general accusation of failure in every part of my life. Even now I struggle to remember a moment of pure joy during that time.

Looking back, I realize the darkness was formed by the shadow of my yardstick. Rather than living under grace, I was trying to live under "the law" (Romans 8:2). But while God's law was intended to show humanity *how* to live, it was and still is powerless to help us do it. That's why Jesus had to come (v. 3).

Trying and failing to fulfill the law's requirements left me feeling like the "wretched man" Paul describes in Romans 7:24. Though I knew what I was supposed to do, I felt incapable of doing it (vv. 18–20).

No matter how hard I tried, my goodest good was never good enough.

But I wasn't the only one who suffered from my yardstick. You can only take so much self-inflicted guilt before you start inflicting it on those around you. Though I tried to be gracious to people outside my home, my family often felt the yardstick of my expectations, especially during those early years.

John needed to be successful so I could be successful. *How do you do it all, Joanna? What a wonderful ministry you guys have!*

My children needed to be good so I could look good. *What an amazing mother you are! Your children are so well-behaved.*

I'm not sure how yardstick expectations show up in your life, but I assure you, they are there. You can find them in the way you respond to these unfinished sentences:

My husband should . . .
My children need to . . .
My friends ought to . . .
My life must be . . .
I can't be happy until . . .

Your answers to these sentences may seem logical and your needs legitimate, but if you believe your happiness lies in their fulfillment, you're looking in the wrong place. Jeremiah 17:5 gives us a solemn warning:

> Cursed are those who put their trust in mere humans,
> who rely on human strength
> and turn their hearts away from the LORD. (NLT)

For it's impossible to put your hope in God if you've already placed it in people.

Laying Down Expectations

As the youngest in his family, David had reason to expect his father would include him in the lineup of sons when Samuel came to anoint the next king. But his father apparently dismissed him as a candidate and left him out in the fields (1 Samuel 16:1–13).

Later, when King Saul's initial favor turned to hatred, David had reason to expect his father-in-law would act honorably. Instead, Saul sought to take his life (chap. 19).

And even later, when David brought back the ark of the covenant to Jerusalem (2 Samuel 6:12–22), he had reason to expect that his wife, Michal, would rejoice at his side. Instead, she ridiculed and despised David's "undignified" worship (v. 20).

But rather than focusing on these and other injustices that marked his life, David took his disappointment to God, something we see him do over and over in the Psalms. Rather than looking to people for affirmation and expecting life to treat him well, David looked to the Lord:

> My soul, wait silently for God alone,
> For my *expectation* is from Him. (Psalm 62:5 NKJV, emphasis mine)

King David wrote these words during a difficult period in his reign. Surrounded by conspirators who wanted to undermine his

LETTING GO OF EXPECTATIONS

Where to begin when letting go of expectations? Melissa Camara Wilkins offers some great places to start. Here's my adaptation of her checklist:

Expectation #1: Other people will think true things about you. Everyone gets to choose their own thoughts, and sometimes people are going to think things about you that just aren't true.

Expectation #2: Others will make the same decisions you would. People will make decisions you don't agree with or even understand. Expecting the world to always work a certain way leads to a cycle of outrage and despair.

Expectation #3: You can't relate to someone if you disagree with them. Consider that you both want to be known and loved. You're both afraid sometimes. Look past the differences and you may find common ground.

Expectation #4: Things will always go your way. Some things may turn out great, but others won't. The more you let go of outcomes, the more you can be present for what is happening in your life.

Expectation #5: Things will never go your way. It's better to expect the worst . . . right? Not really. You're still wasting energy on unhelpful expectations, and you're blocking hope and imagination at the same time.

Expectation #6: Changing things on the outside will fix problems on the inside. Changing your circumstances without changing your heart is just applying a Band-Aid. Expecting people to always meet your needs will leave you frustrated, not fulfilled.

Expectation #7: Eventually you will arrive. Your life is not a Google Maps route. At no point will you "arrive at your destination." Don't let expectations about "getting there" steal your joy in being here and now.[4]

It is better to *trust* in the LORD
than to put confidence in man.

Psalm 118:8 KJV

rule, he had the power to curb the rebellion and destroy the traitors. Instead, David trusted God to work it out.

How can we find such humble patience? It starts by letting go of the desire to control. Rather than demanding a certain outcome, we've got to trust God's ability to make things right in His way and in His time. We've got to place our hope—our "expectation"—in God alone.

The Hebrew word for "expectation" in Psalm 62:5 is *tiqvah*. Though it can also mean "hope," the literal translation of the word is "cord (as an attachment)."[5]

It's the same word used in Joshua 2:21 to describe the "scarlet cord" Rahab the harlot hung out her window after hiding the Jewish spies. "Attaching" her hope to the God they served, she said, "I know that the Lord has given you this land. . . . For the Lord your God is God in heaven above and on the earth below" (Joshua 2:9–11).

Because Rahab put her hope and expectation—her *tiqvah*—in God, she and her family were saved when the walls of Jericho fell. According to Matthew 1:5 she became part of the lineage of Jesus. Her faith and obedience were so remarkable that Rahab is included in the Bible's Hall of Faith (Hebrews 11:31).

Which leads to a question we all must answer: *Where have I placed my hope, and to whom have I attached my expectation?*

I want to be a woman who hopes in God alone.

But to be honest, hope, like faith, has always been a little hard for me to grasp. In today's vernacular, hope seems little more than a wish and a prayer. However, I recently heard a great definition: "Hope is a joyful expectation of something good."

Note the element of trust in that definition. So often we come to God with a list of desired outcomes that we have labeled "good." But, as we've seen, our understanding is limited and our label-maker perception is often wrong. Only God knows what is best in a situation. If we'll submit our requests to Him and then allow Him to have His way, we can joyfully expect that God will bring about what is truly good.

But we need to do the same thing with people. For when we surrender our expectations of others—loving them as they are, not as we want them to be—we make room for the grace of God to work in their hearts just as He's working in our own.

Releasing Others from Expectations

Ruth Bell Graham, wife of the famous evangelist Billy Graham, is often quoted as saying, "It's my job to love and respect Billy. It's God's job to make him good."[6]

That's wise advice for us all. What if we made it a habit to *accept* people rather than *expect* them to be what we want them to be? What if we *graced* them rather than *shamed* them? What if we simply loved people and left their transformation up to God?

My mother graced me like that in so many ways, but one of them proved especially powerful. For a large chunk of my adulthood, I was a terrible housekeeper. But rather than shaking her head at the condition of my home, pointing out that she'd raised me better than that, my mother consistently came alongside me and asked how she could help.

She didn't take over, and she never made me feel as though she was disappointed (though she must have been now and then). Instead, she accepted me where I was. Listening as I shared my struggle to balance ministry and two toddlers. Praying for me when I got discouraged. Offering advice only when asked.

Though it's taken years to get victory over the domestic side of my life, never once did my mother make me feel like a failure. Instead, her love and acceptance created a space of grace where there was room to become the woman God wanted me to be.

Unfortunately, many women haven't had that kind of loving support. Their mothers are professional travel agents—constantly sending them on guilt trips. But while guilt can be a powerful motivator in the short term, it rarely brings true and lasting change.

I find this important to remember when I'm tempted to organize guilt trips for myself or others. As Romans 2:4 reminds us, it is "the kindness of God" that "leads . . . to repentance" (NASB). When we attempt to play the Holy Spirit, our meddling can interrupt what God is doing in people's lives. Rather than hearing the life-giving correction of the Spirit, they hear only condemnation and rejection—from us, and by proxy, from God. As a result, they may rebel and withdraw, building walls in their heart against us, but also against God.

Now that doesn't mean there won't be times when we need to say something about what we observe in another person's life. "If another believer is overcome by some sin," Galatians 6:1 says, "you who are godly should gently and humbly help that person back onto the right path" (NLT). But note that the spirit in which we speak makes all the difference. Are we approaching the situation in gentleness and humility? Or do we come with an agenda and a prideful need to set the other person straight?

"Discernment is God's call to intercession, never to fault finding," Oswald Chambers writes.[7] I think my parenting would have been much more effective had I spent more time on my knees praying for my children rather than constantly giving correction and advice. For the Holy Spirit wants to speak directly to our children so that they, too, learn to make God their "only expectation."

Hanging a scarlet *tiqvah* out the window of their hearts as they learn to trust fully in Him.

Releasing Ourselves from Expectations

As a pastor's wife I'm often asked how I handle other people's expectations. To be honest, it's my own expectations that trouble me most.

I know what kind of pastor's wife I feel called to be. I know the dedication it involves. But all of my *knowing* has never facilitated my *growing*. In fact, most of the time it's only hindered it.

As a young adult, I was afraid of laying down the yardstick for fear that I'd stop caring about holiness and give up trying to be everything God wanted me to be.

But when I stopped pushing away God's grace and learned to receive it, instead of creating apathy the Holy Spirit stirred a deep desire in my heart to please my heavenly Father. As I learned to live out of the security of God's love rather than trying to earn it,

Jesus broke the yardstick of my religious expectations and began to dismantle my cycle of self-hatred and shame.

"Amazing Grace" has always been one of my favorite hymns. But a stanza in the second verse has become especially precious to me, for it sums up the work God has done in my life:

> 'Twas grace that taught my heart to fear,
> And grace my fears relieved.[8]

I'm grateful that grace first instilled in me a holy fear of God and a desire to please Him. Unfortunately, the spirit of fear often highjacked that healthy fear and turned it into "fear of punishment" (1 John 4:18 NLT). My life was forever changed, however, when I came to understand that grace is the power and desire to do God's will (Titus 2:11–12). For it is "God who works in you to *will* and to *act* in order to fulfill his good purpose" (Philippians 2:13, emphasis mine).

Rather than trying to be everything that God wants us to be on our own—trying to meet our self-imposed expectations along with His—the Spirit of grace invites us to partner with Him.

For just as we trusted God's grace to *save* us, we can trust His grace to *change* us.

Releasing God from Our Expectations

In Charles Dickens's famous novel *Great Expectations*, we meet a character who is hard to forget. Miss Havisham wanders around her decrepit mansion like a gray ghost, wearing a decaying wedding gown and only one shoe. She lives frozen in time, as it were, because she once placed her expectations in an untrustworthy man. The grieving woman has left her wedding cake sitting on the dining room table for decades. Hoping—expecting, perhaps—that her beloved would someday change his mind.[9]

Sadly, many people live like this. Unlike Miss Havisham, they appear normal on the outside, but inside they're paralyzed at a point of past pain. Their present happiness is held hostage by the past actions or inactions of other people. But some would say their deepest pain comes from an unfulfilled expectation they had of God.

What do we do when God doesn't answer prayer the way we were taught He would—or thought He should? That's the rub for so many people. Feeling "stood up at the altar," they just can't get past the fact that God didn't heal their child. Didn't save their marriage. Didn't stop the suicide, the rape, the speeding car. I can't begin to imagine how difficult it must be to navigate that kind of pain and confusion.

We all ache for the senseless to make sense. Yet it's at the crossroads of doubt and faith that trust is truly formed. When we make peace with mystery, surrendering our expectations and need to understand, we make room for God to operate in our lives. Though we may never receive the answers we long for this side of heaven, our hearts can still rest in God's goodness and love.

Written during a difficult time in Israel's history, Habakkuk 3:17–18 is an anthem of hope God longs to hear from His people.

> Though the fig tree does not bud
>   and there are no grapes on the vines,
> though the olive crop fails
>   and the fields produce no food,
> though there are no sheep in the pen
>   and no cattle in the stalls,
> yet I will rejoice in the Lord,
>   I will be joyful in God my Savior.

Even in horrible conditions, with no help on the horizon, you and I can choose joy if we'll trust in the Lord and keep our eyes on Him. Listen to how the Classic Edition of the Amplified Bible translates the very next verse:

> The Lord God is my Strength, my personal bravery, and my invincible army; He . . . will make me to walk [not to stand still in terror, but to walk] and make [spiritual] progress upon my high places [of trouble, suffering, or responsibility]! (Habakkuk 3:19)

Your Victory Circle

What not-so-great expectation do you need to let go of, my friend? What disappointment is souring your relationships, your peace, even your friendship with God? Letting go of expectations isn't easy, but it's a spiritual discipline the Holy Spirit wants to help us develop.

Standing in the shadows of that long-ago bonfire, I watched as children and adults stepped forward and relinquished their burdens to the flame. But my expectations had become so embedded, I felt that throwing my wadded-up list into the fire would be like casting my very self into the blaze.

Finally, after everyone left, I stepped out of the darkness.

Tears running down my cheeks, I tossed the list into the flames. But instead of catching fire, the paper ball bounced off a log and rolled to the side. I used a stick to push it toward the blazing embers, but still it wouldn't ignite.

Suddenly I realized that there was something deeper going on. My expectations had become a stronghold, a place where Satan felt comfortable and where Flesh Woman ruled and reigned.

This fresh awareness of the spiritual battle made me determined to relinquish the list more than ever. Pushing it deep into the fire, I prayed, *Lord, I don't want these expectations anymore. I give You my husband, along with my hopes and my dreams. Even if nothing changes, I trust You, God.*

As the paper finally began to burn, God began to rewire my soul. Though it didn't happen overnight, He began the process of restoring my marriage and renewing our love. As I surrendered my idea of how things should be, God was able to replace it with something far better. John and I celebrated our fortieth anniversary recently, and I can tell you that marriage just gets sweeter and sweeter when we do it God's way.

"For I know the plans I have for you," declares the Lord in Jeremiah 29:11, "plans to prosper you and not to harm you, plans to give you hope and a future."

The Hebrew word for "hope" in that final phrase is the word *tiqvah*.

As we put our trust in God, the future He's designed for us is released. With our hearts no longer attached to a specific outcome, we're able to embrace the process and wait patiently for His will to unfold. With our hope placed in God rather than in people, we're enabled to live a life marked by peace rather than panic. Faith rather than fear. Trust rather than torment.

What are you clinging to that needs to be cast into the fire? Whether it's the yardstick of self-imposed requirements that has hung over your heart far too long or a list of expectations that have eroded your ability to love—you can experience a Victory Circle right where you are.

If you'll give Jesus your disappointments and frustrations, the "God of hope [will] fill you with all joy and peace as you trust in him, so that you may overflow with hope by the power of the Holy Spirit" (Romans 15:13).

Enabling you to enjoy the life you've been given—the beautiful *tiqvah* God's designed especially for you.

Six

Upside-Down Kingdom

The secret of the kingdom of God has been given to you.

Mark 4:11

If you've ever read fairy tales or watched a Disney movie, it's not hard to imagine living in a dark kingdom ruined by a curse or ruled by a cruel king.

What was once pure beauty is now shrouded in gray. Where joy and peace once ruled, now chaos and litter fill the space. Evil and corruption pollute even the best of people as hatred and self-interest simmer beneath a thin layer of civility.

Life in the dark kingdom is a slow slog as its citizens trudge around with little hope of anything better. But you rarely notice, because this life is all you've ever known. To you, the gray doesn't seem all that gray. While you're vaguely aware that things aren't as they ought to be, your days seem more or less normal. You don't even know enough to dream there could be anything else.

But then one day you meet a stranger. The kindness in his eyes melts your normal reserve, and so you start a conversation. His gracious words are like none other, so you invite him into your home and eventually into your heart. His presence brings a beautiful light that chases away the shadows and stirs unexpected hope as he tells you what the kingdom used to be like before the dark rebellion.

"I've come to take it back," the stranger tells you. "But my kingdom won't be established by force; it will be a slow invasion of love. Light overcoming darkness. Kindness overwhelming hate. But I need your help," he says. "Will you be my emissary?"

"Of course," you answer eagerly. You want to serve this incognito king. For in the brief time that you've known him, you've felt an inner transformation as "the dominion of darkness" has given way to his "kingdom of light" (see Colossians 1:12–13).

With your agreement comes a promotion. No longer living for your own benefit, you are now an ambassador of the kingdom to come. Your life has been made an embassy for the new king's glory, an outpost of his presence and a dispensary of his love.

There is still one issue, however. Though you're a representative of a new kingdom, you're still a resident of the old. As a dual citizen, you'll likely feel pulled between two loyalties, the incognito king warns. But the conflict of interest can be easily settled by answering this simple question:

From which kingdom will I live today?

The Importance of the Kingdom

If you were asked what Jesus talked about most in the Gospels, what would you say? Would you point to love or grace? Money or forgiveness? Perhaps you'd be as surprised as I was to learn that the number one thing Jesus talked about during His time on earth was the kingdom of God. Depending on the translation you use, that term—along with the "kingdom of heaven" and other miscellaneous references—shows up more than a hundred times in the Gospels alone.[1]

It was the first thing out of Jesus's mouth at the beginning of His ministry. "The time has come. . . . The kingdom of God has come near. Repent and believe the good news!" (Mark 1:15).

It was a key element in His Sermon on the Mount: "Seek first the kingdom of God" (Matthew 6:33 NKJV).

Throughout His ministry, every miracle and healing Jesus performed was intended to show us the power of God and what it looks like when His kingdom comes to earth.

But perhaps nothing reveals the importance of God's kingdom as much as what Jesus focused on after His resurrection. Before ascending to heaven, Acts 1:3 tells us, Jesus appeared to the apostles "over a period of forty days and spoke about the *kingdom of God*" (emphasis mine). Downloading all the important information the men would need to revolutionize the world with God's love.

The kingdom of God isn't just a New Testament concept, however. When you read the Bible carefully, you see that from the beginning of time, God's goal was to create a perfect realm where humanity could flourish and prosper under His loving rule.

From Genesis forward, it's clear that God intended His children to play a part—to serve as sub-rulers of sorts in spreading His kingdom and bringing His reign to the far corners of the world. "Be fruitful and multiply," God told Adam and Eve in Genesis 1:28. "Fill the earth and subdue it; have *dominion* . . . over every living thing that moves on the earth" (NKJV, emphasis mine).

Though the first couple rebelled, God didn't give up on His plan. Instead, most of the Old Testament is a record of His tenacious work. In Genesis 12:1–3, He chose a man named Abraham to father a nation through whom *all* the world would be blessed. Generations later, He faithfully led the man's descendants out of Egypt and into a prosperous land "flowing with milk and honey" (Exodus 3:8).

The promised land was intended to be a visible kingdom filled with God's blessings and presence—a tangible display of His goodness that would woo a broken world back to His love. Of course, we know how that turned out. If the Old Testament was our only record, we'd think that God's kingdom project had failed. But there was a bigger, better plan waiting. Rather than building a physical kingdom on Earth, God sent His Son to dwell inside the human heart.

Establishing an upside-down kingdom God would use to turn a broken world right side up.

The Already and the Not Yet

When Jesus came, the kingdom of heaven invaded earth. God's power broke into the world, bringing healing and salvation. Restoring back to the Garden everyone who receives Him so they can enjoy friendship with God.

But while in that sense "the kingdom has already come," Jeremy Treat writes in his excellent book *Seek First*, "it has not yet come in fullness."[2] As a result, we live in between the "already" and the "not yet."

"The kingdom has already come, but it is not yet fully realized," Treat explains, echoing 1 John 3:2: "We are God's children now, and what we will be has not yet appeared" (ESV). As a result, Treat says, "we should therefore not be surprised by trials, struggle, and opposition."[3]

Unfortunately, living in the "not yet" is difficult, especially when God seems slow to respond to our prayers. As Treat writes, "You might say, 'Lord, I'm ready to be married *now*,' 'Father, I need that job *now*,' 'God, I need you to deal with this difficult person *now*.' But when God says 'not yet' to us, he is inviting us to trust his timing and rely on his sovereignty."[4]

Understanding this dynamic helps me see why not every prayer is immediately answered and why evil seems to triumph more often than it should. Though the kingdom of light has invaded the kingdom of darkness, we live in the tension of the already and not yet.

But this is where our part comes in as followers of Jesus. For just as Adam and Eve and their descendants were appointed to extend God's kingdom to every corner of earth, you and I have been called to do the same. "Go into all the world and preach the Good News to everyone," Jesus told His disciples in Mark 16:15 (NLT).

Instead of expanding His kingdom by military force or a massive revival, Jesus intended to win back the world one soul at a time. And like the disciples, you and I play an important part.

As we surrender our tiny kingdoms to God's mighty rule, our lives become beacons of hope strategically placed throughout the world. Serving as God's ambassadors, we represent His interests, bringing the good news of the gospel to people lost in the slog. And each time we share His love, the kingdom of God advances, pushing back the darkness with tiny yet mighty circles of light.

God's people bringing God's rule back to the world that He created.

The Counterintuitive Life

Living as citizens in God's upside-down kingdom isn't easy. Doing things God's way not only frustrates our Flesh Woman, it directly opposes the ways of the world.

The world says you've got to find yourself. But Jesus says, "Whoever finds their life will lose it, and whoever loses their life for my sake will find it" (Matthew 10:39).

The world says stand up for yourself. But Jesus says, "Love your enemies and pray for those who persecute you" (Matthew 5:44).

The world says do whatever it takes to get ahead. But the Bible says, "In humility value others above yourselves" (Philippians 2:3).

Nothing about Christianity comes naturally to us. The ability to live as Jesus instructs must be formed supernaturally within us by the power of the Holy Spirit. But as we cooperate with grace—choosing to go against our natural instincts, humbling ourselves, and obeying the Father completely as Jesus did—God's kingdom is established in our lives.

I've come to believe that in order to be like Jesus, at times we need to do the *opposite* of what feels natural. For living in the upside-down kingdom of God requires a different way of thinking and acting than how we are wired in our flesh.

If you're a verbal processor like me, for instance, God may ask you to talk less—to "let your words be few" (Ecclesiastes 5:2). If you're quiet by nature, God may ask you to speak up—to be His voice "for those who cannot speak for themselves" (Proverbs 31:8). If you feel a need to be constantly productive, God may call you to a season of rest (Psalm 23:2). If you're more of an observer than an active participant, God may ask you to step up and step out (Deuteronomy 1:21).

In her book *The Opposite Life*, Alex Seeley shares an important lesson she learned after a friend attacked her faith and desire to serve God. Though she initially lashed back, her mother gave her some important advice: "If you really want to be a minister of the gospel who practices what you preach, then you need to understand the principle of moving in the opposite spirit. Kindness would have disarmed the situation, because kindness is not what he was expecting from you." Doing the opposite of what comes naturally would "change the atmosphere and give you authority over the situation," she told her frustrated daughter.[5]

Moving in the opposite spirit requires going against our instincts and leaving our reputation in God's hands. But when we manage to do it, "we activate God to move on our behalf and fight the battle for us in the spiritual realm," Seeley writes. "We defeat the Enemy by doing things God's way, which is what the kingdom of God is all about."[6]

Doing It God's Way

Choose humility.

Those were the words that kept coming to our hearts when John was asked to resign an associate position we dearly loved. A new lead pastor had come to our church in Oregon, and though he was free to create a new staff, he had asked us to stay. We were excited to serve under his leadership because we'd known and admired him for years.

Looking back, perhaps we should have seen it coming. When the initial glow of approval dimmed, there were some subtle signs that all was not well. But John buckled down and worked harder, doing his best to fulfill a double role of music and children's ministry.

However, following our final Christmas production, we received unexpected news. "It's hard to say this after such a great week," the pastor told us, "but I need you to announce your resignation when you get back from Christmas vacation."

We were stunned. Neither of us had thought John's position was in jeopardy, and we didn't know how to respond. When we talked through the situation later, we both acknowledged that one wrong word could damage the church. With that realization came God's words of instruction: *choose humility*.

They confirmed the words the Holy Spirit had spoken to my heart the moment we'd been asked to resign. *This isn't the hand of man, Joanna. This is from Me. Don't be afraid.*

The rejection felt especially personal because the man we served under had been my childhood pastor and helped officiate our wedding. But God reassured us that He was in control.

"Humble yourselves, therefore, under God's mighty hand," 1 Peter 5:6–7 advises. "Cast all your anxiety on him because he cares for you." John and I clung to these verses over the next few months as God gave us the grace to submit to the authority He'd placed over us. But it wasn't easy navigating the emotion. We had to continually bring our hearts back in line with God's Word and choose to believe He was in it all.

We tend to think that the victorious Christian life should be one continuous upward climb. But in God's eyes, we're never so tall as when we bend low and choose to trust Him. Though we'd all prefer a life filled with miraculous stories, I'm convinced God's greatest miracle is the grace and strength He provides to help us walk through trials.

For nothing does more damage to hell's dark kingdom than a man or woman who's trusted God in the furnace and come out the other side shining like gold (see Job 23:10).

A Different Perspective

During World War II the British government designed several posters to encourage a nation weary of battling the Nazis. The most famous one featured five simple words printed boldly beneath a crown: "Keep Calm and Carry On."

A HOLY PARADOX

To live in God's upside-down kingdom, we need to understand the importance of humility as expressed in this Puritan prayer:

> Lord, high and holy, meek and lowly,
> Thou hast brought me to the valley of vision,
> where I live in the depths but see thee in the heights;
> hemmed in by mountains of sin I behold thy glory.
>
> Let me learn by paradox
> that the way down is the way up,
> that to be low is to be high,
> that the broken heart is the healed heart,
> that the contrite spirit is the rejoicing spirit,
> that the repenting soul is the victorious soul,
> that to have nothing is to possess all,
> that to bear the cross is to wear the crown,
> that to give is to receive,
> that the valley is the place of vision.
> Lord, in the daytime stars can be seen from the deepest wells,
> and the deeper the wells, the brighter thy stars shine.[7]

And I will give you *treasures*
hidden in the darkness—
secret riches.
I will do this so that you
may *know* that I am the Lord.

Isaiah 45:3 NLT

If I were to create a poster for God's kingdom, I'd use a variation of David's words found in Psalm 37:3: "Trust God and Do Good."

For in a sense we, too, are under siege. Between the temptations of the world, the flesh, and the devil, the cares of life can choke out our hope until we doubt everything God's promised in His Word (Matthew 13:22). But God's instructions remain steady and dependable—as David learned firsthand.

From his early years as a shepherd boy, David endeavored to trust God and do good. As a result, his intimate friendship with God gave him a heavenly set of standards that were radically different from the people around him. The contrast was never more evident than in his unexpected encounter with a jealous and crazy king.

In 1 Samuel 24:2, we're told that King Saul took three thousand men to help him search for David in En Gedi. As the army closed in, David and his much smaller band of men rushed to take cover in the back of a cave. But when Saul entered the cave alone "to relieve himself" (v. 3), their fear must have turned into glee. The men whispered to David, "This is the day the Lord spoke of when he said to you, 'I will give your enemy into your hands for you to deal with as you wish'" (v. 4).

God had said nothing of the sort, but the thought must have tempted David. With King Saul removed, David wouldn't have to run for his life. There would be no more exile. No more sleeping on hard ground. Surely it wasn't a coincidence that Saul had picked the cave they occupied. Perhaps this *was* the moment God had chosen to fulfill His plan.

David inched his way toward the unsuspecting king and, "unnoticed," cut off a corner of Saul's robe (v. 4). But immediately, the Bible tells us, "David was conscience-stricken" (v. 5). This was God's kingdom. It wasn't David's, nor was it Saul's. God would raise up and take down the king when He saw fit (Psalm 75:7).

When David returned to his men, he told them, "The Lord forbid that I should do such a thing to my master, the Lord's anointed, or lay my hand on him; for he is the anointed of the LORD" (1 Samuel 24:6).

It didn't matter that Saul was seeking to kill David or that David had been chosen to replace Saul. What mattered was God's sovereign right to rule the situation.

Showing God-honoring restraint isn't easy. Perhaps you're walking through an incident of injustice right now. Perhaps it feels like those in authority have misused their power and need to be removed. Perhaps you have an opportunity to be the one who does it.

May I offer a warning? Tread carefully, my friend. Check your motivations. Ask God to reveal the spirit behind your desire to set things straight. For even when we're right, we can be wrong. When we exalt ourselves as judge, jury, and executioner, God may have to exalt Himself against us. For, as James 4:6 reminds us, "God opposes the proud but gives grace to the humble" (ESV).

When we rush to take matters into our own hands, we take them out of the hands of God. Putting us on a dangerous path of self-reliance and making it difficult for the Holy Spirit to convict those who need to be convinced of their wrong.

When David revealed to Saul how close he'd been to death (1 Samuel 24:8–15), the king was stunned by the mercy he'd been shown. "You are more righteous than I," Saul admitted. "The LORD delivered me into your hands, but you did not kill me. When a man finds his enemy, does he let him get away unharmed?" (vv. 17–19).

"May the LORD reward you well for the way you treated me today," Saul told David in verse 19. But then he made an extraordinary confession: "I know that you will surely be king and that the kingdom of Israel will be established in your hands" (v. 20).

When we trust God to defend and avenge us—living from a different kingdom than the kingdoms of this world—something beautiful is released. Heaven breaks in and accomplishes more than we could ever do on our own.

Trust God and do good—these are our marching orders. When we follow them, God does the rest.

The Blessing in the Beatitudes

"Imagine how the world could be impacted if followers of Jesus all moved in the opposite spirit to that which we find in our cultures," Alex Seeley writes. "Imagine if Christians actually practiced what we are instructed to do in the Bible."[8]

More than ever, I'm convinced this simple principle can change the world. Because nothing is as revolutionary as the opposite spirit Jesus describes in the Sermon on the Mount:

> Do good to those who hate you, bless those who curse you, pray for those who mistreat you. If someone slaps you on one cheek, turn to them the other also. If someone takes your coat, do not withhold your shirt from them. Give to everyone who asks you, and if anyone takes what belongs to you, do not demand it back. Do to others as you would have them do to you. . . .
>
> Love your enemies . . . and lend to them without expecting to get anything back. (Luke 6:27–31, 35)

Living contrary to the world is difficult, for nothing awakens our Flesh Woman like injustice. Without the power of God at work within us, we will naturally default to the patterns of our fallen nature. Trading slap for slap and insult for insult. Meeting evil with evil rather than overcoming it with good (Romans 12:21).

But as we allow the Holy Spirit to help us form different responses, a powerful blessing is released. This is affirmed in Luke 6:20–23 and Matthew 5:3–12 (often called the Beatitudes). In these passages, Jesus tells His listeners that those who are often pitied—the poor, the hungry, the heartbroken, the hated—are actually "blessed."

According to the Passion Translation study notes attached to Matthew 5:3, the Aramaic word for "blessed," *toowayhon*, means "enriched, happy, fortunate, delighted, blissful, content, blessed." But there's more: it also means "to have the capacity to enjoy union and communion with God."[9]

Isn't that amazing! The very thing Satan uses to drive a wedge between our heart and God can actually draw us closer to Him.

It's the beautiful grace John and I experienced after resigning that long-ago January in Oregon.

With little to do except prepare our house for market and send out résumés, John and I had a lot of time on our hands. The Lord's comforting presence during that period was sweet, but we still had no idea of what lay ahead.

"We've found nirvana," I told John after our house sold. With no job on the horizon and little money in the bank, it seemed we'd reached the state of "perfect nothingness" the Buddhists are so keen about. "It's highly overrated," I told John with a smile.

But unbeknownst to us, God was working behind the scenes in ways we'd only dreamed of. For more than a year, God had been stirring a desire in John's heart to pastor a church of his own. Though we were willing to go anywhere, we longed to go back home to Montana. In fact, there was a specific church God had laid on our hearts, a small church in the resort town of Whitefish. The position wasn't open at the time of our resignation, but a month later the pastor unexpectedly resigned.

John had a résumé waiting, addressed to the church that had been long in our hearts. And so began a great adventure. I wish I had time to fill you in on the details, for God did so many unbelievable things to get us where He wanted us to go. Though the journey had its ups and downs, the Holy Spirit was faithful to lead us, giving us a beautiful congregation to grow with and love for the next fifteen years.

No more "nirvana"—our hearts had found a home. Our state of perfect blessedness.

Looking back, I can see God's wisdom in every twist and turn. Had John not been asked to resign his position, we would have been too busy preparing for an Easter production to even think about applying for the church. God had been in control the whole time. It *was* His hand and not the hand of man.

I don't know what you're going through, my friend, but let me reassure you: God knows what He's doing. What looks like the end may well be a new beginning. What seems terribly wrong just might be gloriously right. For God often uses vehicles of injustice to reposition His people—His ambassadors—to new places in His kingdom.

So don't be fooled. No matter the broken pieces, God has a plan and a purpose for your life. If you'll refuse to be derailed by bitterness and if you'll trust His power to redeem the devil's darkest schemes, the hardship you've faced will open doors to your future. Though you may feel as though you're walking in the dark, the Holy Spirit will illuminate your soul with God's glory, so that you become like the people described in Philippians 2:15: "blameless and pure, 'children of God, without fault in a warped and crooked generation.'"

Shining "like stars in the sky as you hold firmly to the word of life" (vv. 15–16).

Our Pledge of Allegiance

Several years ago, I had the privilege of attending a citizenship ceremony for a friend. Though it wasn't easy to renounce all ties to her homeland, she understood that she had to let go of one country to fully embrace the other. I watched with tears in my eyes as she and dozens of others from around the world raised their right hands and repeated this solemn vow:

> I hereby declare, on oath, that I absolutely and entirely renounce and abjure all allegiance and fidelity to any foreign prince, potentate, state, or sovereignty, of whom or which I have heretofore been a subject or citizen; that I will support and defend the Constitution and laws of the United States of America against all enemies, foreign and domestic; that I will bear true faith and allegiance to the same. . . . and that I take this obligation freely, without any mental reservation or purpose of evasion; so help me God.[10]

It was a powerful moment. Solemn and holy. Packed with meaning as men and women of different nationalities became part of one nation under God, leaving their old identities behind.

Recently, as I was meditating on the Lord's Prayer found in Matthew 6:9–13, it was as though the first few sentences lifted off the page. *This*, I thought, *is the Christian's pledge of allegiance.* Before presenting our needs or asking for forgiveness, Jesus teaches us to declare our loyalty to God and welcome His rule—both in our hearts as well as the world.

> Our Father in heaven,
> hallowed be your name,
> your kingdom come,
> your will be done,
> on earth as it is in heaven. (vv. 9–10)

To help unpack the meaning, let's examine these lines phrase by phrase.

"Our Father in heaven."

Don't pass over these words too quickly, for they contain a revolutionary truth. Because of Jesus, you and I are invited to call God our Father. It's a term rarely used for Yahweh in the Old Testament. When Jesus came, however, He introduced us to a God who wanted to be up close and personal with His people. We're not only able to call Him "Father," but as Romans 8:15 tells us, because of the Spirit's work uniting our hearts to God, we can use the intimate term Jesus used: *Abba*—which essentially means "Daddy God."[11]

When we pray the words "our Father in heaven," we claim the privileged status of being part of His inner circle. Sons and daughters deeply loved by the Most High God.

"Hallowed be Your name."

To "hallow" God's name is to reverence it as holy. To exalt and set it apart in our hearts as being "worthy of complete devotion as one perfect in goodness and righteousness."[12] But it's hard to be a good ambassador if you don't know the king. Gratefully, God has given us His Word which includes His many names to show us who He is, including,

- *Jehovah-jireh*, "The Lord-Will-Provide" (Genesis 22:13–14).
- *Jehovah-rapha*, "I am the Lord who heals you" (Exodus 15:26).
- *Jehovah-shalom*, "The Lord our Peace" (Judges 6:24).
- *Jehovah-shammah*, "The Lord is there" (Ezekiel 48:35).
- *Jehovah-ra-ah*, "The Lord is my shepherd" (Psalm 23:1).[13]

You'll find other names to study in Appendix B. For God's names reveal His character. As we get to know the God we can trust, we'll more accurately reflect His likeness to a waiting, watching world.

"Your kingdom come."

Though we live on a beautiful planet, it's so very broken. We don't have to look far to see the evil effects of the fall. But each time we pray, "Your kingdom come," we invite God to invade the brokenness with His presence. Yes, we're praying for Christ's second coming, but we're also asking God to break into the world right here. Right now. Right where we live.

In a sense we are saying, "Your way is better, God. Come establish the kingdom of heaven in my heart and push out the darkness with Your glorious light. Fill me with Your likeness so that I can represent Your kingdom accurately and effectively."

As God's kingdom is established in us, He will invade the world through us. For we'll carry His presence every place that we go.

"Your will be done."

With this phrase we align our hearts to the heart of our Father. Rather than expressing our opinions and desires, we pray for His perfect will to be done in us and then through us. Serving at the pleasure of our Master, we echo the words of Jesus in Gethsemane as we make ourselves available to God: "Not my will, but yours be done" (Luke 22:42).

Though Jesus wrestled with His humanity the night before He died, asking, "If it is possible, may this cup be taken from me"

(Matthew 26:39), He followed those words with a declaration of allegiance to God's most perfect plan. We do the same every time we pray, "Your kingdom come, your will be done."

". . . on earth as it is in heaven."

While I don't understand it fully, God has linked His work on earth to you and me. As someone once said, "You're the only Jesus some will ever see. You're the only Word of life some will ever read."

When we fully surrender our lives and make ourselves available to Him, heaven breaks in and releases God's power. Though we may not witness it with our own eyes, we become part of the "already," though we live in the "not yet." Our involvement may be as small as a kind smile or an encouraging word, but when we share it, people are given a glimpse of God's goodness and glory. As a result, the kingdom of God advances and heaven comes to earth.

These familiar phrases that Jesus taught have become my daily prayer and a pledge of allegiance to God's rule and purposes in my life:

Your kingdom come . . . in me.

Your will be done . . . through me.

That's how Jesus brought God's kingdom to earth two thousand years ago. As we humble ourselves before God and obey what He asks us to do, we make our incognito King visible—displaying the light and life of Jesus as we seek first the kingdom of God.

All because we've chosen to live by heaven's mandate to "Trust God and Do Good."

Seven

Smashing Idols

You shall have no other gods before me.

Exodus 20:3

It was quite a victory for the Philistines. They'd not only triumphed over the Israelites; they'd captured their God as well. At least that's what they thought.

When they'd first been told that Israel had brought the ark of the covenant to the battlefield, the Philistines were terrified. "The gods have come into their camp!" they called out to one another. "This is a disaster! We have never had to face anything like this before!" (1 Samuel 4:7 NLT).

They had reason to be afraid, for the God of the Israelites had a fierce reputation. Bringing His people out of Egypt by parting the Red Sea and destroying Pharaoh's army. Causing the walls of Jericho to fall down, and helping the Israelites defeat other cities with barely a battle. With this mighty God now part of the skirmish, what sort of destruction did He have planned for the Philistines?

Surprisingly, however, they were able to easily defeat the army of Israel and capture the golden box that supposedly contained their deity. The polytheistic Philistines must have congratulated themselves when they placed the ark in the temple of their god Dagon in Ashdod. Surely if one god was good, two were better. With the presence of Yahweh under their control, now His blessings would belong to the Philistine nation.

But when the people of Ashdod visited the temple the next morning, 1 Samuel 5:3 tells us, "There was Dagon, fallen on his face on the ground before the ark of the LORD!" The idol appeared to lay prostrate in worship.

Just a strange coincidence, the people probably thought as they lifted their lifeless idol back into place. But the next morning the same thing happened. Their small-g god lay "on his face," bowing once again before the big-*G* God of Israel—only this time the idol's "head and hands had been broken off and were lying on the threshold" (v. 4).

The Philistines had underestimated the God they'd captured, and Dagon wouldn't be the only one who suffered. First Samuel 5:6–12 outlines the severe judgment God brought on the Philistines—afflicting people with tumors and their cities with rat infestations, causing death and panic everywhere the ark was sent.

Finally, the Philistines were forced to admit that Israel's big-*G* God was beyond their control. So they returned the ark to Israel along with an offering of "five gold tumors and five gold rats" (6:4), expensive symbols of the plagues they'd suffered. Hoping perhaps, that these offerings would appease the God of Israel and convince Him to remove the punishment their ill-conceived idea had brought.

A God Who Can't Be Controlled

I think all of us would like a God we can manage. A jolly Santa-Claus-in-the-sky who winks at sin and hands out candy-cane blessings. A vending-machine God who always responds to the right amount of prayer mixed with the right amount of faith. A formula

God who works according to our spiritual computations: if we do A and we do B, then God has to do C.

Instead, the God we worship is wild and untamable. Rather than bowing to us, He insists we bow in submission to Him. Though faithful and always loving, our big-G God is beyond our understanding and always outside our control. He says as much in Isaiah 55:8–9:

> My thoughts are not your thoughts,
> neither are your ways my ways. . . .
> As the heavens are higher than the earth,
> so are my ways higher than your ways
> and my thoughts than your thoughts.

My pastor husband is fond of saying, "Christianity isn't a democracy. We don't get to vote what God should or should not do." Though we're invited to bring our requests in prayer, when our heavenly Father says no, it is just as much an answer as when He chooses to say yes. Which means we've got to trust God's character and embrace mystery when we don't understand His ways. Stepping through confusion and fear when He asks us to do something that doesn't make sense. Bowing our will to His will in every circumstance.

That isn't an easy pill for us humans to swallow. Perhaps that's why the satanic lure to "be like God" proved irresistible to Adam and Eve (Genesis 3:5). And why, from the very beginning, the biggest temptation God followers face is the gravitational pull of idolatry.

Many years ago I saw a small notice in our local newspaper announcing a "Build Your Own Theology" workshop. The organizers invited people to bring their ideas of God and promised to provide overviews of other world religions. With a buffet of god options spread before them, people could create their own notion of deity.

Obviously, the workshop had nothing to do with theology—the study of the one true God. Instead, it was a chance to "Build Your Own Me-ology." An invitation to carve out a god in your own image.

A god who'll do your bidding without you having to listen to his.

Idol-Making Hearts

God doesn't take idolatry lightly. In fact, He hates it with a passion. For He knows the evil that's released when humans put their trust in lesser gods. In Exodus 20:3–5, the first part of the Ten Commandments, God makes His feelings clear:

> You shall have no other gods before me.
>
> You shall not make for yourself an image in the form of anything in heaven above or on the earth beneath or in the waters below. You shall not bow down to them or worship them; for I, the LORD your God, am a jealous God.

It's a theme God repeats time after time in the Old Testament because of humanity's idolatrous nature. We see the sad pattern even among the people God had chosen to be His own. Israel would trust Yahweh for a season and experience great blessings, but then their hearts would "turn away and worship other gods" (Deuteronomy 11:16). Despite repeated warnings, their continual rejection forced God to punish them. In two notable instances, He actually handed them over to captivity (2 Kings 17 and 25). Eventually they'd repent and God would deliver them. But the heartbreaking cycle was repeated countless times.

The issue of idolatry is also addressed strongly in the New Testament (emphasis in verses is mine).

> You have had enough in the past of the evil things that godless people enjoy—their immorality and lust, their feasting and drunkenness and wild parties, and their terrible worship of *idols*. (1 Peter 4:3 NLT)

> The acts of the flesh are obvious: sexual immorality, impurity and debauchery; *idolatry* and witchcraft. . . . Those who live like this will not inherit the kingdom of God. (Galatians 5:19–21)

> Therefore, my dear friends, flee from *idolatry*. (1 Corinthians 10:14)

If we take Scripture seriously and believe it applies to our lives today, we cannot escape the fact that idolatry is forbidden for those who follow Jesus. But how do we guard against it? After all, who worships idols anymore—at least in the Western world?

Back in Bible times, idolatry was out in the open. High places and altars, sacred stones, and Asherah poles[1] dotted the Old Testament landscape (see, for instance, Exodus 34:13). Later, when persecution spread the gospel beyond Israel to neighboring regions, Christians often found themselves surrounded by carved images and massive temples dedicated to pagan gods.

Unfortunately, today's idolatry is less visible and harder to identify, because it rarely takes a blatant physical form. Instead, idolatry tends to be housed in our hearts and worshiped in our minds.

In his book *Counterfeit Gods*, Timothy Keller defines an idol as "anything more important to you than God, anything that absorbs your heart and imagination more than God, anything you seek to give you what only God can give. . . . Anything so central and essential to your life that, should you lose it, your life would feel hardly worth living."[2]

It's a sobering definition. Because even good things can become small-g "god things" if we allow them to become the central focus of our hearts.

The Adultery of Idolatry

In a very real sense, idolatry is adultery. When we look for satisfaction and meaning in people, possessions, positions or power, we break our marriage vows to Jehovah.

"God is jealous for your heart, not because he is petty or insecure, but because he loves you," Kyle Idleman writes. "The reason why God has such a huge problem with idolatry is that his love for you is all-consuming. He loves you too much to share you."[3]

But avoiding spiritual adultery can be difficult because, as John Calvin once wrote, the human heart is a "perpetual factory of idols."[4] Though it may be unconscious, every time we look to lesser things, we're telling God, "You are not enough for me."

In Colossians 3:5, Paul writes, "Put to death, therefore, whatever belongs to your earthly nature: sexual immorality, impurity, lust, evil desires and greed, which is idolatry." At first glance, we might not think we have a problem with the items listed. Yet lust—the "I must have it now" greedy desire for people and things—often fuels our desire for a god we can control.

The word "greed," which Paul identifies specifically as idolatry in Colossians 3:5, comes from the Greek word *pleonéktēs*. It means "to be covetous . . . a defrauder for gain."[5] The word denotes a willingness to go to any length to get what we want, no matter whom we hurt along the way. Even if God is the One we hurt the most.

Covetous lust always undermines trust. It steals our affections and tells us that true happiness can be found only in other lovers, in small-g gods. But rather than satisfying our greedy appetites, idolatry only makes us hungry for more.

The Idol of More

Several years ago I had the privilege of visiting Singapore. It's a beautiful place with beautiful people and amazing food. Celebrated as the "shopping capital of the world," each of the city-state's many subway stops features a giant mall, many of them filled with glittering jewels, designer clothes, and everything a woman could want or imagine. Even a seasoned shopper like me felt a little overwhelmed.

In one of those shops I saw a T-shirt that summed up the experience. It read, "All I want is more of what I want."

And isn't that the issue? It turns out the human heart is a gaping, ravenous hole. Enough is never enough. But the "more" of idolatry never manages to fill our emptiness. Just ask the "wisest" man who ever lived.

When God singled out Solomon to follow David as the next king of Israel, the young man seemed like a perfect fit. Invited to request anything he desired from God in 1 Kings 3:5–9, he asked for "a discerning heart to govern your people and to distinguish between right and wrong" (v. 9).

God honored Solomon's humble, selfless request by giving him the great wisdom he desired and astonishing wealth as well. "The whole world sought audience with Solomon to hear the wisdom God had put in his heart," 1 Kings 10:24 tells us. "Year after year, everyone who came brought a gift—articles of silver and gold, robes, weapons and spices, and horses and mules" (v. 25).

While Israel flourished during Solomon's reign, unfortunately, his famous wisdom didn't. Though the king lived "according to the instructions given him by his father David," 1 Kings 3:3 adds a disclaimer, "*except* that he offered sacrifices and burned incense on the high places" (emphasis mine).

Except. It's such a small word, yet filled with so much impact.

You can be a good Christian and attend church every Sunday, *except* . . .

You can be a good wife and a loving mother, *except* . . .

You can be a good employee and a hard worker, *except* . . .

Compromise can pollute even the godliest intentions. Starting out small and seemingly unimportant, one concession leads to another, causing us to do things that God has clearly marked out of bounds.

Solomon's "exceptions" eventually led to his downfall. But his most damaging compromise includes another small word: *however*. We find that part of his story in 1 Kings 11:1–6:

> King Solomon, *however*, loved many foreign women besides Pharaoh's daughter—Moabites, Ammonites, Edomites, Sidonians and Hittites. They were from nations about which the Lord had told the Israelites, "You must not intermarry with them, because they will surely turn your hearts after their gods." Nevertheless, Solomon held fast to them in love. He had seven hundred wives of royal birth and three hundred concubines, and his wives led him astray. As Solomon grew old, his wives turned his heart after other gods, and his heart was not fully devoted to the Lord his God, as the heart of David his father had been. He followed Ashtoreth the goddess of the Sidonians, and Molek the detestable god of the Ammonites. So Solomon did evil in the eyes of the Lord; he did not follow the Lord completely, as David his father had done.

What a sad ending to a promising life. In Solomon, I see the "Downward Ds of Idolatry" that can infect and pollute the purest of hearts:

- Divided attention
- Diluted devotion
- Detestable idolatry

If you secretly believe that the key to happiness is "more"—that if you had more money, more power, more love, or more fame, then you'd be satisfied—I hope you'll remember Solomon's story . . . and the bleak words he wrote at the end of his life:

> I denied myself nothing my eyes desired;
> I refused my heart no pleasure. . . .
> Yet when I surveyed all that my hands had done
> and what I had toiled to achieve,
> everything was meaningless, a chasing after the wind.
> (Ecclesiastes 2:10–11)

Divided attention dilutes our devotion toward God, making us prone to idolatry. But Jesus came to show us a better way—the way of trust.

"Do not worry about your life, what you will eat; or about your body, what you will wear," He tells us in Luke 12:22. Jesus sums up the issue in verses 30–31: "For the pagan world runs after all such things, and your Father knows that you need them. But seek his kingdom, and these things will be given to you as well."

A Home of My Own

We all have legitimate longings. For some it's a successful career, maybe a corner office with our name on the door. For others it's a life of service and the sense we're making a difference in the world. For still others it's marriage and a house filled with kids.

No matter the longing, it hasn't escaped the Father's notice. In fact, the desire you feel may have been planted in your heart by God Himself.

Unfortunately, legitimate longings can be twisted into abnormal or "deformed desires,"[6] especially if they haven't been surrendered to the Lord. For only Jesus can purify our longings so that they draw us closer to His heart rather than luring us away.

Rachel knew she was deeply loved by her husband, Jacob, yet her childlessness weighed heavily on her heart. For years she'd watched her sister (and rival wife), Leah, bear Jacob one child after another. The frustration of her inability to conceive must have been excruciating. But her legitimate longing twisted into an obsessive desire.

"Give me children," she demanded of her husband, "or I'll die!" (Genesis 30:1).

Poor Jacob didn't know what to say. "Am I in the place of God?" he asked her (v. 2).

It's an important question for us all and a key to discovering our own idolatry: *Have I put this dream, this job, this relationship, this possession in the place of God?*

For several years we lived in the parsonage connected to our church in Whitefish, but eventually the growth of the church made it necessary to find a home of our own. Unfortunately, everything in the resort community was out of our price range.

Determined to find something, I combed weekly real-estate ads and drove side streets looking for an empty lot to build on. I day-dreamed about how we'd decorate and how often we'd entertain. In fact, I might have become the teeniest bit obsessive. The way I saw it, we needed a house, and I was going to make it happen.

But one morning, as I read Rachel's words in Genesis 30:1, I heard the echo of a recent prayer: "Lord, give me a house! Please give me a house." Though I hadn't added the words "or I'll die," I felt them subconsciously.

Without realizing it, my dream had become an idol. An obsession I thought about constantly and believed was necessary to my joy.

6 IDOL-SMASHING STRATEGIES

Rather than being overwhelmed by the realization you might be serving idols unaware, bring your heart to Jesus. Just as He removed the money changers from the temple (Mark 11:15), He knows how to cleanse the temple of your heart where He dwells in you.

1. ***Ask the Holy Spirit to reveal any idolatrous connections.*** Don't try to dig them up on your own, but don't explain them away. If God points out an area and you feel yourself pushing back, you have a clear indication that His diagnosis is correct.

2. ***Confess that you've relied on this idol more than you've relied on God.*** Allow your heart to grieve over the pain your adulterous rejection has caused the Father. Ask God to help you hate your idolatry, for we never forsake what we secretly love.

3. ***Renounce any power you've given to lesser things.*** Call out the idolatry by name and declare its power broken by the name and blood of Jesus. Ask God to give it a holy stench so that you recognize idolatry when it tries to return.

4. ***Demolish lies and enthrone Jesus.*** Ask, "What lie have I believed about God that has led to this idolatry?" Take time to reflect and then consciously reject the lie. Enthrone Jesus in the place where your idol once dwelled and allow His truth to dissolve the lie.

5. ***Get rid of anything related to the idolatry.*** In order to destroy idols, we must stop feeding them. So delete apps, go on a shopping fast, even turn off the internet—do whatever it takes to starve the stronghold while providing healthy food for your soul.

6. ***Add a declaration of trust to your worship.*** It isn't the songs we sing; it's the trust we bring that touches the Father's heart. Declaring our faith out loud not only dethrones idols, it shakes the gates of hell—for trust is God's love language and it releases His power to work.

> They will never again pollute themselves with their idols . . . for I will *save* them from their sinful apostasy. I will *cleanse* them. Then they will truly be my people, and I will be their *God*.
>
> *Ezekiel 37:23 NLT*

Give that desire to Me, Joanna, I felt the Lord whisper to my heart. *Trust that I know what you need.*

The battle to let go was fierce, but I knew I needed to make a decision.

"Lord, I want to want You more than I want a home," I finally prayed. "Your will be done—in Your time and in Your way."

As I relinquished my dream to Jesus, I felt a weight lift off my shoulders. I hadn't realized how tightly I'd gripped my "household [god]" (Genesis 31:19).

Though I had to reaffirm my decision the next day and several days after that, eventually even Flesh Woman relinquished the dream of home ownership. So we were both shocked when, less than a month later, God miraculously opened the door for us to build a new home.

I wonder how often you and I fall into idolatry because we don't understand how much God longs to bless us. According to Philippians 4:19, He really does want to "supply all [our needs] according to His riches in glory" (NKJV). But until we empty our hands, God cannot fill them. For He will not allow anything or anyone to usurp His rightful place in our hearts.

Recognizing Idolatry

If you wonder whether you've been flirting with idols, consider these four questions proposed by Jeffery Curtis Poor:

- *Where do I spend my time?*
- *Where do I spend my money?*
- *Where do I get my joy?*
- *What's always on my mind?*[7]

These are great questions, but I'd like to suggest two more:

- *Where do I run for refuge?*
- *Who has the most influence in my life?*

If we look to Google for wisdom more than we look to God's Word . . . if we seek approval on social media rather than seeking the approval of God . . . if we allow "influencers" to shape our lives more than the influence of Scripture . . . then we have a problem, my friend.

The internet (and other forms of popular culture) can easily become our personal Tree of the Knowledge of Good and Evil. If we look to it too often, we'll find ourselves disregarding the Tree of Life. To navigate the snares of the enemy, we must be wise and discerning, for lurking below the wisdom of the world is a dark host of idols.

Including the idolatry of self—the very root of Adam and Eve's original sin.

It used to be that we idolized celebrities, rock stars, and sport standouts. But now, with the rise of social media, it seems a lot of us are chasing fame for ourselves. In a 2017 survey, nearly three in four kids, ages 6–17, said they wanted to be YouTube stars, vloggers or bloggers, musicians or actors.[8] Perhaps that's why a recent online beauty campaign targeting teens chose this alarming slogan: "Worship yourself. The world will follow."[9]

If we're not careful, even as Christians, we can find ourselves bowing down to idols manufactured by the world.

The god of hustle.

The idol of beauty and influence.

The golden calf of money and success.

The not-so-new-age philosophy that says everything you need can be found within yourself. Just speak it out "to the universe," they say, and your destiny will "manifest" itself.

Sadly, I'm hearing Christians use this verbiage. At times, it seems they have more faith in the universe than in the One who created it. Of course, God wants us to flourish, but He never intended that we'd do it apart from Him.

But there's another kind of idolatry that's even more dangerous—it's our idolatry of God. Rather than allowing God to define Himself and set the boundaries of our lives, we can subconsciously try to reshape Him into our image.

Keeping God confined to a box made of our preferences, we assume He thinks like us and wants the same things as us. As a result, we build an incomplete theology around our pet doctrines, spiritual experiences, or the latest Christian fad. Unbeknownst to us, we're no longer worshiping the true and living God—just a pale imitation we've made with our own hands.

Sadly, the idolatry of God can fool us into thinking that spiritually we're in a good place. But in reality, it's just another attempt to camouflage self-worship with religion, relegating God to the role of servant and making ourselves the deity.

I can't help but think of Paul's warning in 2 Corinthians 11:3–4:

> I am afraid that just as Eve was deceived by the serpent's cunning, your minds may somehow be led astray from your sincere and pure devotion to Christ. For if someone comes to you and preaches a Jesus other than the Jesus we preached, or if you receive a different spirit from the Spirit you received, or a different gospel from the one you accepted, you put up with it easily enough.

Dear friend, don't be dazzled by the world's offerings or blinded by the false gods that lurk in your soul—even when they come dressed in religious garb. Anything that divides your attention and dilutes your devotion will eventually lead to destruction. When you mix the holy with the unholy, you run the risk of "being deceived by the serpent's cunning" as Eve was. Just one idolatrous bite away from rejecting God.

It was the sin that toppled Eden. And it will topple us as well.

Idolatry Unmasked

I can't imagine what the people of Israel were thinking when they abandoned their big-*G* God to serve the small-g gods of the nations around them. For many of these foreign gods seem sourced by hell itself. Unpredictable and selfish, evil and downright cruel, they demanded unspeakable acts of those who bowed down to worship them.

"At times of crisis, Baal's followers sacrificed their [firstborn] children . . . to gain personal prosperity," Ray Vander Laan writes,[10] as did the worshipers of Molek and Chemosh, the Ammonite and Moabite gods. But that wasn't the only "detestable" sin required by pagan worship. "Believing the sexual union of Baal and the [Canaanite goddess] Asherah produced fertility," Vander Laan adds, "their worshipers engaged in immoral sex to cause the gods to join together, ensuring good harvests."[11]

Isn't it interesting that these ancient forms of idolatry targeted two things that are most precious to God—the sanctity of life and the holiness of marriage? Sadly, too often, both are still being sacrificed on idolatrous altars today.

But God's people can fall prey to idolatry in other areas. Remember how the Philistines thought they could add Yahweh to their worship of Dagon? Well, later the Israelites began doing the same thing, but in reverse. Absorbing the customs of the nations around them, they tried to mix the many with the One, going so far as to erect Asherah poles beside holy altars (2 Kings 23:15). Polytheism became so rampant at one time that some Jewish sects considered Asherah to be God's wife.[12]

Sadly, this confusion may have started with the very man who built God's temple. Remember how King Solomon gave in to the pleadings of his foreign wives to build temples and high places for their pagan worship? In his later years, the not-so-wise king actually worshiped the false gods himself, thus setting the stage for idolatrous worship to take over Israel.

This was the situation King Josiah inherited when he came to power three hundred years later. By that time God's ways seemed all but forgotten—but not by Josiah. From an early age the young king "began to seek the God of . . . David" (2 Chronicles 34:3).

When a copy of the law was discovered during repairs to the temple, Josiah was appalled to see how far his nation had strayed from God's commands. Repenting on behalf of his people, the king called them to worship God alone (see 2 Kings 22–23).

He also set out to systematically purge the land of all idolatry—destroying altars to Baal, burning Asherah poles, and desecrating the high places where sacrifices had been offered to pagan gods.

Sadly, Josiah's purge had to include God's temple. For it was filled with items made for pagan worship, including an Asherah pole. All of it had to be removed, along with the living quarters that had been constructed *inside* the temple to house "the male shrine prostitutes" (2 Kings 23:4–7).

How could God's people have fallen to such depths of depravity? It all started with compromise. A concession in one generation that led to all-out acceptance of evil in the next. A dark "family recipe" Satan still uses today.

Rejecting Idolatry

Though we're not obligated to repeat it, idolatry is often passed down from generation to generation. Our father worshiped money, so we worship money. Our mother built her life around her kids, so we do the same. Patterns of addiction, sexual immorality, and ungodly behavior can influence our children and their children as well. For as King Josiah discovered, idolatry that isn't dealt with only grows worse.

If we don't search our hearts and repent of any wickedness, we run the risk of handing down a compromised religion. The kind of diluted and polluted Christianity that Paul describes in Romans 1:21–22 and 25:

> For although they knew God, they neither glorified him as God nor gave thanks to him, but their thinking became futile and their foolish hearts were darkened. Although they claimed to be wise, they became fools. . . .
>
> They exchanged the truth about God for a lie, and worshiped and served created things rather than the Creator—who is forever praised. Amen.

It's been said that what we do in moderation, our children may do in excess. I can't think of a better reason to start cleansing the temple of my life. To remove any false religions or worldly philosophies I may have tried to mix with my Christianity. To leave behind any form of spiritual "prostitution" I may have dabbled with in pursuit of success. To dethrone myself and topple any false image of God I may have created so that the one true God rules over my heart and my mind.

For I want my children to inherit a pure and "genuine faith" like the one passed down to Timothy by his mother and grandmother (2 Timothy 1:5 NLT).

Most of all, I want Jesus to be my King of kings and Lord of lords.

With absolutely no rivals. No lesser gods.

Eight

The Unoffendable Heart

> A person's wisdom yields patience;
> it is to one's glory to overlook an offense.
>
> Proverbs 19:11

For most of his life, my friend has worn his offended heart like a shield.

Something happened in childhood that he can't get past. He can't forgive. A dark, simmering resentment boils just below the surface, making him difficult to be around. Prickly and a bit hard to please.

What happened to this man was wrong, terribly wrong. But in his refusal to forgive, the abuse sadly continues. Though he never talks about it, he lives as though it happened yesterday. He's constantly on the defensive and braced for the next blow.

On the outside, he seems to have it all—a beautiful home and a successful business. But inside, he's angry. Really, really angry. And just when he thinks he might be able to get past it, a new slight or betrayal—real or imagined—comes along. A new reason to lash out. A new brick added to the wall he's built around his heart as fresh wounds combine with old hurts, confirming and reinforcing the belief that you can't trust anyone.

Not even God.

What's Tripping You Up?

Have you noticed it's easy to talk about the importance of forgiveness when you're not the person who needs to forgive?

The Lord reminded me of this while working on this chapter. I hadn't realized I was approaching the subject a bit flippantly with a holier-than-thou attitude. Like, "Come on, you guys—you know you need to forgive. Just do it!"

But then God allowed me to have two disturbing dreams, one after the other. I woke up fuming over the separate situations and what people had done. The dreams felt so real that I found myself nursing my anger and rehearsing what I would say if I had the chance to confront the perpetrators—never mind the fact none of it had happened! I'm embarrassed to say it took at least fifteen minutes just to cool down.

Aren't you grateful Jesus understands our humanity?

Rather than judging us from the viewpoint of His perfect divinity, Jesus was willing to spend thirty-three years battling the same sort of things we battle. As a result, "This High Priest of ours understands our weakness, for he faced all of the same testings we do" (Hebrews 4:15 NLT). Jesus knows what it's like to be betrayed and rejected, hurt and offended—even when it's just a bad dream.

Growing up in a small town, Jesus probably overheard whispers about His questionable parentage. Throughout His ministry, Jesus was insulted and attacked by religious people who continually questioned His authority (Mark 2:6–12). Even His own family expressed doubts about the way He did ministry, attempting to intervene by claiming, "He is out of his mind!" (Mark 3:21).

Left to our humanity, it's only natural to become rigid and defensive when people mistreat us. If we're not careful, it can become a habitual way of life. Retreating from relationships to self-protect, we build high walls, dig deep moats, and engage spiky defensive measures in the hope of never being wounded again.

But that approach never works. For as Jesus pointed out in Luke 17:1, "It is impossible that no offenses should come" (NKJV).

If we haven't learned to trust that God can use everything that touches our lives, we'll feel obligated to hold on to bitterness, believing that people's actions have ruined our lives. We'll forget that "our struggle is not against flesh and blood" (Ephesians 6:12), and we'll end up living in a state of perpetual war, battling people rather than taking our "stand against the devil's schemes" (v. 11).

In Luke 17:1, the word for "offense" comes from the root word *skandalon* and can be translated "stumbling block" or "snare."[1] It refers to "the part of a trap where bait was attached," which is why John Bevere calls offense "the bait of Satan."[2]

Live long enough and you're going to be hurt—not once or twice, but multiple times, sometimes within the same day and by the same people. Inevitably, we will say and do things that hurt them as well. If we're not careful, we can all fall for Satan's bait of offense, swallowing it hook, line, and sinker.

But with the Lord's help, we can escape the snares of the enemy by choosing to forgive. "It is to one's glory to overlook an offense," Proverbs 19:11 reminds us.

Though forgiveness isn't easy, it's incredibly important. For an offended heart not only shuts out people, it shuts out God as well.

The Propensity for Offense

It's one of the oldest tricks in the Book.

After derailing Adam and Eve's relationship with God, Satan started working on their children. You can read the entire story in Genesis 4, but verses 4–5 sum up the problem: "The LORD looked with favor on Abel and his offering, but on Cain and his offering he did not look with favor."

Rather than expressing his hurt to God over the rejected offering, Cain focused his resentment on the other person—something we're all prone to do when we feel passed over or unappreciated.

Mercifully, God called the matter to Cain's attention—just as He does when bitterness threatens to take over our hearts. "Why are you angry? Why is your face downcast? If you do what is right, will you not be accepted?" the Lord asks Cain in verses 6 and 7. "But if you do not do what is right, sin is crouching at your door; it desires to have you, but you must rule over it."

Sadly, Cain ignored God's warning and allowed sin to have its way—nursing his anger and self-pity until murdering his brother seemed a logical choice (v. 8). Quite an overreaction, if you ask me. But that's the nature of offense. When hurt is allowed to grow into hatred, there's no telling what we might do or where we'll end up.

In reality, Cain was angry with God, but it was his brother who felt his wrath. Why such an extreme response? Who knows? Perhaps a long history of animosity between the two brothers provided fertile ground for Satan's plot. It's just one of several factors that can feed our own propensity toward offense:

- *Personality*. If we're highly sensitive by nature, a painful experience can be perceived as a personal attack. But God wants to give us a tough hide to accompany the tender heart we're called to nurture (Ephesians 4:32 ESV).
- *Family of origin*. If the people who raised us were prone to holding grudges, we can also be quick to judge and slow to give mercy. But God can rewire our souls so that other people's actions don't determine our response.
- *Past trauma*. If we've been abused or misused by people who should have known better, everyone's actions become suspect. But God wants to heal our hearts and shelter us in the security of His love, freeing us from the need to self-protect.
- *Mismanaged hurt*. If we sweep pain under the rug or refuse to forgive, it often comes out sideways—affecting our mental and physical health, making us prone to anger and destructive behaviors. But God can help us get past the hurt if we'll give it to Him.

Of all the things that make us susceptible to offense, I believe it's the last one that trips us up the most because we don't always recognize it. Mismanaged hurt likes to camouflage itself behind a myriad of excuses, rationalizations, avoidance, and even paranoia:

- "I've forgiven, but I'll never forget."
- "After all I've been through, I've got a right to be angry."
- "That's the past! I don't ever want to talk about it again."
- "You've got to get them before they get you."

If we don't deal with underlying pain, mismanaged hurt will affect all of our relationships, causing us to view people through a suspicious lens. Though many of us try to deal with the hurt on our own, until we get honest with God (with the help of a godly counselor if needed), the hurt will eventually surface.

So rather than minimizing your pain, telling yourself to put on your big-girl pants and move on, bring your wounded heart to our Wounded Healer. Jesus knows how to help you process your hurt so that pain from your past no longer affects the present or your future.

The Problem of Mismanaged Hurt

I admire King David in so many ways. His honesty before God invites me to be transparent. His passion for God inspires me to worship unrestrained. His refusal to take revenge on his enemies is something I want to emulate. For the Bible is clear that as God's people, we must leave room for God to act. "It is mine to avenge; I will repay," the Lord says in Deuteronomy 32:35.

However, when it came to dispensing vengeance, David wasn't above giving God a few suggestions. Consider his prayer request concerning an enemy in Psalm 109:9–10:

> May his children be fatherless
> and his wife a widow.
> May his children be wandering beggars;
> may they be driven from their ruined homes.

Wow. I've faced significant betrayals in my life, but I don't think I've ever prayed for the destruction of my enemy's family.

But that's the difference between living under the old covenant and the new covenant. In the Old Testament, we rarely read of one person forgiving another. Instead, forgiveness seems to be God's domain—with yardstick-grudges being the most common human response.

When David cried for vengeance in Psalm 109, he followed the pattern of other Old Testament prayers, such as the one Jeremiah prayed against his enemies (Jeremiah 18:23). But David's words seem especially laced with pain, and perhaps with good reason.

Raised by a distracted father (1 Samuel 16:11). Rejected by his brothers (17:28). Pursued by a cruel king (chaps. 19–30). Criticized by his wife (2 Samuel 6:20). Betrayed by a friend (Psalm 55:12–14). Temporarily overthrown by his son (2 Samuel 15). The list went on and on. One unresolved grief laid upon another.

All of which led to some unbelievable actions as David's mismanaged hurt made itself known. I can't help but wonder if early rejection wasn't part of the reason David sought comfort in the arms of another man's wife (2 Samuel 11). Later, when one of his sons raped his daughter (chap. 13), perhaps it was guilt over his own sinful past that caused his passive response.

Gratefully, because of what Jesus did on the cross, we are no longer locked in a cycle of unforgiveness and vengeance—even vengeance against ourselves. For His blood covers every type of sin—the sins we've committed and the sins committed against us. But He provides even more. By His grace, we are forgiven. And by His grace, we have the strength to forgive.

Radical Forgiveness

When Jesus declared in Matthew 5:44, "Love your enemies, bless them that curse you, do good to them that hate you, and pray for them which despitefully use you, and persecute you" (KJV), He was calling us to a depth of love and forgiveness unlike anything the world had ever known. Once again, Jesus upped the ante by calling us to live from a different kingdom response. A wholehearted and total forgiveness that's impossible apart from His enabling grace.

Rather than waiting for people to come to their senses and repent of their actions, Jesus calls us to bless them, to do good to them, and to pray for them. It was the same radical mercy He displayed on the cross when He prayed, "Father, forgive them; for they know not what they do" (Luke 23:34 KJV).

Unfortunately, rather than receiving God's help to forgive, we often default to the world's logic and subscribe to one of the following myths:

- *Myth #1*: I can't forgive until I feel like forgiving.
- *Myth #2*: I can't forgive until the person apologizes.
- *Myth #3*: I can't forgive because that's saying what the other person did doesn't matter.
- *Myth #4*: I can't forgive because someone needs to make that person pay.

These often-unconscious thoughts may seem reasonable and are certainly believed by many people. But when we choose to live by our understanding rather than by the truth of God's Word, we walk through life chained to our offenders. Dragging our hurt wherever we go, unbeknownst to us, we've made ourselves the real prisoner.

But, praise God, you and I can choose a different response. Because of Jesus, we don't have to wait for someone to apologize, and we don't have to work up the desire to forgive. Instead, we can offer the mercy given to us by Jesus (Ephesians 2:4–5). For He wants to empower us to look beyond the offense like He did when falsely accused and sentenced to die. Here's how 1 Peter 2:22–23 describes His response:

- "He committed no sin, and no deceit was found in his mouth."
- "When they hurled their insults at him, he did not retaliate."

- "When he suffered, he made no threats."
- "Instead, he *entrusted* himself to him who judges justly" (emphasis mine).

That's the secret: Jesus entrusted Himself to the only righteous Judge. Rather than lashing back at those who mistreat us and trying to avenge every wrong—or living behind a shield of prickly defensiveness—we can trust that God is at work even in our pain.

Though it may take time, as we choose to let go of offense—and do it again and again—the Spirit develops within us what Francis Frangipane calls the "unoffendable heart of Jesus."[3] A heart that doesn't wait for another person's repentance to bestow mercy, but follows the instructions found in Colossians 3:13 (NLT): "Make allowance for each other's faults, and forgive anyone who offends you. Remember, the Lord forgave you, so you must forgive others"

Hammering Out Forgiveness

Many years ago, a church friend and I had a falling out. I don't remember the details, but I do remember the pain. Her rejection felt so undeserved. I'd lie in bed at night trying to come up with ways I could remedy the situation. But my friend wasn't interested in continuing our friendship. She was done with me, she said, and that was the cruelest blow of all.

I tried to forgive her, but to be honest, I was offended at her offendedness. The fact we attended the same church where my husband pastored made the situation especially awkward. But somehow we managed to avoid each other without revealing our unspoken feud. Or at least we thought we did. Looking back, I'm pretty sure our fellow church members felt the tension. They must have sensed the distance between us and heard the shift in tone at the mention of the other person's name.

For when "one part [of the body] suffers," 1 Corinthians 12:26 tells us, "all the parts suffer with it" (NLT). We can't harbor a grudge against another Christian without it affecting—and eventually infecting—the body of Christ. Which is another reason the New Testament places so much emphasis on forgiveness.

"See to it that no one falls short of the grace of God and that no bitter root grows up to cause trouble and defile *many*," Hebrews 12:15 warns (emphasis mine). Like poisonous ground cover, the dark spirit of offense sends out tendrils seeking validation, and those tendrils can easily take root. Whether in the form of a prayer request, a not-so-innocent "asking for advice," or the simple "need to vent," we spread bitterness when we ask people to choose sides.

Worst of all, when we hold a grudge, it spreads to our other relationships. For you can't harbor offense against one person without becoming suspicious and cynical of everyone else.

Though God was patient with me as I navigated the broken relationship, He made it clear I couldn't remain angry with my friend and still fulfill His purposes. Not because I was the pastor's wife, but because I was His child.

Together, God and I began the hard work of letting go. But it wasn't easy. Forgiveness is rarely a one-time decision. Instead, it's a process—and it *always* takes longer than we think it will. At least that was my experience. Just when I thought I had worked through the hurt and released the offense, something new would happen, and I'd pick it up again.

"Forgiveness vacillates like this," Max Lucado reminds us in his book *You'll Get Through This*. "It has fits and starts, good days and bad. Anger intermingled with love. Irregular mercy. We make progress only to make a wrong turn. Step forward and fall back. But this is okay. When it comes to forgiveness, all of us are beginners. No one owns a secret formula. As long as you are trying to forgive, you are forgiving. It's when you no longer try that bitterness sets in."[4]

Hard as it was to work through to forgiveness, I was determined to keep trying. And as I continued to ask the Lord to change my heart, He began to give me perspective on our situation. Rather than focusing on my hurt and anger, I started to consider that my friend might be hurting as well. My prayers took on a new tone as God began to give me a fresh love for her that didn't require reciprocation. Gratefully, she also allowed God to work in her heart, and over time our relationship healed.

I came out of that experience with a fresh determination not to be so vulnerable to the *skandalon* traps of the enemy. For I want the unoffendable love described in 1 Corinthians 13:5: "It is not irritable or touchy. It does not hold grudges and will hardly even notice when others do it wrong" (TLB).

Just think how different our friendships, our marriages, our relationships with our children and coworkers would be if we focused on these three things:

- not being irritable or touchy
- not holding grudges
- hardly noticing when others do it wrong

We'd not only be more like Jesus, we'd also be free to "love and let live." Rather than umpiring people's lives, constantly calling strikes and foul balls on their actions, we'd be able to leave the judging up to God. Trusting that He would work in the hearts of other people because we've allowed Him to work in our own. And in the process, opening our hearts to a love that "always trusts, always hopes, always perseveres" (v. 7).

Reflecting the unoffendable love of Jesus that has been so richly lavished on us.

Being a Good Forgiver

"I wish you were dead." That's basically what the prodigal son told his father in the familiar story found in Luke 15:11–32.

I imagine the words must have hit hard, nearly knocking the father over. Teenage logic assumed, "I'll get an inheritance one day; why not now?" But I have a feeling the tension and disrespect had been building for months, if not years.

The boy couldn't wait to get away—far, far away.

9 WAYS TO CULTIVATE AN UNOFFENDABLE HEART

As Jesus said in Luke 17:1, "It is impossible that offenses won't come" (NKJV). So how do we cultivate the unoffendable heart of Jesus? Here are some things that have helped me avoid the enemy's *skandalon* traps:

1. ***Ask God to rewire your soul.*** We all have emotional triggers and weak spots that make us irritable and touchy. Ask the Lord to help you identify them and come up with ways to respond rather than react. He wants to give you a patient, genuine love that isn't easily ruffled, rewiring your soul so that you hardly notice when someone says or does something wrong (1 Corinthians 13:5).

2. ***Ask the Holy Spirit to reveal unresolved issues.*** Sometimes overreactions in the present are rooted in the past. (For instance, authority issues with your dad might transfer to your boss.) When something awakens a charged response in you, ask the Lord to show you what's really going on (Psalm 139:23–24). If needed, talk to a godly counselor to help you work through your past so you can move forward into your future.

3. ***Try to deal with hurt as it happens.*** Don't let offenses pile up. Though it takes time to work through emotions, don't try to do it alone. Take your hurt to Jesus. Together, determine if the pain is legitimate (sometimes it's not), and whether it requires biblical confrontation (Matthew 18:15). Either way, allow God to help you walk toward forgiveness quickly so the offense doesn't grow and spread.

4. ***Choose not to remember the sins done against you.*** To "forgive and forget" isn't humanly possible, but with the Holy Spirit's help, we can choose not to "remember" just as God does with our sin (Hebrews 8:12). Rather than rehashing a wrong that's been forgiven, when a painful memory reemerges, take it to Jesus and purposefully place it under His blood. Each time you lay down the hurt, its power and sting will lessen.

5. ***Refuse to be defensive.*** Be open to correction and criticism—even when it hurts (Proverbs 27:6). Seek to understand where people are coming from. Listen as they share their side of the situation and, if appropriate, calmly share your own side. When

someone offers an opinion, don't immediately reject it. Ask for time to prayerfully consider what they've said, for God Himself may be trying to speak to you.

6. ***Try to believe the best about people.*** If we're not careful, mismanaged hurt can make us cynical about everyone. But negativity bias causes us to miss potential gifts. Determine to give grace in every situation. For our love should be "ever ready to believe the best of every person, its hopes are fadeless under all circumstances" (1 Corinthians 13:7 AMP-CE).

7. ***Refuse to pick up other people's grudges.*** When we get offended on behalf of someone else, we run the risk of making matters worse for everyone—especially ourselves. While we should pray for the situation and, if possible, promote reconciliation, our primary role is clear: "As far as it depends on you, live at peace with everyone" (Romans 12:18).

8. ***Memorize related Scriptures.*** Part of rewiring my responses has included repeating James 1:19 often: "Be quick to listen, slow to speak and slow to become angry." Our fallen nature is reactionary, allowing people and situations to determine our responses rather than God's Word. Look for verses to strengthen any weak places so that you become more like Christ.

9. ***Pray blessings over your "enemies."*** It's completely counterintuitive to our flesh, but we've been called to bless, not curse (1 Peter 3:9). Learning to bless and pray for those who've hurt me rather than complain about them to God has revolutionized my life and my heart. Rather than waiting for people and situations to change, God has used the exercise of "repaying evil with blessing" to change me!

Be *kind* and *compassionate* to one another, *forgiving* each other, just as in Christ God *forgave* you.

Ephesians 4:32

Swallowing his hurt, the father did what his heart said to do. He emptied his savings, liquidated his stocks, and gave a share of the proceeds to the brash young man standing before him. The same son he'd cradled on his lap. The child who'd sung him silly songs and promised to love him forever.

The transaction was done almost before it began. With his bags already packed, as soon as he received the money, the young man set off to a far and distant country with no plans to ever come back.

Months passed, then a year. Time softened the pain, but it didn't diminish the father's love, which kept him watching and waiting for his son's return. Until that day when he saw a familiar shape moving toward him on the horizon.

The father stepped off the porch and made his way down the road. Was it him? Could it be? Slowly but steadily, the figure came toward him. Head downcast. Feet bare, shuffling in the dust. Clothing ragged and dirty, hanging on an impossibly skinny frame. Though the young man had changed and was still far away, somehow the father knew it was his son.

And so the father ran. Heart bursting, feet pounding, he ran. He threw his arms around the dusty stranger as he kissed him and cried.

At first the son melted into the father's arms. But then, as if remembering something he'd come to do, he dropped to his knees before his father and tried to speak between his tears—something about sinning against heaven and no longer being worthy of his family's name.

But the father heard nothing. His heart was dancing too loud.

"Quick! Bring some clothes!" he cried to his servants as he pulled the boy to his feet. "Don't forget the shoes, and remember the ring!"

"But father—I mean sir . . . ," the shamed son said, stumbling over the words. "I'm so very sorry . . ."

The father took the tear-streaked face in his hands. "Oh, my boy . . . plenty of time for all of that," he said with a smile. "Right now it's time to celebrate.

"You're home, my son. You're home."

Forgiveness Available for All

This story moves me so deeply because it depicts the family reunion available to every one of us. It's a picture of the ever-reaching love of God that is ours when we "come to our senses" and finally head home.

But it's also an example of the grace God gives to the offended and the offender alike when we choose to do life His way. Grace to forgive and grace to repent. As we access His power to look beyond our hurt and love the person, we no longer seek vindication but work for reconciliation instead.

The father's forgiveness didn't happen the day his son came home. It started the moment the boy walked away. It followed the young man to a distant country. It watched with sad eyes as he squandered his wealth. Though the son was absent and rebellious, forgiveness was already planning a reconciliation. Watching and waiting for the prodigal to come home.

When the young man finally repents in Luke 15:21 and suggests he be made a servant instead of a son, the father interrupts with these words:

> Quick! Bring the best robe and put it on him. Put a ring on his finger and sandals on his feet. Bring the fattened calf and kill it. Let's have a feast and celebrate. For this son of mine was dead and is alive again; he was lost and is found. (vv. 22–24)

Each item the father bestows indicates God's heart of radical forgiveness, for the gifts restored everything the young man had lost.

The robe reinstated his *dignity*.

The ring reestablished his *authority*.

The sandals returned his *identity*.

The fattened calf declared his *worth*.

Sadly, such mercy isn't always appreciated. Especially when it's granted to somebody else. In Luke 15:25–32 we read the response of the older brother, the son who'd stayed at home to take care of the fields. Deeply offended by the lavish love showered on his undeserving brother by his father, the older son spewed out his own mismanaged hurt.

> Look! All these years I've been slaving for you and never disobeyed your orders. Yet you never gave me even a young goat so I could celebrate with my friends. But when this son of yours who has squandered your property with prostitutes comes home, you kill the fattened calf for him! (vv. 29–30)

The father's reply was one of infinite patience and understanding. "My son," he says in verse 31, "you are always with me, and everything I have is yours."

With those words, I hear the heavenly Father reassuring our hearts that His love for others in no way diminishes His love for us. Instead of living at a distance, "slaving" in the fields to earn our Father's favor, older brothers are also invited to come home.

No need to compete. No need to compare. No need to be offended. For there are more than enough robes, rings, sandals, and fattened calves to go around. Enough love, forgiveness, and grace to restore everyone.

The Bible doesn't tell us how the story ended. We don't know if the older son joined the celebration or if he added another brick of offense to the wall in his heart. I think perhaps God left it open-ended so that you and I can determine our own response.

When offense comes knocking—when the bait of Satan appears—how will we respond? Will we trip over the actions of other people, allowing them to create bitterness and distance in our souls? Or will we allow God's grace to create the heart of Jesus within us?

One choice brings torment and frustration. The other brings transformation and joy.

For we are never more like Jesus than when we choose to have an unoffendable heart.

Nine

Living Beyond Your Dreams

Until the time came to fulfill his dreams,
the LORD tested Joseph's character.
Psalm 105:19 (NLT)

It started in my early twenties—a burning desire to speak to women.

While I loved being in full-time ministry with my husband, I often felt as though God might have something more for me. Sometimes during church services—especially at women's conferences—a passion to preach would well up within me like "fire shut up in my bones" (Jeremiah 20:9).

With the desire, however, came clear direction that I wasn't to do anything about it. If speaking was part of God's will for my life, it would be God who made it happen.

At the close of a women's gathering in Oregon, I worked up courage to ask the director what I should do with the stirring. She patted my hand and told me to pray.

But I'd been praying for months, asking God to purify my motives and clarify that my dream was more than a passing whim or a prideful fancy. The Lord had confirmed both the call and the fact that I needed to wait. But what to do in the meantime? Was there something I should be doing to prepare my heart and my mind?

Little did I know it would be nearly two decades before God opened the door for me to speak.

And when He did, it would be in a completely unexpected way.

Navigating Dreams

Dreams can be wonderful, glorious things. They can shape our lives and give us direction. They can energize and propel us out of our comfort zones and into God's will. But they can also be dangerous if we assume it's up to us to make our dreams come true.

"Do nothing out of selfish ambition or vain conceit," Philippians 2:3 tells us. "Rather, in humility value others above yourselves." This verse has been an ever-present balance in my life, for, as I've said before, the call of God can be fancy food for the flesh. God dreams can turn into human schemes if we're not careful. Especially in the #dreambigdreams, #fulfillyourdestiny world in which we live.

Find yourself. Push yourself. Exalt yourself. It's been Satan's siren call from the beginning. *You deserve more than you currently have.* Even the disciples fell for the devil's lies—and at the Lord's Supper, no less.

Jesus had just served the Passover meal, saying, "This is my body given for you; . . . This cup is the new covenant in my blood, which is poured out for you" (Luke 22:19–20). After the symbolic laying down of His life at dinner, Jesus took the position of a lowly servant and washed the disciples' feet (see John 13). But rather than being inspired by Christ's humility, the disciples started arguing among themselves "as to which of them was considered to be greatest" (Luke 22:24).

Raised with the Jewish dream of a coming Messiah, the men were eager to secure a position of power in Jesus's new kingdom.

They expected Him to overthrow Rome and take His rightful place on the throne. It was the moment they'd dreamed of since childhood. They couldn't fathom that God would do it any other way.

Clearly, they didn't understand what Jesus had been telling them about God's upside-down kingdom, and we can find it confusing as well. For the kingdom of heaven doesn't operate like the systems of this world. To be part of God's dream for humanity, we must understand that the way up is the way down.

"Men of authority in this world . . . are obsessed with how others see them," Jesus told His competitive disciples in Luke 22:25–26. "But this is not your calling. You will lead by a different model. The greatest one among you will live as one called to serve others *without honor*" (TPT, emphasis mine).

Such selfless anonymity grates against our human need for significance, which is probably why God has set it up this way. For some of God's most important work is done in the shadows, with heaven as its only witness.

My friend Kim Milstead is serving her husband like this. He suffers from multiple forms of dementia, and his decline has been fast on one hand yet agonizingly slow on the other. Kim is one of the most talented people I know, with a gift of administration and organization that blessed our church for years. But now she serves Jesus by ministering to her husband 24/7 in the confines of their home.

Serving in the shadows isn't easy. To be faithful when nobody notices is hard on our flesh. For all of us need to be appreciated now and then. But if our goal is the approval of others, we may miss the approval of God. Perhaps that's why the Bible tells us to "give your gifts in private" (Matthew 6:4 NLT). To pray in secret (Matthew 6:6) and resist self-promotion (Luke 14:11).

Whenever I feel my Flesh Woman rising up and demanding to be significant, I remember a quote I once read from an anonymous pastor: "I was never of any use to God until I made peace with being ordinary."

What a contrast to the current wisdom of the world! Even our Christian culture has exalted excellence and extraordinary living to the point that we often devalue the beauty of an ordinary but faithful life. Yet for every named person in the Bible, there are many more unnamed individuals who served God in significant ways.

For every Elijah, there's an unnamed widow who fixed him dinner and offered her last bit of bread (1 Kings 17:9–16).

For every Peter, there's an unnamed man who made his upper room available for Jesus's last meal on earth (Luke 22:7–13).

For every Paul, there were scores of unnamed followers who risked their lives to spread the gospel (Acts 8:4).

God used every one of them—the named as well as the unnamed, the ordinary yet extraordinary people who simply gave God what they had. And He still uses that kind of willingness today.

"God seems interested in little things," John Duckworth writes. "A widow's coin. The washing of a foot. The surrender of a small boy's loaves and fish. . . . He may call us to move mountains once in a while, but the rest of the time He has plenty of molehills to be relocated. He probably wants more encouraging notes sent than books written, more sandwiches shared than sermons preached, more Band-Aids applied than edifices built."[1]

Duckworth concludes, "That's good news for those of us who have only little things to work with. Like a cup of water. Or a chicken. Or a word or deed so tiny it can't even be remembered—except by the recipient, who may never, ever forget."[2]

Our Dream-Giving God

While we, like the disciples, must guard against the flesh-feeding tendencies of our dreams, God does want to use us. And that includes you, my friend! You were created for a purpose. Your life is not a mistake, nor is it inconsequential. What you do with the days, months, and years you've been given matters to God, for He's strategically placed you to be used in His kingdom.

In her classic devotional *Springs in the Valley*, Mrs. Charles E. Cowman writes, "You are God's opportunity in your day. He has waited for ages for a person just like you. If you refuse Him, then God loses His opportunity which He sought through you, and He will never have another for there will never be another person on the earth just like you."[3]

It's humbling yet gratifying to realize that we've been invited to be part of God's work on the earth—and that what He has in mind isn't dependent on our abilities or hampered by our limitations. Our only responsibility is to make ourselves available and trust that God will lead us.

But what does that look like? How do we become "God's opportunity" in our little corner of the world? And what do we do with the feeling that God might have something more for us than we're currently experiencing?

The Lord gave me a direct answer to those questions at another conference several years after the one I told you about in the beginning of this chapter. The keynote speaker made a statement that would forever change my life.

"Deepen the message. Let God broaden the ministry."[4]

Suddenly I knew. This. This was God's will for my life—to deepen my relationship with Jesus by tending my connection to the Vine (John 15:1–8). To spend time in His Word and allow the Holy Spirit to transform my heart and mind. That's how the life of Jesus would flow in and through me, so that any fruit that came from our relationship would be His doing and not mine. (To help deepen your walk with God, see resources at JoannaWeaverBooks.com/grow.)

So often, we tie ourselves in knots trying to discern God's will for our lives. But if we're walking close to Jesus, we won't have to find our purpose; our purpose will find us.

For God wants to work through you, my friend. Right now, in your realm of influence, as you wait to see what will happen with your God-sized dream. Soothe a screaming baby so a tired momma can attend a church service. Share lunch with a coworker and get to know each other better. Visit a shut-in, fast and pray for a friend going through a difficult time. It's all ministry. It all affects eternity. And all of it touches the heart of God.

But don't be surprised if your dream ends up being bigger than you are. And don't be disappointed if it requires multiple

DREAMING GOD-SIZED DREAMS

If you feel God stirring your heart to do something for Him, but you're not sure what it is, Holley Gerth invites us to pray this prayer:

> God, your thoughts are not my thoughts (Isa. 55:8).
>
> What you have planned for me is beyond all I can ask or imagine (Eph. 3:19–20).
>
> Yet you have also promised to reveal it to me through your Spirit (1 Cor. 2:8–10).
>
> So I open my heart, mind, and life to more of you—to whatever you have for me. Where there is ongoing fear in my life, please replace it with faith. Where there is a desire to hold back, give me the strength to move forward. Where there is a desert, lead me into the Promised Land you have prepared for me.
>
> I embrace that my part is to pray, plan, and most of all seek you. And yours is to get me where you want me to go (Prov. 16:9 and 19:21). Wherever that is, that's where I want to be too. Because there's no better place in this world or the next than with you (Ps. 84:10).
>
> Your kingdom come, your will be done, on earth (especially my little corner of it) as it is in heaven (Matt. 6:10).
>
> In Jesus's name, amen.[5]

For we are his *workmanship*,
created in Christ Jesus for good works,
which God prepared beforehand,
that we should *walk* in them.

Ephesians 2:10 ESV

generations to complete. For God is writing *His*-story across eternity, a beautiful story of redemption that requires everyone's involvement.

"Watch to see where God is working and join Him," Henry Blackaby advises in his powerful book *Experiencing God*.[6]

As we do our part, God will be faithful to do His.

The Long, Twisting Way

"Did you ever hear of anyone being very much used for Christ who did not have some special waiting time, some complete upset of all his or her plans?" Frances Ridley Havergal wrote as she looked back on her life journey.[7]

A prolific author of poetry and hymns, including one of my favorites, "Take My Life and Let It Be," Frances spent most of her short life (1836–1879) battling recurring illness and constant weakness, to the point a doctor told her she would have to choose between writing and living. Her health wouldn't permit her to do both.

But Frances persevered despite many tests and setbacks. "Her American publisher went bankrupt," Warren Wiersbe writes in his excellent book *50 People Every Christian Should Know*, and two years later "the offices of her British publisher burned down." The fire destroyed the manuscript as well as the plates of a hymnal she'd recently completed. Without a copy of either material, she had to begin all over again, rewriting the words of the book as well as the hymnal music.[8]

Of the first upset, Frances wrote a friend, "Two months ago, this would have been a real trial to me, for I had built a good deal on my American prospects; now, 'Thy will be done' is not a sigh but only *a song*! . . . I have not a fear, or a doubt, or a care, or a shadow upon the sunshine of my heart."[9]

Something had changed inside Frances, and she credited it to an experience she'd had after reading a little booklet called *All for Jesus*. Stirred to deeper consecration, Frances laid down her life as well as her dreams. "There must be full surrender before there can be full blessedness," she wrote of the experience.[10]

Oh, how I want the blessedness of total consecration. For my plans have suffered many upsets, and my timetable has rarely coincided with God's. But to receive delays and detours with the gracious patience Frances displayed, I'm going to have to learn how to cooperate with the Holy Spirit and choose to persevere. For our heavenly Father seems fond of the long, twisting way.

Perhaps it's because people in the Bible who enjoyed shortcuts rarely did well. Take King Saul and Samson, for instance. Both men experienced immediate success in their careers, but their walk with God was nearly nonexistent. Maybe that's why God often frustrates our plans.

Because of His love, God is willing to appear cruel in order to be kind. He knows how to tame our ambition, temper our motives, and strip away the flesh from around our call. And often He uses a waiting period to do it—consider the following people:

- *Abraham* waited twenty-five years before Isaac was born.
- *Moses* spent forty years in exile before leading God's people out of Egypt.
- *Paul* didn't begin his missionary journeys until twelve years after his conversion.
- *David* endured at least ten years of injustice as God molded him into a king He could trust.

In case you think the Lord was punishing these men, think of the long wait Jesus endured. Raised in obscurity, the Son of God didn't even begin His earthly ministry until He was thirty years old. Which proves that God is never in a hurry, and we need to make peace with that. What we view as obstacles may well be part of our preparation. For no one apart from Jesus is born fully prepared to do God's work. In fact, it may take a lifetime for us to become people God can fully use.

Unfortunately, most of us grow impatient with God's patience. We prefer the fast track and a straight line to God's plan. But God in His wisdom often takes us the long way around. He knows we need the battle, the wilderness, and extended stretches of difficulty to grow into the people He wants us to be. Shortcuts can actually short-circuit God's work in our lives, which is why He often uses delays to prepare us for his purposes.

I think David understood that, which is why he encouraged us to "wait" on God fifteen different times in the Psalms, including "wait patiently for the Lord" (27:14 NLT). But how do we do that? How do we wait patiently when it seems the *wait* will never end? I think the answer can be found in one of the most well-known verses in the Bible: "Be still, and know that I am God" (Psalm 46:10).

I love what Lloyd John Ogilvie has to say about this verse. "In Hebrew the word 'still' is not passive, but active. It carries the implications of 'let loose, leave off, let go.'"[11]

Being still isn't easy. Nor is waiting on the Lord. For both require that we "cease striving" (Psalm 46:10 NASB 1995) and relinquish control. But even there, God is willing to help us. As Ogilvie writes: "The reason we can be still is because of Yahweh. His name means 'to make happen.' Our God makes things happen."[12]

Do you catch that, my friend? When we still our hearts and cease striving, we allow *the God who makes things happen* to work on our behalf! Not only in the situations around us, but also in the place we need it the most. Deep down in our souls.

A Necessary Death

When God first stirred a desire in my heart to speak to women, Flesh Woman was quick to offer advice. Perhaps I could print out brochures and send them to churches. Or call national ministries and let them know of my availability to speak.

"You've got to get yourself out there," she advised. "How will they know you exist if you don't tell them?"

But the Holy Spirit didn't agree. Instead, He chose to keep me on a short leash. While others might be free to self-promote, I sensed that wasn't to be my method.

Occasionally—very occasionally—a speaking opportunity would present itself. And when it did, Flesh Woman would turn a fifteen-minute devotional into the catalyst for an entire speaking career. Perhaps a rep from *Women of Faith* would be in the audience. Perhaps Billy Graham would hear about my message and invite me to share his stage.

Of course, none of my "vain . . . imaginations" (Romans 1:21 KJV) panned out. Instead, year after year, God seemed to confound my dreams rather than fulfill them. And it wasn't just my desire to speak. It happened in nearly every area of my life.

I found it all very confusing—until I attended a seminar that talked about the sequence of necessary experiences God uses to prepare people for their calling. Using the life of Abraham, the speaker walked us through the birth, death, and fulfillment of a vision experienced by the patriarch and other great heroes in the Bible.

For me, the life of Joseph illustrates this concept so powerfully. We not only see the birth, death, and fulfillment of a vision in his life but we also learn how to navigate the often-confusing process in our lives. Here's how the pattern unfolded for Joseph:

- *Birth of a vision.* God gave Joseph not one but two dreams showing a future of power and authority (Genesis 37:5–11).
- *Death of a vision.* Betrayed by his brothers and sold into slavery, Joseph was then falsely accused and thrown into jail (37:12–36; 39:1–20).
- *Fulfillment of a vision.* Joseph was elevated to a position of leadership in Egypt that saved the known world—including his family—from starvation (chaps. 41–43).

Perhaps you find yourself locked in a dream sequence—feeling stuck somewhere between the birth, death, and fulfillment of a vision you thought was from God. I know how hard that can be, for I've experienced it many times in my own life. Maybe that's why I find Joseph's story so compelling. Though it's filled with twists and turns, injustice and betrayal, trials and triumphs, ultimately it's the story of God's faithfulness to a man who chose to fully surrender and trust the Lord with all his heart.

Because sometimes the most important thing we can do with a dream is to give it back to God.

The Care and Feeding of a Dream (Lessons from Joseph)

I'm amazed at the grace and patience Joseph showed during the twenty-year stretch between his dreams and their fulfillment (Genesis 37, 39–50).[13] His life offers many lessons, but here are seven that have helped me.

Lesson #1: Don't parade your dream before people; ponder it before God.

It's easy to get excited when the Lord gives us a glimpse of what He might do through our lives. Joseph couldn't wait to share his dreams with his family (Genesis 37:5–11). Unfortunately, his brothers were already jealous over their father's blatant favoritism (exemplified by the gift of an "ornate robe" in verse 3). But even his father was offended when Joseph's second dream involved his entire family bowing down to him (vv. 9–11).

So when God gives you a dream, don't be quick to share it with others. Instead, follow the example of Mary, who, after having her newborn baby worshiped by shepherds and proclaimed Messiah by angels, didn't feel a need to share her side of the story. Instead, she simply "treasured up all these things and pondered them in her heart" (Luke 2:19).

If the dream is from God, you can trust Him to fulfill it. You don't need people's approval or help to make it happen. Just keep your eyes on Jesus and remain willing to do whatever He asks. The Holy Spirit will go before you and open the necessary doors.

But don't be dismayed if life suddenly goes sideways and your dreams take on a nightmarish hue. For even then, as Joseph learned, God is in control.

Lesson #2: God never wastes our pain. He uses it for His purposes.

I can only imagine the emotions that raced through Joseph's mind as he stood on the slave block in Egypt. Gone was the fancy coat of his father's favor. Gone were the dreams he'd thought were from God. Instead, Joseph was about to be auctioned off to the highest bidder—a man named Potiphar who was an official in Pharaoh's court (Genesis 39:1).

I'm pretty sure the broken teen had no idea that God was shaping him for a specific purpose. As a pampered rich kid, he definitely wasn't prepared for the life of a slave. According to one commentary, Joseph's "coat of many colours" (37:3 KJV) may have indicated a favored status that didn't require the boy to work.[14] But instead of giving up in despair or resentment, the seventeen-year-old kid made the best of a difficult situation: choosing to serve his new master with all of his might.

Lesson #3: You can prosper in difficult times if you are willing to work hard and serve well.

I marvel at Joseph's transformation as he had so many things stacked against him. Somewhere along the dusty road to Egypt, I'm convinced he connected with God. Receiving grace to forgive his brothers as he surrendered his dreams and chose to trust God. There's no other way to explain Joseph's willing attitude or the tangible blessings that came as a result.

"The Lord was with Joseph so that he prospered," Genesis 39:2 tells us. The young slave served with such skill and determination that "Potiphar put him in charge of his household, and he entrusted to his care everything he owned" (v. 4).

But Joseph's troubles weren't over. After rejecting the advances of Potiphar's wife, she falsely accused Joseph of rape. Suddenly the faithful steward found himself in prison. Chained once again by betrayal (vv. 19–20), he had yet another reason to grow bitter and give up all hope.

But Joseph refused the slippery slope of self-pity. Instead, he bowed his knee and chose to trust God, then once again, got up to serve.

Lesson #4: Don't let other people's bad behavior determine your own actions.

Despite the unfairness of the situation, once again the young slave rose up through the ranks—this time in prison. "The warden put Joseph in charge," Genesis 39:22–23 tells us. "[He] paid no attention to anything under Joseph's care, because the LORD was with Joseph and gave him success in whatever he did."

Do you see the common denominator in Joseph's situations?

"*The LORD was with Joseph* so that he prospered" in slavery (39:2, emphasis mine).

"*The LORD was with Joseph* and gave him success" in jail (v. 23, emphasis mine).

The Lord is with you in the middle of your captivity, my friend. Though moved with compassion as you grieve your shattered dreams, if you'll trust Him, He wants to give you the grace to endure and even prosper. For as you choose a different response than the one that is expected, God will help you succeed and the people around you will be blessed.

Lesson #5: God uses trials to prepare and position us.

Sometimes we're so overwhelmed by trouble, we can't see God at work in the big picture. We don't realize He's strategically positioning us to be in the right place at the right time to do the right work.

Had Joseph not been in prison, he wouldn't have been available to interpret the dreams of Pharaoh's baker and cupbearer (Genesis 40:1–19).

Had the cupbearer remembered Joseph's request to "mention me to Pharaoh" (v. 14), Joseph might have been out of prison and unavailable to interpret Pharaoh's dreams (41:1–14).

Had Joseph not cultivated a close relationship with God, he wouldn't have had the skill to interpret the dreams or point to God as the source (v. 16).

And had Joseph not selflessly outlined clear solutions to the coming famine (vv. 28–36), Pharaoh might not have appointed him to oversee the preparations.

"Can we find anyone like this man," Pharaoh asked in verse 38, "one in whom is the spirit of God?" His officials agreed, and Joseph was made second-in-command to Pharaoh. Clothed in fine robes, he was also given everything he'd need to save the Egyptian nation (vv. 42–49).

Lesson #6: Be willing to serve someone else's dream.

Sometimes, as David Santistevan points out, "the best way to prepare for the fulfillment of your own vision is to serve someone else's, even for a season."[15]

Joseph's willingness to help those around him is so amazing. Rather than chasing his dreams, he interpreted the dreams of others. Rather than doing only what was required as a slave and then as a prisoner, Joseph served his masters willingly and with great skill (Genesis 39:4, 23). The young man had no idea that God was using it all to prepare him for his destiny.

For it was the time spent in Potiphar's house and the prison that prepared Joseph for the palace. Both situations gave Joseph the needed skills to administrate preparations for the lengthy famine (41:47–49). His wise management of seven years of plentiful harvest stored up so much grain there was more than enough to feed Egypt and the starving world around them (vv. 56–57).

So while you're waiting on your dream, be faithful to serve God where He's placed you and be sure to support the dreams of others. Attend Bible study and encourage the teacher. Offer to clean up after the next women's retreat. Engage and take notes during your pastor's sermon rather than checking Facebook. Be a "first clapper," as my friend Jodi Detrick puts it,[16] and cheer other people on.

If you're willing to serve the God-sized dreams of others as faithfully as you would serve your own, God will take notice.

More importantly, He will be glorified. Which brings us to the final lesson.

Lesson #7: You can trust God's methods, His timing, and His plans.

Joseph's dream came true twenty years after being sold into slavery. Forced to travel to Egypt to purchase grain to save their family, his brothers bowed before the Egyptian magistrate not knowing the powerful ruler was the brother they'd betrayed (42:1–6). Though the next chapters imply that Joseph had to work through some intense emotions, Genesis 45:1–3 records a beautiful reunion as Joseph revealed himself to his brothers.

Of course, the men were "terrified at his presence" (v. 3). But Joseph responded gently and invited them to draw close (vv. 4–5), for he had some important discoveries he wanted to share—a God-centered perspective on his journey that we need as well. Listen to the gracious mercy displayed in his words:

> I am Joseph, your brother, whom you sold into slavery in Egypt. But don't be upset, and don't be angry with yourselves for selling me to this place. It was God who sent me here ahead of you . . . to keep you and your families alive and to preserve many survivors. So it was God who sent me here, not you! (45:4–5, 7–8 NLT)

This was God's idea . . . not yours. Though it may be hard to receive, allow this truth to sink deep in your heart. It may feel as though your life has been disrupted and forever derailed by the actions of others, but consider the story of Joseph. Nothing thwarts God's purposes—He uses everything to perform His will. You can be confident of that, my friend.

Trusting the Dream Giver

"Not until history has run its course will we understand how 'all things work together for good,'" Philip Yancey writes. "Faith means believing in advance what will only make sense in reverse."[17]

When I look back at my own life, I can see the incredible wisdom of God in every deferred hope and every delayed dream. What

I perceived as slowness on God's part was actually His mercy, for He alone knew what was best for my life.

When I laid down my dream to speak, I had no idea God would replace it with a call to write. But even then His pace has differed from mine.

It was six long years between my first book and the release of my second. But when it finally appeared, *Having a Mary Heart in a Martha World* had risen to the top of the Christian bestseller list, largely by word of mouth. During that time, God used the first book to open opportunities to speak—making the dream I'd surrendered come true.

I've had the privilege of sharing God's heart with women around the nation as well as the world. But even then, the Lord has kept my dream on a short leash. To be fully available to our family and church, He's limited the amount of invitations I'm able to accept.

You see, we have a good and gentle Shepherd. A wise and loving Father who prepares us for His purposes and never sets us up to fail. Because He knows what's best for us, He takes us at a pace we can go. I love the way theologian Kosuke Koyama explains it:

> God walks "slowly" because he is love. If he is not love he would have gone much faster. Love has its speed. It is an inner speed. It is a spiritual speed. It is a different speed from the technological speed to which we are accustomed. . . . It goes on in the depth of our life, whether we notice or not, whether we are currently hit by storm or not, at three miles an hour. It is the speed we walk and therefore it is the speed the love of God walks.[18]

So don't be discouraged at the slow unfolding of your dream, my friend. For the Dream Giver is also your Dream Fulfiller.

Rather than running ahead and trying to make it happen on your own, surrender to the pace of the Good Shepherd. Allow the Holy Spirit to write God's message deep in your heart and trust Him to open the doors for broader ministry. Don't get caught up in the need to do something big for God. Just be available. Prosper where you are planted. Live fully—right here and right now.

That way, when it's time to call you forward, you'll be prepared and ready.

Fully equipped by God and available to make His dreams come true.

PART THREE

Holding On

Lord . . . I finally understand I don't have to fully understand each thing that happens for me to trust You. I don't have to try and figure it out, control it, or even like it, for that matter. In the midst of uncertainties, I will just stand and say, "I trust You, Lord" . . .

You are the perfect match for my every need.
I am weak. You are strength.
I am unable. You are capability.
I am hesitant. You are assurance.
I am desperate. You are fulfillment.
I am confused. You are confidence.
I am tired. You are rejuvenation.

Though the long path is uncertain, You are so faithful to shed just enough light for me to see the very next step . . . So, I'm seeking slivers of light in Your Truth just for today and filling the gaps of my unknown with trust.

Lysa TerKeurst[1]

Ten

Believing God

Did I not tell you that if you believe, you will see the glory of God?

John 11:40

Remember being little and learning to swim?

My dad would stand in the water several feet from the edge of the pool with outstretched arms. "Come on, honey! Jump!" he'd say. "I'll catch you."

But I'd just stand there shaking my head, teeth chattering and knees knocking together as my polka-dot swimsuit dripped puddles on the concrete ledge.

Jump? I'd think. *Is he crazy?* Wasn't it enough that I'd let him take me into the water up to my armpits? If I jumped, my head might go under water, and if that happened, a little girl could drown. The fact that he kept spitting water out of his mouth like a whale and grinning like a maniac did nothing to inspire confidence.

But finally, with a few more assurances and promises of ice cream, I took the leap. Arms flung out wide, I launched myself from the safety of concrete into the liquid unknown. It was all or nothing now—everything committed, no turning back.

It felt like eternity, but it was only a moment before I found myself safe in Daddy's arms. Oh, there was water in my eyes, and I was spitting like a whale. My head felt suspiciously wet, as though I'd gone under. But all my hesitation was swallowed up by one glorious realization: That was fun! Really fun!

Why in the world had I held back? My father had caught me just as he'd promised.

"Do it again, Daddy!" I shouted. "Let's do it again."

Our Trustworthy Father

I wonder how many adventures we miss simply because we don't trust God. How much joy and wonder we forfeit because we don't believe that He can "do exceedingly abundantly above all that we ask or think, according to the power that works in us" (Ephesians 3:20 NKJV).

With evidence of God's power all around us—from the complexity of the universe down to the intricate nature of the human cell—you'd think we'd spend most of our time bragging about God like the kid down the block. "You think your dad is great? Well, you ought to see mine! He can do absolutely *anything*!"

Instead, I've spent a lot of my life playing it safe, venturing only as far as what seemed plausible in my own strength. Only believing for things within reach. Trusting God as long as I could see Him, feel Him, and understand Him, but not daring to leap beyond my comfort zone because at some level I wasn't sure He would catch me. Plus, I was afraid I would do it wrong.

I think somewhere along the way to adulthood, most of us have lost our childlike innocence and faith. Perhaps something happened, and we deemed God unreliable. Perhaps people ridiculed our religious fervor, and we stopped bragging about our Father and His power to save. Or perhaps we never quite managed to relinquish control long enough to leap into His arms.

Whatever the cause, I think we'd all agree: we don't believe God the way we should.

Oh, we may believe *in* God—in the sense of acknowledging His existence. But according to James 2:19, that isn't enough. For "even the demons believe—and shudder!" (ESV).

As Christians, we've believed *on* Jesus and trusted Him for our salvation. But if that's the sum total of our belief, we may miss the "joy and peace in believing" (Romans 15:13 NKJV) that the Bible promises.

We need to determine what we believe *about* God so that our minds line up with Scripture—something we'll discuss later in this chapter. But we don't have to understand in-depth theology to prove our faith. For it isn't right thinking that gets us gold stars in heaven—as Abraham found out way back in Genesis.

"Abram believed the LORD, and he credited it to him as righteousness." This statement appears first in Genesis 15:6, but the same thought is repeated three times in the New Testament—Romans 4:3; Galatians 3:6; and James 2:23—as if to emphasize its importance.

Abraham *believed* God—that's what counted most in God's book. And if we want to please the Lord, we need to do the same.

In the first half of this book, I focused on the importance of letting go in surrender. But now, my friend, it's time to learn how to hold on in faith. Believing God with all that we are—heart, mind, and soul. Fully trusting He's everything He says He is and that He will do everything He's promised in His Word.

Unfortunately, that kind of faith doesn't come naturally. We need the Lord's help to believe as we should.

Learning to Believe

Both of our older children and their spouses struggled with infertility—John Michael and Kami for eight years, Jessica and Loren for five. Most of that time the topic was so painful we rarely talked about it. But oh, how we prayed. Both couples had committed their lives to Jesus as children. Both loved the Lord and served Him in ministry. Yet as hard as it is to grasp, obedience doesn't necessarily guarantee blessing—at least the tangible, outward blessing we often desire.

"I know God can give us a baby," Jessica told me several years ago as we talked over lunch. "But what if He doesn't want to?" She bit her lip to keep back the tears. "Can I be okay with that? I'm trying to be."

Tears streamed down both our faces as I grabbed her hand across the table. There are promises in Scripture concerning the blessing of children (Psalm 128:3) and the gifts of a godly lineage (127:3–5), but we both understood that doesn't happen for everyone. Jessica and Loren were open to the idea of adoption and had served as foster parents for several years. But their desire for biological children just wouldn't go away.

So together we took that desire to the Lord and laid it before Him. Asking for a miracle, but also requesting strength to believe in His goodness no matter how He chose to respond.

For honestly, that's the bottom line when it comes to belief—especially considering David's words in Psalm 27:13.

> I would have despaired unless I had believed that I would
>   see the goodness of the LORD
> In the land of the living. (NASB 1995)

I'm grateful for this beautiful promise, but we need to be careful where we put the emphasis. If we're looking for *good things* rather than the "goodness of the LORD," when life goes wrong and stays wrong, despair will be the result.

But when we look for God in our situation—trusting that His love and perfect wisdom are always at work—we won't get mired in the quicksand of unbelief or desperation. For whether He answers our specific requests, we'll still be able to see God's goodness.

And if we'll ask, He will even supply the faith we lack.

"Everything is possible for one who believes," Jesus told the father of a demon-possessed boy (Mark 9:23). But rather than going away dejected, believing the miracle was dependent on him,

WHAT TO DO WITH DOUBT

Honest doubt doesn't cancel honest faith. The pendulum of hope often swings wildly between belief and unbelief. But while God isn't threatened by our questions, I do believe there's an important boundary we must not cross if we want to stay close to the Lord.

Pastor and author Barnabas Piper identifies two types of doubt: "unbelieving doubt" (which leads us away from faith) or "believing doubt" (which leads us to deeper faith). As you read through the following pairs of statements by Piper, check the one you think is most true of you right now.

___ Unbelieving doubt asks questions in order to challenge.
___ Believing doubt asks questions in order to learn.

___ Unbelieving doubt takes questions to anyone but Jesus.
___ Believing doubt takes questions directly to Jesus.

___ Unbelieving doubt questions God's character because He is beyond our understanding.
___ Believing doubt trusts in God's character because He is beyond our understanding.

___ Unbelieving doubt says, "not Your will, but mine be done."
___ Believing doubt says, "not my will, but Yours be done."[1]

The difference may be subtle. But consider how one type of doubt presses you close to the Father's heart, while the other drags you away. Invite the Holy Spirit to reveal any other unbelieving doubt that may be affecting your faith. Repent of any unbelief and ask God to bring His truth to that place. For just as He did for Thomas, Jesus wants to help you "stop doubting and believe" (John 20:27).

But I have prayed for you that
your *faith* may not fail.

Luke 22:32 ESV

the father looked to Jesus for the healing of his son and help to increase his faith. "I do believe," he said; "help me overcome my unbelief!" (v. 24).

As the father trusted in the Lord and His ability to heal, Jesus rebuked the demons, and the boy was delivered (vv. 25–27). For it wasn't the *strength* of the man's faith but the *object* of his faith that made the difference.[2]

It's an important thing to consider when we are struggling to believe. *Am I placing my faith in a specific outcome, or am I placing my faith in God alone?*

A System of Belief

"You may be a Christian," evangelist Randy Ruis told the crowd gathered at our state ministry conference, "but are you a believer? A true believe-er?"[3]

His question hit something deep in me and still lingers today.

In chapter 3 we talked about the Greek word *pistis*. It means faith or trust, but can also be translated "belief," which adds another facet to our discussion of trusting God. Just as I've come to think of faith as a *possession*—something I have—and trust as an *action*—something I do—it helps me to consider belief as the *system of thought* by which I live.

Deeply held beliefs form the core of who we are—which can be good or bad, depending on what we've embraced as truth. For our belief system shapes our attitudes and behaviors, our values and convictions. It filters our thoughts as well as our words. Proverbs 23:7 tells us, as a person "thinks in his heart, so is he" (NKJV). Which means, as Christians, we've got to learn how to *think* biblically in order to *live* biblically.

This is where it gets a little tricky—for the human mind is a battlefield. Because our thought life affects our will as well as our emotions, it is here that Satan works to undermine our faith.

Consider the power of our thoughts. The things that happen to us aren't nearly as influential as what we make those events mean in our minds. The stories we tell ourselves can become self-fulfilling prophecies. For instance, childhood abuse can be carried into adulthood, causing us to repeat self-destructive patterns because we're convinced that we're damaged goods. We can even let the stories we've created affect our relationship with God, believing that He could never love us or set us free from guilt and shame.

That's why we as Christians need to invest in our mental and spiritual infrastructure by saturating ourselves in Scripture and getting to know Jesus in a deep and personal way. The Tree of Knowledge continually pits itself against the knowledge of God in our lives. But we are not helpless in this battle, as 2 Corinthians 10:4–5 explains:

> For the weapons of our warfare are not of the flesh but have divine power to destroy strongholds. We destroy *arguments* and every *lofty opinion* raised against the knowledge of God, and take every thought captive to obey Christ. (ESV, emphasis mine)

We often think of this verse in the context of spiritual warfare. But it's invaluable when it comes to the battle Satan wages for our minds. When we build our belief system around the whole counsel of God's Word, we're able to recognize renegade thoughts and counterfeit truths when they appear. We learn to "take every thought captive" rather than allowing those thoughts to captivate us. As we sort through them with the help of the Holy Spirit, the arguments of the enemy and the lofty opinions of our flesh lose their power as they're made to bow to the authority of Christ.

Here's what it looks like for me. When unbelief starts rising in my heart, I'm learning to pause and ask, *What argument is exalting itself "against the knowledge of God" in this situation?*

When I'm tempted to doubt, I ask, *What lofty opinion have I believed more than the opinion of God?*

When a thought seems to have extra power or influence, I evaluate it by asking, *Where did this thought come from and where is it going?*

Here's the deal—not every thought we think comes from ourselves. Satan loves to use personal pronouns when he plants ideas in our minds. "*I* am a loser . . . *My* life is a mess . . . There's no hope for *me*." For he knows that if we're convinced the thoughts come from us, he won't have to condemn us—we'll do it ourselves.

But we also need to recognize when renegade thoughts try to lead us astray. Detours of resentment. Cul-de-sacs of self-pity. Ruts of unbelief meant to keep us circling the wilderness so that we never enter the promised land.

While not every thought requires such intense interrogation, monitoring what we think about requires diligent work. But if our belief structure is scripturally sound, we can test our thoughts against what we know about God and discard what doesn't fit. As we think about what we're thinking about, inviting the Holy Spirit to renew our minds, you and I receive supernatural understanding. For we've been given "the mind of Christ" (1 Corinthians 2:16).

As a result, we're able to recognize and destroy mental arguments—the ones planted in our heads by Satan and the ones we come up with by ourselves—including the lofty opinions of Flesh Woman. For we have a zero-tolerance policy when it comes to thoughts that exalt themselves against God's rule in our lives.

To Believe or Not to Believe

Aren't you glad God didn't tidy up the Bible to only include stories of people who always did it right? People of faith who never wavered in their trust or faltered in their obedience? Men and women who were never tripped up by the troubles of life?

David chronicles his story with clear-eyed honesty that's kind of shocking. Rather than revising history as ancient rulers used to do, purging it of less-than-stellar references, David admitted his mistakes honestly. He even turned them into songs.

I believe God included these unvarnished reflections in the Bible so that you and I could be encouraged, especially on those less-than-stellar days when doubt creeps in and our faith begins to weaken.

In 1 Samuel 19–20, the conflict with King Saul had escalated to a point that David had to flee Jerusalem. Sadly, in his rush to leave the city, David appeared to leave his faith behind as well, which led to some questionable decisions.

Afraid for his life, David fled to the city of Nob where he convinced the head-priest to give him a weapon (21:1–8). The only thing available was the sword that had once belonged to Goliath—the one David had used to take off the giant's head (v. 9). With the massive weapon in hand, David did something strange. He ran north to Philistine territory—to Goliath's hometown (v. 10, see also 17:4).

What was David thinking? Who in their right mind goes to the enemy for protection? And why would you take along the sword of the hometown hero you'd destroyed?

Well, I submit that David *wasn't* thinking. He was panicked and running scared. Rather than looking to God for protection, he was trusting in his own devices and ill-conceived plans.

We do the same when we allow doubt and fear to exalt themselves against the knowledge of God's faithfulness in our lives. It's almost as if we lose our minds, forgetting all the many ways the Lord has delivered us in the past. With renegade thoughts running wild, we often run straight into the arms of the enemy in search of help.

Perhaps David thought the Philistines would be elated when he defected to their side. But the opposite thing happened. With his motives called into question, David was forced to feign madness to save his life. The Philistine king wanted nothing to do with a crazy man and allowed David to leave (1 Samuel 21: 10–15).

The frightened man ran to the cave of Adullam and hid there. As he stilled his heart before God in that quiet place, a no-longer-panicked David was able to write these beautiful, believing words:

> I will take refuge in the shadow of your wings
> until the disaster has passed.
>
> I cry out to God Most High,
> to God who vindicates me. (Psalm 57:1–2)

Rather than striving and conniving, David started resting and relying. Rather than leaning on his own understanding, he took his thoughts captive and made them center on God. In response, the Lord provided everything David would need for the long journey ahead. Including four hundred unlikely men who would become a mighty army (1 Samuel 22:1–2).

All of it made possible because David chose to exalt God above his fear-driven thoughts.

Nurturing Belief

Beth Moore has become a beloved mentor to me through her Bible studies, especially the bestselling *Believing God*. I recently watched a video where Beth talked about the crisis of faith that led to the writing of that study. "I came to a point where if God wasn't more than I thought He was, I wasn't going to make it."[4]

As God revealed Himself to her in the Word, Beth narrowed down what she'd learned into a list of essential truths. She summed them up in a "five-statement pledge of faith" that I've memorized and repeat often, especially when doubt and unbelief try to exalt themselves against the knowledge of God.

1. God is who He says He is.
2. God can do what He says He can do.
3. I am who God says I am.
4. I can do all things through Christ.
5. God's word is alive and active in me.[5]

She ends the pledge with three simple but powerful words: "I'm believing God."[6]

Some people might find the exercise too simplistic, but I've found it revolutionary. It puts rebar into my belief system and steel into my soul, anchoring me to the unchanging truths of who God is and all that He wants to be to me.

I don't know about you, but I'm tired of settling for less than God offers—believing little and missing much. I want my belief in God's character to be so solid that I'm ready to leap into His arms and follow Him anywhere He leads. Which brings us back to Abraham, who really did leave everything he knew because he "*believed* the LORD" (Genesis 15:6, emphasis mine).

The Hebrew word translated "believed" is *aman*. It's the word from which we get the *amen* we say at the end of our prayers.[7] It means to "confirm or support," but the meaning goes deeper than that. It can be translated to "foster as a parent or a nurse" and involves being "faithful, to trust."[8]

Belief, you see, isn't something that happens overnight. We have to cultivate it. For some people it takes years. For others it takes a lifetime.

How do we say *aman* to God's promises when life keeps throwing us curveballs and His promises seem delayed? We find several clues in Romans 4:18–22, where Paul writes about Abraham's life:

> Against all hope, Abraham in hope believed and so became the father of many nations, just as it had been said to him, "So shall your offspring be." Without weakening in his faith, he faced the fact that his body was as good as dead—since he was about a hundred years old—and that Sarah's womb was also dead. Yet he did not waver through unbelief regarding the promise of God, but was strengthened in his faith and gave glory to God, being fully persuaded that God had power to do what he had promised. This is why "it was credited to him as righteousness."

In this portion of Scripture, I see five ways we can nurse, parent, and foster our faith just as Abraham did.

"Against all hope, Abraham in hope believed."

After watching my kids struggle with infertility, I can't imagine what it must have been like for Abraham and his wife, Sarah.[9] After fifty-plus years of marriage, they'd surely given up hope of having children. So when God told Abraham he would be the "father of many nations," but nothing happened for twenty-five more years, trusting God must have been incredibly difficult. But Abraham kept believing.

"When everything was hopeless," Romans 4:18 tells us in The Message, "Abraham believed anyway, deciding to live not on the basis of what he saw he *couldn't* do but on what God said he *would* do. And so he was made father of a multitude of peoples."

If you're facing a hopeless situation, I encourage you to find out what God says about it. Don't live on the basis of what you see or what you feel. Refuse to allow your personal or situational limitations to limit what you believe about God.

"Without weakening in his faith, he faced the fact[s]."

Abraham wasn't in denial about his situation as he waited for God's promise. He could look in the mirror, state the facts, yet still acknowledge God's power: *I'm old. My wife is old. It looks impossible . . . but I'm believing God.*

Rather than focusing on his problem, Abraham kept his eyes on the Lord. What God said overruled every obstacle—Sarah's inability to conceive, her skepticism about the promise, even the age on his driver's license. "And so from this one man," Hebrews 11:12 tells us, "and he as good as dead, came descendants as numerous as the stars in the sky and as countless as the sand on the seashore."

"Yet he did not waver through unbelief regarding the promise of God."

Because I'm familiar with Abraham's story, I do find myself objecting to this "did not waver" part. Genesis 16 describes a time when Abraham and Sarah tried to help God by using a servant, Hagar, to bear a son for Abraham: Ishmael. Later, when the promised child, Isaac, finally arrived, the ensuing power struggle between the two women resulted in heartache for everyone.

Yet God didn't sum up Abraham's life by his worst mistake. And He doesn't discount our faith when, in a weak moment, we lean on our own understanding and pull an "Ishmael" by trying to fulfill His promise through human means. God doesn't reject us. He *will* challenge us, however.

I can't count the times I've felt God's loving exasperation in my spirit: *After all the ways I've helped you, Joanna, how long are you going to waver between belief and unbelief? Isn't it time to trust Me?*

Of course the answer is yes. Gratefully when we respond in repentance, God not only forgives but He also gives us the grace we need to trust Him. Even when the promise involves a long wait.

"[Abraham] was strengthened in his faith and gave glory to God."

When Isaac was finally born, how Abraham and Sarah must have rejoiced! It's easy to be strengthened in our faith and give glory to God when our prayers are answered. But then, many years later, God said to Abraham, "Take your son, your only son, whom you love . . . [and] sacrifice him there as a burnt offering on a mountain I will show you" (Genesis 22:2).

I can't imagine what went through Abraham's mind. Waiting for the promise is one thing, but when God asks us to give the promise back—well, that requires an extraordinary kind of faith.

Reading the story, I'm stunned by Abraham's obedience. He didn't argue with God. He got up "early the next morning" and headed with Isaac toward the place of sacrifice (v. 3). For Abraham understood that "God is too good to be unkind and too wise to be mistaken. And when we cannot trace His hand, we must trust His heart."[10]

"Being fully persuaded that God had power to do what he had promised."

When Abraham and Isaac reached the place of sacrifice, Abraham bound his son and laid him on the altar, fully prepared to give back what God had graciously given him. To be honest, this part of the story is disturbing. If I didn't know God the way I do, I'd question His love, and I'd certainly argue with His methods.

But this story is bigger than one man's obedience. For it foreshadows the heart of our Father and the willingness of His "one and only Son" (John 3:16) to lay down His life for our salvation. It also gives us a glimpse of the sacrifice involved if we want to live a life of faith.

The thought of losing Isaac must have crushed Abraham's heart, but the man loved God more than he loved God's gifts. Because he trusted God's character, he didn't question God's ways. As he raised the knife to slay his son, God interrupted the sacrifice, saying, "Now I know that you fear God, because you have not withheld from me your son, your only son" (Genesis 22:12).

When God gives us an "Isaac," we don't have to be afraid to give it back to Him. For fulfilling the promise is God's job. Our part is to trust and obey.

Hoping against hope.

Facing facts without weakening.

Not wavering in unbelief (and repenting when we do).

Strengthened in our faith so we bring Him glory (even though it involves sacrifice).

Because we're fully persuaded that God will accomplish all that He's said He will do.

Holding the Promise

"Never believe anything bad about God."[11]

This advice from theologian and author Dallas Willard may be the most important thing you'll ever read. For it addresses the tension we feel living between the already and not yet—the challenge of believing in God's goodness though we live in a world filled with pain.

When I started to work on this book, Jessica was still struggling with infertility, trying to decipher what God would have her and her husband do. The doctors had said the best way for them to have biological children was in vitro fertilization, or IVF.[12] But would using a medical procedure to have a baby be taking the situation out of God's hands?

"It seems strange," Jessica told me, "but for me it's taking a lot of faith to consider IVF. It costs so much money, and what if it doesn't work?" In her mind it seemed safer—at least emotionally—not to try. But as she and Loren continued to pray, pushing through the fear and surrendering the results to God, they felt a release to try the procedure.

A few weeks from the time I'm writing this, we will celebrate Thanksgiving with our grown kids and their spouses. Best of all, John and I will get to cuddle four precious grandbabies. God used the miracle of IVF to give Jessica two sons and John Michael a set of twins—a boy and a girl. Our hearts and arms will literally be overflowing with gratitude.

But I hope we'd still be grateful this Thanksgiving had the procedures not worked. For God's goodness isn't measured by our perceived blessings nor by our lack of them. Jesus already proved the greatness of God's love when He went to the cross.

Perhaps you're one of the thousands of couples praying to have children—or one of the many wannabee grandmas interceding on their behalf. Or perhaps you struggle with another unresolved issue. An ongoing illness. A relationship change. A financial dilemma. Such painful circumstances may tempt you to stop believing, but I urge you to press through the doubt and choose to hold on to your forever-faithful God.

I can't promise that if you trust the Lord and actively believe, everything will turn out the way you want. But I can promise you this: if you'll take every thought captive and choose to exalt God over your fear, you'll find that Jesus is walking with you every step of the way.

Are you ready to start believing, my friend?

Your heavenly Father's waiting for you in the deep end—and He's fully capable of catching you if you'll take a leap of faith. So grab your polka-dot swimsuit and a pair of goggles. For He wants you to experience abundant life right here and right now.

As you leap into His love—choosing to believe that He's faithful—God will take you on a great adventure as you continue to trust in Him. And you'll find yourself saying, "Do it again, Daddy! Let's do it again!"

Eleven

Content in His Love

I have learned the secret of being content in any and every situation.

Philippians 4:12

When I found out I was pregnant a few months before I turned forty, I didn't handle it well.

I'm grateful to report that my first response was a trusting and heartfelt surrender like that of Jesus's mother, Mary: "Let it be to me according to your word" (Luke 1:38 NKJV). I was even able to echo Paul's words in 1 Corinthians 6:19–20 and say, "[I'm] not [my] own; [I've been] bought at a price."

I meant both statements from the bottom of my heart, but it wasn't long before Flesh Woman began to freak out. *You're just a few years away from an empty nest, Joanna! This will completely ruin my plans—I mean, your life.*

I tried to deflect her arguments, but they made a lot of sense. The math alone was enough to set my head and heart spinning. None of my high school essays had included the goal "I want to actively parent for thirty-five years." But that's what I was facing.

According to my calculations, I'd probably need a walker by the time this baby graduated.

But what really did me in was the idea of having to start over. Sleepless nights and endless laundry. Playdates and T-ball. Parent-teacher conferences and not-so-voluntary volunteering. Plus the big one: five years of lukewarm meals due to cutting up a little person's food. (Yes, I'm just that self-centered.)

With John Michael graduating the next year, I told a friend, "I never thought I'd be shopping for cribs and colleges at the same time."

"Yeah," she countered dryly. "But it could be worse. You could be shopping for diapers and Depends."

I wish I could say that I immediately made peace with the idea of having a baby—that after the initial shock wore off, I embraced it as a wonderful blessing. I tried to be okay with it. I really did. I spent a lot of time asking God to adjust my attitude and make me happy about the life-changing event. But for the first time, I couldn't make myself want what God wanted for my life, and that scared me.

It helped that I didn't feel His displeasure. Instead, I felt His presence. *I realize this is hard for you, Joanna*, I felt the Father whisper, *but I know what I'm doing. You can trust Me.*

Though it took me months to work through the shock, during that time I learned a life lesson I hope I never forget.

Our heavenly Father loves us so much, He gives us what we need. Even when it doesn't line up with what we want.

Learning Contentment

As Christians we are called to contentment—which Joni Eareckson Tada and her husband define as "an internal quietness of heart . . . that gladly submits to God in all circumstances."[1] But, as I discovered, that kind of restful trust can be hard to come by.

Especially if our definition of *contentment* is anything like the world's.

Most dictionaries link the word contentment to positive circumstances. The Cambridge Dictionary defines it as "happiness and satisfaction, often because you have everything you need."[2] Another dictionary says it's "the happiness you feel when you have everything you want and you enjoy your life."[3]

If those definitions are correct—if our contentment is determined by our possessions and how much we enjoy life—most of us Americans should be overwhelmingly content. For never in human history has a group of people had more resources and more ways to enjoy them than we do here in the United States.

According to journalist Dick Meyer, in recent decades we've been "healthier, better fed, longer-lived, safer, sent fewer young people off to war and forged one of humankind's greatest technological revolutions." And yet "social science shows that Americans on the whole have found it harder to garner contentment, connection and optimism during these prosperous years."[4]

Though "humans have never had it so good, we don't feel so good," Meyer concludes.[5] Which raises the question: If having everything we want isn't the secret to contentment, then what is?

Scripture gives an answer from a man uniquely qualified to speak on the subject. As a Roman citizen, Saul (later to be known as Paul) seems to have been raised in a wealthy home. Sent to Jerusalem to study under the famous rabbi and scholar Gamaliel, he was on the fast track to prominence in the Sanhedrin, the Jewish supreme council of his day. And his influence skyrocketed when he decided to rid the world of Christians.

But then, while on a trip to Damascus to do just that, Saul encountered Jesus, and his life forever changed (Acts 9). Laying aside privilege and prestige, the former persecutor of Christians became an itinerant missionary, preaching the gospel throughout the Roman world. It wasn't an easy job, to put it mildly. In 2 Corinthians 11:23–28, we read about the difficulties Paul faced:

- enduring long hours of hard work and numerous imprisonments
- surviving five whippings with thirty-nine stripes, three beatings with rods, one stoning

- being shipwrecked three times, stranded in the open sea for a day and a half
- moving constantly, sharing the gospel and escaping enemies
- facing danger from bandits, both Jews and Gentiles, and false believers in the city and in the country, on land and at sea
- suffering from weariness, hunger, thirst, nakedness, and cold
- feeling overwhelming pressure in caring for all the churches

Yet despite decades of rejection, insult, and hardship, Paul was able to write these words from a prison cell:

> I have learned to be content whatever the circumstances. I know what it is to be in need, and I know what it is to have plenty. I have learned the secret of being content in any and every situation, whether well fed or hungry, whether living in plenty or in want. (Philippians 4:11–12)

Read those lines again and let them sink in. "I have *learned* to be content." Contentment doesn't show up fully formed in us, no matter our personality. It's a skill that must be practiced, a mindset that must be learned. It's a quality that is cultivated by a continual trust in God as we look to Him to be our source of peace and joy.

I can't help but think of my friend and life coach Joy Schroeder. Though paralyzed and confined to a wheelchair due to a severe car accident thirty-five years ago, Joy is one of the most productive, purpose-filled people I know.

"I love my life, Joanna!" she told me during one of our coaching sessions. Despite being dependent on the assistance of others, Joy mentors college students and coaches ministry leaders around the world from an iPad propped up on her kitchen table.[6]

While this isn't the life Joy and her husband, Dick, had expected, God has used the couple to literally shape a generation through a ministry called Chi Alpha. All because, like Paul, they learned "the secret of being content in any and every situation" (v. 12).

What is that secret? It's found in the next verse: "I can do everything through Christ, who gives me strength" (v. 13 NLT).

Tapping Into the Source

The world says we can't be content unless we're happy. But happiness is based on happenings, and what happens in our lives is largely out of our control. That's why the Holy Spirit offers us joy instead—an underlying sense of "okayness" that reassures us God is working on our behalf. Though we may not be content *with* our situation, God can help us be content *in* it.

After struggling to make peace with being pregnant at a relatively advanced age, I worried that the battle might continue after the baby was born. With my previous births, I hadn't felt that immediate connection some women enjoy. Instead, it had felt like I was babysitting for several weeks after they were born.

Then Joshua came along. And despite my months of pregnant wrestling, the moment he was placed in my arms, God flooded my heart with love and an overwhelming sense of peace. It was as though something in my heart had finally come home.

Tracing his tiny face and caressing his shock of thick, black hair, I knew with certainty that this baby was a gift from God. Though the doctors warned that Joshua might have developmental issues, my concern and even my fears were tempered by a sense of destiny on his life. Our unexpected child had been purposed and formed in the Father's heart. The Lord would help us help our son become all that he was meant to be.

I had no idea that Joshua would do the same thing for me. But he has. From the very beginning of his life, Josh has shown me what contentment looks like—especially as it relates to trusting God.

As a baby, Josh cried when he needed food or a clean diaper, but as soon as he saw me moving toward him, he would stop whimpering and simply wait. Even his doctor remarked on my baby's ability to "self-calm"—a quality that is still evident in Josh as a teenager. When he gets frustrated or angry (which isn't often), he rarely stays in a bad mood. Instead, he takes it to God and gives himself a good talking-to. "It's going to be okay, Josh," I'll hear him say quietly. "Just breathe."

In this increasingly hectic and angry world, the ability to self-calm seems more important than ever. I was fascinated to find that when Paul speaks of being "content" in Philippians 4, he uses a compound word in Greek—*autarkēs*. A combination of "self" (*autos*) and "sufficiency" (*arkeō*), it means to be "sufficient or adequate in one's self—completely apart from or independent of the circumstances of life. It stresses the idea of being satisfied in one's own inner being—no matter what one's external lot in life may be."[7]

This word for "content" or "self-sufficient" would become popular a few centuries later among the Stoics, followers of a Greek school of philosophy. According to Jack L. Arnold, Stoic "philosophy taught that a man should be self-sufficient in all things in his own strength. He should strive to the utmost of his might, by the arm of the flesh, to submit to situations without grumbling. Yet, it was by gritting his teeth and [adopting] a grin and bear it attitude."[8]

Sadly, that's how many of us live, even as Christians—gritting our teeth no matter what happens and trying not to grumble. Holding on until Jesus comes, but without hope of contentment or peace in this troubled world.

When Paul used the word *autarkēs*, however, he was referring to a different kind of self-sufficiency. A confidence based on the One who loves us rather than on our ability to persevere.

Listen to how the Amplified Bible (Classic Edition) translates Philippians 4:13:

> I have strength for all things in Christ Who empowers me [I am ready for anything and equal to anything through Him Who infuses inner strength into me; I am self-sufficient in Christ's sufficiency].

Don't you love that? "Self-sufficient in Christ's sufficiency." This is self-calming at its best, my friend. Just as Josh trusted me to meet his needs as an infant, we can trust God to supply our needs. For "those who seek the LORD lack no good thing" (Psalm 34:10). As we "wait on the LORD" for His provision, He promises to "renew [our] strength" (Isaiah 40:31 NKJV).

Just another reason to rest our hearts in these four trust-inspiring facts: God is good. He loves us. We belong to Him. And He takes care of His own.

Chasing Contentment

Do you have a "happy place"—a location or memory you visit in your mind when things get hard? A mental spot where you feel completely peaceful and content?

For years my happy place was a seaside massage I'd enjoyed during our twenty-fifth anniversary trip to Puerto Vallarta. With soft, gauzy curtains blowing in the breeze and the sound of soft music mingled with waves crashing below, it was a little slice of heaven.

Today, my happy place is with my grandchildren. When I hold them, it feels as though my heart will burst. But the truth is that even in the happiest of places, the "happy" part can be fleeting. For it isn't long before the twins, Jaxson and Quinley, want down off my lap. Or Nathaniel begs for a snack while I'm in the middle of changing baby Josiah's diaper.

I'm pretty sure that if I went back to Mexico, I'd probably be let down as well. For that's the nature of earthly contentment. It's like a butterfly that lands softly on our shoulder—beautiful and magical, but all too temporary. We should enjoy the moment with breathless wonder. But just as babies fill their diapers, butterflies eventually fly away.

If our contentment is based on having everything we want and enjoying life, we'll lose it when our circumstances change. And even if we were able to make our happy place more permanent, chances are it still wouldn't satisfy.

Just ask the wisest man who ever lived.

After building a temple for God, David's son set his sights on building his kingdom, pursuing pleasure, and amassing unimaginable wealth. Solomon's success was remarkable. Yet at the end of his life he wrote,

> When I surveyed all that my hands had done
> and what I had toiled to achieve,
> everything was meaningless, a chasing after the wind.
> (Ecclesiastes 2:11)

Earthly contentment is fleeting, as Solomon discovered. But godly contentment endures.

Paul shared that truth with his young friend Timothy as the apostle neared the end of his life. "Godliness with contentment is great gain," he writes in 1 Timothy 6:6. "If we have food and clothing, we will be content with that. Those who want to get rich fall into temptation and a trap and into many foolish and harmful desires that plunge people into ruin and destruction" (vv. 8–9).

When we allow the disappointment of *what isn't* to swallow the joy of *what is*, we miss the blessings God has already showered upon us. Blindly pursuing this world's riches, we risk "ruin and destruction" rather than the satisfied life God calls "great gain."

The Problem of Discontentment

Back in the 1960s, Pastor Ray Stedman shared a set of statistics with his congregation that I found interesting. "At the beginning of [the 1900s] the average American wanted 72 things, 18 of which he regarded as necessary. But by the mid-century mark, 1950, the list of American wants had grown to 496 things, 96 of which he regarded as absolute necessities."[9]

With all the recent advances in technology and next-day delivery to our front door, just imagine what our list of "necessities" might look like today.

Strangely, instead of making our lives easier, this embarrassment of riches has made them more complex. The moment you purchase the latest gadget, something better pops up in your newsfeed. You finally donate the flare-leg jeans you've held on to since high school, only to see them all over Instagram. With the last pieces added to your living room remodel, a design expert declares that "farmhouse" is on its way out.

With every click or scroll, we're convinced that everyone else has a shinier, happier, more beautiful life than we do. So we buy more things in an effort to make ourselves happy, hoping to impress people we'll never meet.

I believe this unholy discontentment, though perpetuated by the advertising industry, is fed by hell itself. Designed to keep us unsettled and dissatisfied, distracted from the life we have and the God we need.

If I could just get there and have that, I would be content, we tell ourselves. But "there" keeps moving as we encounter more and more things that we just can't live without.

The constant diet of mental stimulation afforded by our various devices doesn't help matters. In his book *Chasing Contentment*, Erik Raymond writes, "Many can scarcely engage in the menial tasks of life for very long without checking their phones. It's as if we're saying, 'I have learned in whatever situation I am in to be discontent.'"[10]

But as Socrates is quoted as saying and King Solomon found out, "He who is not contented with what he has, would not be contented with what he would like to have."[11] We can have a perfectly wonderful life, and still crave more.

It's a dangerous condition. Just ask David.

The Prolonged Stare

Scripture doesn't tell us why David decided to sit out the battle against the Ammonites, described in 2 Samuel 11:1. It only tells us, "In the spring, at the time when kings go off to war, David . . . remained in Jerusalem."

Perhaps he felt he'd earned a vacation. After years of leading his men into battle and choking down his fair share of army rations,

David probably looked forward to relaxing around the palace, spending time with his wives, and enjoying some great meals.

But downtime doesn't always refresh us—especially if our heart isn't in the right place. Instead, it can open us up to all kinds of temptations. Especially when those temptations are fed by a simmering discontent.

I know I may be reading between the lines here, but 2 Samuel 11:2 tells us David had trouble sleeping. Perhaps he was frustrated by the competitive nature of his too-many wives. (Polygamy baffles me. John and I find one wife more than we can handle, even on my best days.) Or perhaps David's restlessness was fed by boredom. As a man of action, he needed something to do.

Whatever the reason, we know that "David got up from his bed and walked around on the roof of the palace" (v. 2). It was a common pastime in Jerusalem, where flat roofs provided a perfect spot to cool off after the heat of the day. But on this particular evening, as David looked out over the city from his high vantage point, "he saw a woman bathing." This was no ordinary woman. Verse 2 tells us she "was very beautiful."

The moment could have passed without incident. David could have averted his eyes and kept on walking. But he didn't. Even after the king learned Bathsheba was married to Uriah the Hittite (listed as one of David's "mighty warriors" in 1 Chronicles 11:41; see vv. 26–47), the lust that often accompanies discontentment led him to clearly violate God's law: "David sent messengers to get her. She came to him, and he slept with her" (2 Samuel 11:4).

We'll talk about the ramifications of David's sin in a later chapter, but let's not miss the warnings found in the story thus far:

- Discontentment makes us believe we deserve more than we have.
- Discontentment emboldens us to take what isn't ours.
- Discontentment casts off restraint in favor of momentary pleasure.

- Discontentment blinds our hearts to the effect of our sin on others.
- Discontentment normalizes sin and ignores God's commands.
- Discontentment makes us willing to break God's heart to get what we want.

The Language of Discontent

"You don't understand, Joanna," a woman told me years ago as she tried to explain the rightness of her extramarital affair. "We pray before we make love."

I don't know about your reaction, but that statement absolutely terrifies me. To justify our sin by spiritualizing it is blasphemy. I can't imagine how much it hurts the heart of God. But that's the nature of sin. It sears our consciences and opens us up to satanic deception—like the kind expressed by the "adulterous woman" in Proverbs 30:20 who

> eats and wipes her mouth
> and says, "I've done nothing wrong."

Beware, my friend, of that not-so-innocent email or that out-of-the-blue phone call. The fact that your old boyfriend suddenly appeared in your social media feed isn't a sign you're supposed to reconnect.

But sexual sin isn't our only temptation. The satanic hiss of discontent that lured Adam and Eve to the forbidden can keep us circling the wrong tree as well. Discontentment can lead us to pad a résumé to get the position. Or tear down a rival to prop up our worth. Or use discretionary funds to fund a vacation. Or any other number of destructive behaviors.

Even if we manage to resist blatant sin, we can become fluent in the language of discontentment, camouflaging our grumbling and murmuring against God behind a string of "if-onlys" and "when-thens":

- *If only* I had a husband, then I'd be content.
- *If only* I had a decent house, then I'd be satisfied.
- *If only* I had children . . .
- *If only* I didn't have children . . .
- *When* I get my degree, *then* I'll be happy.
- *When* my kids leave home, *then* I'll finally have a life.
- *When* I retire, *then* I'll do what God's been asking.

If we believe our contentment is contingent on having something different from what we currently have, we'll live in a poverty mindset that makes us greedy and stingy all at the same time. Rather than trusting God to meet our needs, we'll spend our lives attempting to hoard happiness. Not realizing we're trying to fill our emptiness with things that will never satisfy.

That's why having a true understanding of God is so important. If we don't understand how much He wants to bless us, we'll see God as a cosmic killjoy and miss all the Scriptures that declare His love and good intentions toward us. One of my favorites is found in Psalm 37:4 (ESV).

> Delight yourself in the LORD,
> and he will give you the desires of your heart.

You and I were created for blessings, but not at the expense of our souls. When we place the desires of our heart in the hands of Jesus and choose to find joy in Him alone, He will fulfill our longings in a way that causes us to flourish. Giving us an "unsatisfiable satisfaction" that fills us with His presence yet leaves us wanting more.

The Psalm 131 Woman

I love Psalm 131. Written by David, these three short verses give us a picture of a blessed and contented life that finds all it needs in God alone.

SECRETS OF A SETTLED SOUL

Aren't you tired of chasing blessings and coming up empty? True fulfillment requires daily decisions to be

- *Content with who you are*. God made you on purpose, my friend. There is no one else like you, so you need to be fully present just as you are. God wants to use your personality, physical body, intellect, and talents to display His glory in the world—even as He continues to transform you into the likeness of His Son.
- *Content with where you live.* God has placed you exactly where He wants you—including your address, your job, the family you were born into, and so on. While God may change some of that in the future, right here and right now, by faith, you can choose to say, "The boundary lines have fallen for me in pleasant places" (Psalm 16:6).
- *Content with what you have.* God has entrusted this one life to you. Refuse to squander it by grumbling or complaining. Choose to be grateful for what you've been given and look for ways to use it for His kingdom. Live from the abundance of God's provision rather than the poverty of always wanting more.
- *Content to trust God for everything else.* Because God knows you best, only He can provide what you need. When blessing comes, rejoice in His goodness. When trouble comes, trust that it's passed first through His hands. Don't let your joy and peace be determined by your circumstances.

You're *blessed* when you're content
with just who you are—no more, no less.
That's the *moment* you find yourselves
proud owners of everything
that can't be *bought*.

Matthew 5:5 MSG

My heart is not proud, LORD,
  my eyes are not haughty;
I do not concern myself with great matters
or things too wonderful for me.
But I have calmed and quieted myself,
  I am like a weaned child with its mother;
  like a weaned child I am content.

Israel, put your hope in the LORD
  both now and forevermore.

The "Proverbs 31 Woman" is often held up as a great role model—and rightly so, for we should all try to emulate the loving, industrious woman the proverb describes. However, if I had to choose, I'd rather be known as a "Psalm 131 Woman":

- *A woman whose "heart is not proud."* Instead of trying to be first, she's willing to go last. She seeks to understand others rather than always needing to be understood. You don't have to agree to be considered her friend. When she makes a mistake, she's quick to admit it rather than deflect blame. Instead of looking for approval from people, she seeks it from God.
- *A woman whose "eyes are not haughty."* Rather than viewing people who are different with judgment or disdain, she meets them with the love of God. She's quick to pray and slow to criticize. Believing the best in people rather than suspecting the worst, she never despairs of another person, for she's experienced God's transforming power.
- *A woman who isn't obsessed by "great matters or things too wonderful" for her.* Though she's competent and willing to use the gifts God has given her, she's content to stay in her lane. When He assigns a "great" and "wonderful" task to someone else, she doesn't let self-pity make her question His love. She isn't plagued by worry over world events, for she knows that God is in control.

- *A woman who has "calmed and quieted" her soul "like a weaned child."* Trusting God to meet her needs, "with thanksgiving, [she presents her] requests" to Him and allows the "peace of God" to guard her heart and mind (Philippians 4:6–7). Rather than wailing and flailing, she waits patiently for God's provision, confident that His love is working on her behalf.

Though the Psalm 131 Woman has a childlike faith, it isn't childish. Rather than making demands, she trusts that her Father knows best. As a result, she's content and displays a calm maturity. For she rests in this truth: *If God doesn't provide it, I don't need it. And if I need it, He'll provide it at just the right time.*

The Weaned Soul

The reference in Psalm 131 to being a "weaned child" may seem a bit graphic, but it helps us understand why God often allows frustration and delay in our lives. Just as I had to wean my little ones, God takes us through a weaning process as well. Making us wait a little longer between feedings. Introducing solid food to our diet when we'd much prefer milk.

Growing up is a confusing process for a toddler, and it can be confusing for Christians as well—to the point we want to cry:

Why would God withhold something I so desperately need?

Why doesn't He answer my prayers? I've tried to be faithful.

Weaning is painful, but without it, we can become addicted to God's blessing without being addicted to God. If we're to become "self-sufficient in Christ's sufficiency," we're going to have to leave our "childish ways" behind (1 Corinthians 13:11 GNT).

When Paul talks about learning to be content in Philippians 4:11–12, most English translations use the word *learned* twice. The original Greek, however, involves two different words. In verse 11, *learned* basically means "to understand."[12] But verse 12 uses another Greek word which "has the idea of being 'initiated' into something, much as the mystery religions would 'initiate' someone into their secret practices through a process."[13]

Learning contentment is a skill and a holy art. It starts with a *choice* of the will that changes the *condition* of our heart, which in turn creates a new *pattern* for life. As we find meaning and purpose in Jesus, looking to Him to provide our every need, we are initiated into an exclusive club—something Pastor Alan Carr calls "The Secret Society of the Satisfied."[14] A growing, thriving group of people who've learned that true peace and joy are only found in trusting God.

Rather than pounding on the Father's breast, demanding nourishment, these contented folks have learned how to feast on the meat of God's Word. Sitting quietly on His lap, they trust His provision. Secure in the Father's love, they're at peace in spite of their needs.

You and I are invited to join this select society. To be satisfied and contented people who are led and fed by the Good Shepherd. So filled with His goodness, we can't help but lie down in green pastures. Our thirst so quenched by His love, we walk beside still waters without needing to drink. People of the weaned soul—no longer driven to want more, always more.

For like David, we've discovered the beautiful truth of Psalm 23:1, "The LORD is my shepherd, I lack nothing."

Interestingly, this settled-soul contentment may bring our heavenly Father more glory than anything else we do. For as John Piper says, "God is most *glorified* in us when we are most *satisfied* in Him."[15]

What a wonderful reason to become a lifetime member of the Secret Society of the Satisfied!

Twelve

The Gift of Discipline

My dear child, don't shrug off God's discipline,
 but don't be crushed by it either.
It's the child he loves that he disciplines;
 the child he embraces, he also corrects.

Hebrews 12:5–6 MSG

When it comes to physical fitness, let's just say it isn't my spiritual gift.

I'm not one of those girls who loves working out. The kind who rolls out of bed eager to pound the pavement as the sun comes up. Most mornings you'll find me rolling over in bed trying to find a more comfortable position. I have no desire to post records at spin class or display an exquisite Zumba technique. I'm more selfless than that. Because I don't want to make others feel bad about themselves, I just don't show up. It's better for us all.

The truth is, I'm not fond of sweat. I have yet to experience the endorphin rush people gush about when they exercise hard. Instead, I just feel tired. Really tired. And ravenously hungry.

Gratefully, the Lord helped me lose forty pounds many years ago and I've kept it off by being careful of what I eat. But I still need help to overcome my resistance to exercise. For it might help defeat the inner rebellion I feel toward any kind of discipline that requires long-term commitment.

I'm an event girl, you see. Give me a project and I'm all over it. But ask me to do maintenance—the routine of having to do the same work over and over—and I want to scream.

But life, it turns out, *is* maintenance.

When we faithfully show up and do things we don't want to do just because they need to be done—well, that's the stuff of greatness, my friend. Especially when we trust the Holy Spirit to help us, seeking to do it all "as working for the Lord" (Colossians 3:23).

Discipline Is Not a Four-Letter Word

You may have noticed I want life to be easy. I think we all do. But Adam and Eve gave up the pleasant path when they chose to distrust God. In His mercy, however, God reversed the curse and turned it into a blessing, using the difficulties of life outside the Garden to strengthen, correct, and train us as we submit ourselves to Him. That's why Proverbs 3:11–12 advises,

> Do not despise the LORD's discipline,
>   and do not resent his rebuke,
> because the LORD disciplines those he loves,
>   as a father the son he delights in.

God's discipline and correction isn't rejection. It's direction. But how we respond to it determines whether we will benefit from it. As I see it, we have three choices.

Resisting God's Discipline

If your Flesh Woman is anything like mine, she doesn't like being corrected or being told what to do. Sometimes when the

Holy Spirit drills down on a wrong attitude, I attempt to deflect blame. *But what about those other people? They shouldn't have done what they did.* When He points out an issue in my life, I try to rationalize it away. *I know I shouldn't have had the second piece of cheesecake, Lord, but I'm really stressed out.*

At times resisting discipline involves ignoring God's voice entirely, much as my three-year-old granddaughter did on a recent visit when she picked up something breakable. "Please set it down, Quinley," I told her calmly. But instead of obeying, my sweet baby girl continued to play with the object, turning her head away slightly with a sly little smile. Pretending I hadn't corrected her, she acted as though I hadn't said a word.

"Do not despise the Lord's discipline," Proverbs 3:11 tells us. The word translated *despise* means "to spurn," "cast off," or "reject." But it can also mean "disappear" or "melt away."[1] When we ignore the discipline of the Holy Spirit—whether corrective or instructive—in a sense, we are rejecting God. But unlike an indulgent grandparent who winks at our sin with a smile and a sigh, our heavenly Father loves us enough to take action. For He knows that disobedience left unchecked only grows.

Resenting God's Discipline

Cloaked in self-righteousness, our Flesh Woman gets offended when God points out a weakness or sin. The idea that she might be anything less than wonderful awakens self-pity. *I was only trying to help, God. No one appreciates me!* When that doesn't work, self-preservation rises up. *I didn't do anything wrong. I will not apologize for defending myself.*

But resenting God's discipline can also involve despair. *I'm such a loser! What's the point of trying? I'll never change.* Proverbs 3:11 tells us to "not resent his rebuke." The word translated *resent* means "to be [or make] disgusted or anxious, abhor, be distressed, be grieved, loathe, vex, be weary."[2] You see, we can become so "grieved" by our sin that self-loathing takes over, causing us to *obsess* about our failure rather than *confess* it to the Lord. Regret and shame only keep us tied to our sins.

Receiving God's Discipline

Until we *receive* discipline from the Lord rather than resisting or resenting it, we can't access the power of the Holy Spirit to break the power of sin. On our own, we can't develop the new patterns of life God wants us to have. But when we trust that His perspective on our life is more accurate than our own, receiving His discipline and choosing to repent, the Holy Spirit enables us to choose a better way of life. Though patterns formed by our sin and weakness may linger for a time, as we cooperate with God's grace, He will help us truly change.

For the discipline of the Lord is always for our benefit. Intended to strengthen, correct, and train us so that we become more like Him.

Discipline That Strengthens

My son Josh was a happy observer for the first ten months of his life. He giggled and cooed at everything the family did. But due to low muscle tone, Josh was slow to make measurable progress in many areas. Finally, his doctor suggested an in-home physical therapist. Leslie Hayden came faithfully to our home for more than two years, putting Josh through his paces and teaching us exercises to help build his stamina and strength.

"Normal muscles are interlocked as layers, even at rest," Leslie told us during our first meeting, holding up her hands with the fingers interlaced. "But Josh's muscles are separate," she explained, pulling her hands apart. "So we have to awaken and bring the muscles together before we can begin to strengthen them."

And awaken them she did. Once a week, Leslie made my one-year-old absolutely miserable. Though she tried to make it fun for Josh, it was a lot of hard work. As his underdeveloped muscles were challenged, he'd sweat profusely and grunt and groan, fuss and moan in a manner eerily reminiscent of his nonathletic mother.

Baby Josh had to be taught every movement. How to roll over. How to sit up. How to crawl. How to pull himself up on furniture.

He would be two and a half before he started to walk, four years old before he started to talk. Nothing came instinctively for my child. Everything had to be learned. But as Josh cooperated (though reluctantly at times), we saw him grow in ability and strength.

As parents, John and I could have accepted our child's limitations and allowed him to stay weak. But Leslie told us Josh had potential for more, so we faithfully pushed and prodded him. Though we loved our son as he was, we loved him too much to leave him that way.

Is it any wonder that God does the same thing with us? Pushing and prodding us beyond our perceived capabilities. Requiring, nearly forcing us at times, to obey His commands. Because our Father knows the potential He's placed within us, His love won't let us settle for anything less.

"Endure hardship as discipline," Hebrews 12:7 tells us, "God is treating you as his children. For what children are not disciplined by their father?" The word translated *discipline* in this verse carries the idea of "tutorage, i.e. education or training," even "nurture." But it also carries the sense of "disciplinary correction."[3]

Had Josh been able to talk in those early years and you asked whether he felt loved or punished during physical therapy, he would have probably answered, "Punished." He had no idea the depth of love and dedication behind our actions. Unfortunately, like Josh, we often misinterpret our education by God. But as Hebrews 12:10–13 explains, if we'll cooperate with God's prescribed exercises, we'll become the strong, resilient, capable people we were born to be:

> [Our human fathers] disciplined us for a little while as they thought best; but God disciplines us for our good, in order that we may share in his holiness. No discipline seems pleasant at the time, but painful. Later on, however, it produces a harvest of righteousness and peace for those who have been trained by it.
>
> Therefore, strengthen your feeble arms and weak knees. "Make level paths for your feet," so that the lame may not be disabled, but rather healed.

Now nineteen, Josh is thriving. Though he still has some limitations, he's a testimony to the value of consistent discipline that, while painful, is administered in love.

So don't resist God's strengthening regimen, my friend, and don't resent it. Instead, receive it as a sweet gift to your soul. For no matter how exhausting it feels, you can trust that God's discipline is always for your benefit.

Even when it points out a wrong that needs to be made right.

Discipline That Corrects

My poor mother had her hands full with two little girls born eighteen months apart. Linda and I were so headstrong, she feared we'd be juvenile delinquents by the time we were six. But between my parents' prayers and their loving but firm discipline, God turned our willfulness into a stubborn determination to follow Him. And the healthy "fear of God" they instilled in our hearts definitely helped.

"Be sure your sin will find you out," my mother often said, quoting Numbers 32:23 (NKJV). You can hide your sins from people, she told us. But "nothing . . . is hidden from God" (Hebrews 4:13 NLT).

I wonder how long David thought he could continue his cover-up. From the start, he'd involved several of his staff in the Bathsheba affair. When one servant warned that the object of his interest was already married, David sent other "messengers" to get the bathing beauty (2 Samuel 11:3–4).

Later when he received word that Bathsheba was pregnant (v. 5), David attempted to hide his indiscretion by bringing her husband back from the battlefield (v. 6). But loyal Uriah didn't feel right sleeping in his wife's arms while his fellow soldiers slept outside on the ground. When David encouraged him to go home the next night, Uriah still chose to sleep outside the palace rather than go home to his wife (v. 8–9).

Unfortunately, David didn't show the same kind of integrity. Desperate to cover his sin, he sent instructions for his general to place Uriah "out in front where the fighting is fiercest" and then "withdraw from him so he will be struck down and die" (v. 15).

The dark plan worked. Uriah was killed in battle.

Perhaps, like me, you've wondered how a "man after God's own heart" became an adulterer and murderer. Though I can't presume to know the process, I do know the nature and effects of sin. I've watched it harden the hearts of committed Christians, searing their consciences to the point they not only sin against people but blatantly sin against God. And God takes that very seriously—as David would soon find out.

Once the prescribed time of mourning for Uriah was over, David and Bathsheba were free to marry. The king must have sighed in relief, thinking his cover-up had worked. But deep inside he must have known that what he "had done displeased the Lord" (v. 27).

When the prophet Nathan asked for an audience with the king, I wonder if David welcomed his friend or came to the meeting slightly guarded. But when Nathan opened the conversation by talking about a property dispute, David must have relaxed. *This isn't about me at all.* It appeared a rich man had stolen a poor man's beloved lamb (2 Samuel 12:1–4), and as Nathan told him about the unjust situation, the former shepherd began to fume.

"As surely as the Lord lives, the man who did this must die!" David erupted. "He must pay for that lamb four times over, because he did such a thing and had no pity" (vv. 5–6).

I wonder if Nathan allowed a silence to settle around the conversation before he looked deep in his friend's eyes and spoke the words God sent him to say: "You are the man!" (v. 7).

Shock waves must have hit David's soul as he sat back on his throne. Stripped bare of his excuses, the darkness of his heart was exposed by four little words. *You are the man.*

David's sin had finally found him out.

Though it might not be as dramatic when God brings correction to our souls, one way or another our sin will be exposed. For as Jesus says in Luke 12:2, "The time is coming when everything that is covered up will be revealed, and all that is secret will be made known to all" (NLT). He makes it clear in Revelation 3:19: "Those whom I love I rebuke and discipline."

When the Holy Spirit puts His finger on sin in our lives, we need to be quick to repent. For complete honesty before God is the only thing that can break the deceptiveness of sin.

We don't know exactly when David wrote Psalm 32:1–2, but it certainly describes the relief David must have felt after coming clean with the Lord. The freedom that is ours when we receive the Holy Spirit's correction and repent.

> Oh, what joy for those
> whose disobedience is forgiven,
> whose sin is put out of sight!
> Yes, what joy for those
> whose record the Lord has cleared of guilt,
> whose lives are lived in complete honesty! (vv. 1–2 NLT)

When you and I uncover our sins before Jesus, He covers them with His blood. And in responding to His rebuke, we are set free.

Discipline That Trains

In 2016, gymnast Simone Biles won four Olympic gold medals for her performances in individual all-around, vault, floor exercise, and the team all-around, plus a bronze medal for the balance beam.[4] She made everything seem effortless, successfully performing maneuvers that other accomplished gymnasts wouldn't even try.

But five years later, during the Tokyo Olympics, the world watched and commented as Biles made the excruciating decision to withdraw from the team competition. A bad case of "the twisties"—a loss of body orientation—had hit her while performing a vault. The condition lingered, causing her to miss most of the events she'd been expected to medal in.[5] But Simone remained on the floor and cheered on her teammates, finishing the games with two medals[6] and a record as "the most decorated gymnast of all time."[7]

What has been Simone Biles's secret? Natural talent honed by years of discipline—early mornings and long practices where she was pushed beyond strength and stretched beyond measure. Simone said no to an easy life and yes to discomfort in order to perfect her double back flip with a triple twist—just one of four gymnastics skills named for her.[8]

Though I've always dreamed of being a gymnast, I've never wanted to do the work required. Give me Simone's skill and make me look great in a sequined leotard and I'll be happy. I don't even need a gold medal.

But life doesn't work that way. And that, in a nutshell, is the issue when it comes to spiritual maturity and growth. Diligent training is the only way to release the potential God's placed within us. For it's the strain that produces strength—just as disciplined practice perfects needed skill.

Over and over in his epistles, Paul compares our spiritual journey to the work of an athlete whose goal is to win.

> Everyone who competes in the games goes into strict training. They do it to get a crown that will not last, but we do it to get a crown that will last forever. Therefore I do not run like someone running aimlessly; I do not fight like a boxer beating the air. No, I strike a blow to my body and make it my slave so that after I have preached to others, I myself will not be disqualified for the prize. (1 Corinthians 9:25–27)

Just as Olympic coaches help athletes create routines and perfect their form, the Holy Spirit helps us shape a better way of life. Convicting us of sin and teaching us more about Jesus, the Spirit pushes and prods us beyond all comfort with one goal in mind—to make us mature believers, "equipped for every good work" (2 Timothy 3:17).

As you and I show up and do the work, embracing God's discipline as a gift, Jesus Himself—the world's best Coach—releases

8 PRACTICES FOR SPIRITUAL MAINTENANCE

Just as our bodies require regular and diligent upkeep, you and I need to maintain our souls. In addition to the classic spiritual disciplines of prayer, Bible study, and meeting together with fellow believers, the following practices can help you stay in good spiritual shape.

1. ***Ask the Holy Spirit to increase your spiritual hunger.*** We can't want God without His help. So when He stirs your spirit, don't ignore His prompting. The Lord is wooing you to Himself and releasing grace to want Him more.

2. ***Fill your home or office with worship.*** When you don't have time or strength to worship God, turn on praise music and allow it to change the atmosphere—in your inner life as well as your outer circumstances.

3. ***When it comes to Scripture, read less and reflect more.*** Spend time soaking in Bible passages. Read until God speaks, then record what He's saying to you. The Holy Spirit wants to make the Bible come alive to you.

4. ***Remain tender to the checks and conviction of the Spirit.*** If you don't have peace about a situation, don't move forward. If God puts His finger on sin in your life, be quick to repent. Converse with God about everything and avoid quenching the Spirit.

5. ***Take Jesus everywhere you go***. He's with you whether you realize it or not—but acknowledging His presence and bringing Him into daily decisions keeps you Christ-centered and Spirit-led.

6. ***Practice regular spiritual housekeeping***. Don't let sin linger; with the Lord's help, deal with it. Ask God to adjust your attitude. Repent of any jealousy or pride. And don't put off obedience; instead, do your best to quickly obey.

7. ***Check your spiritual temperature.*** If you're feeling dry or distant from God, don't ignore the condition. But don't let condemnation

create more distance in your soul. Ask Jesus to awaken your heart and rekindle your soul. He loves to reveal Himself to people who recognize their need of Him.

8. *Make time for spiritual maintenance*. There's something powerful about an extended time alone with God. Find a quiet spot and unplug from outside voices. Be still and allow your heart to reconnect to the heart of your Father. Then with your Bible and journal in hand, start a holy conversation.

We ask God to give you complete knowledge of his will and to give you spiritual *wisdom* and *understanding*. Then the way you live will always honor and please the Lord, and your lives will produce every kind of *good fruit*.

Colossians 1:9–10 NLT

His power within us. Supercharging us by His Spirit so that we're able to perform "every good thing that is pleasing to him" (Hebrews 13:21 NLT).

Training in Godliness

"Train yourself to be godly," Paul advises in 1 Timothy 4:7–8. "For physical training is of some value, but godliness has value for all things, holding promise for both the present life and the life to come."

Just as physical training requires maintenance, we're called to consistently work toward holiness as children of God. However, trying to do it apart from the Holy Spirit is impossible. Believe me, I've tried. But all my best efforts at perfecting myself have only led to a bad case of the spiritual "twisties"—a severe disorientation that leaves me spinning helplessly and feeling far from God.

So how do we cooperate with the Holy Spirit's work in our life? Well, just as Simone Biles started at a young age, learning one gymnastic skill before adding another, we, too, must grow in grace and Christlikeness.

Peter outlines a training schedule to help us do that:

> Make every effort to add to your faith goodness; and to goodness, knowledge; and to knowledge, self-control; and to self-control, perseverance; and to perseverance, godliness; and to godliness, mutual affection; and to mutual affection, love. For if you possess these qualities in increasing measure, they will keep you from being ineffective and unproductive in your knowledge of our Lord Jesus Christ. (2 Peter 1:5–8)

Each element of this plan builds on the previous, but it all starts with this mandate: "Make *every effort* to add . . ."

Growing our faith isn't a passive activity. It requires an investment of energy and focus to work out what God has so graciously worked in (Philippians 2:12–13). As we make *every effort* to learn these important skills, God will give us a holy determination that's willing to practice and work hard to bring forth the life of Christ already within us (Galatians 2:20).

I had to smile when I learned the history behind the word translated *add* in 2 Peter 1:5. *Epichoregesate* comes from the root word *choros*,[9] from which we get our words *chorus*, *choreograph*, and *choreography*.[10] Isn't that beautiful? As we add one godly quality to another, perfecting one skill at a time, the Holy Spirit helps us choreograph a life that's worthy of God.

Let's take a moment and break down the routine:

- *"Add to your faith . . ."* This is where we start—with the all-out surrender of our lives to God. Believing that

Christ's work on the cross has provided all we need, we reject self-reliance and trust His power at work within us.

- *"Add . . . goodness."* Our deep trust in God should lead to a life marked by moral excellence. Not just right *doing*—that is, "good" on the outside. But right *being*—infused with God's goodness all the way through.
- *"Add . . . knowledge."* "The Spirit of wisdom and revelation" (Ephesians 1:17) wants to help us know Jesus better. An experiential knowledge of Christ and God's Word that goes beyond our own intellect and transforms the way that we live.
- *"Add . . . self-control."* As we relinquish control to God, He gives it back to us in a purified discipline that helps us master our passions and subject our appetites. Helping us live a life that's worthy of Christ's name.
- *"Add . . . perseverance."* The ability to "stay under,"[11] to carry a load or finish a task without giving up or giving in.[12] The endurance of Jesus displayed on the cross now works in us to make us strong and able to persevere.
- *"Add . . . godliness."* As image bearers of God, we are meant to bear a striking resemblance to our Maker. As we stay close to Jesus—"the pioneer and perfecter of faith" (Hebrews 12:2)—it will be His likeness that people see.

The first six spiritual "Olympic skills" have to do with our inner life and relationship to God, but the last two Peter recommends involve our relationship with others.

- *"Add . . . mutual affection."* This word denotes a "brotherly" love or kindness. Rather than focusing on ourselves, we're called to care about "the interests of others" (Philippians 2:4)—to be Jesus with skin on to everyone we meet.
- *"Add . . . love."* No ordinary love, this *agape* love desires the highest good of others and serves them selflessly. It's

> the kind of love Jesus exhibited when He laid down His life for us. We are called to do the same (1 John 3:16).

All of these skills are important to our maturity in God. As we add one skill to another skill and practice them regularly, the Holy Spirit will help us shape and perfect every move until we're doing intricate floor routines marked by God's presence. Vaulting over obstacles. Navigating the uneven bars of life. Moving confidently along the balance beam—the narrow way we've been called to walk as Christians (see Matthew 7:14).

Doing it all with a well-trained, submitted heart that is unafraid of falling. For we've been coached by a God "who is able to keep [us] from stumbling and to present [us] before his glorious presence without fault and with great joy" (Jude 24).

Embracing Discipline

Discipline strengthens. Discipline corrects. Discipline trains.

It really is God's gift to us. But we've got to humble our hearts in order to benefit. That's what David did when God used Nathan to bring him face-to-face with his sin.

Stunned into silence, David listened to the prophet's lengthy rebuke from the Lord (2 Samuel 12:7–12). But he didn't just listen. The chastened king responded with repentance. And we can learn a lot from his teachable heart.

"I have sinned against the LORD," David confessed in verse 13, cutting to the heart of the matter. No more spinning his story. No more ignoring his immense sins. Just raw, real, no-longer-adulterated repentance.

Though God forgave the sin, its consequence would be costly—the death of David and Bathsheba's infant son (vv. 14–19). But the Lord graciously allowed the couple to have other children—four more sons to be exact.

The first one they named Solomon (v. 24), perhaps derived from the Hebrew for "peace"—*shalom*.[13] I like that.

But it's the name of their second son that really speaks to my heart. In 1 Chronicles 3:5, we find a list that appears to record their offspring from youngest to oldest. And there we see that the second son born to David and Bathsheba (after Solomon) was given an unexpected name.

Nathan. Named after the prophet who had revealed their dark sin.

Rather than resenting the man and trying to forget the painful moment, David and Bathsheba honored both him and God. Receiving the correction of the Lord as a blessing, they commemorated it in the name of their son.

How to Recognize Discipline

What will our response be when the discipline of the Lord comes to us? Will we resist it or resent it? Or will we receive it as a gift to our souls?

To get to that point, we must first recognize when God is trying to get our attention—whether its discipline intended to correct, strengthen, or train. Here are a few ways I've come to recognize the Lord's work in my life:

- *Has God been dealing with an issue from multiple standpoints?* For instance, if my short temper has become an issue at work and at home, out of love, God allows consequences of my behavior to *correct* me.
- *Are there warning signs in my life that all is not well?* For instance, if my health is declining because of lack of self-care, God may allow me to experience weakness so I'm willing to do what is needed to build *strength* (even if it means exercise!).
- *Am I experiencing a drift in my devotion or unease in my soul?* For instance, if life's busyness has taken my focus from God, He may allow a difficult trial to draw my heart back to Him. At times, He'll stir a holy dissatisfaction

> inside to make me pursue *training* that will deepen my faith and strengthen my walk with Him.

No matter the form of discipline, it's important to remember that God's not looking at the *perfection* of our life but the *direction* of our heart. When we set our minds on pleasing God and knowing Him better, we can be "confident of this, that he who began a good work in you will carry it on to completion until the day of Christ Jesus" (Philippians 1:6).

So if God corrects you, receive the rebuke and repent.

If Jesus points out a weak place He wants to strengthen, be willing to cooperate with grace.

And if the Holy Spirit is trying to train you, be teachable and willing to do the work.

For God wants to prepare you and me for our place on heaven's Olympic team. Sparkling with His glory as we represent Jesus to the world. Trained, strong, and disciplined people.

Able to stick our landings—with no twisties in sight.

Thirteen

Faith over Fear

> They will have no fear of bad news;
> their hearts are steadfast, trusting in the Lord.
>
> Psalm 112:7

My boot heels clicked against the tile floor as I rolled my carry-on through the crowds of passengers at the Minneapolis airport. Bending close to my phone, I tried to hear John's voice over the noise.

"I'm going to share what's been happening with the congregation tomorrow," he told me. We'd just moved into our new church building in Whitefish debt free but, as it often happens, the pressures of a building campaign had taken a toll. Disagreement between John and some of the leadership was finally coming to a head. But instead of fear, all I felt was relief that the division would soon be out in the open. Perhaps now God could heal it.

The enemy was working the same havoc I'd experienced with our women's ministry team several years before (something I talk about in *Having a Mary Spirit*). But God had done such a work in me during that "crucible" time that I knew He would use this trial as well. We had enjoyed thirteen beautiful years of pastoring this church. Surely God would help us weather a few difficult ones.

I'd always believed (and still do) that church conflicts don't have to end in church splits. Yet there we were.

On the precipice.

John and I prayed together at the end of our call. But as soon as I hung up, the enemy attacked with fear. *What if it's all your fault?* he insinuated. *What if there's something going on that you don't know about? What if it all blows up tomorrow at church?*

Immediately I imagined every terrible possibility: theological error, financial irresponsibility, lack of integrity or moral failure—all the things people tend to assume when a church is in turmoil.

But with the swirling fear came advice from my friend Alicia Chole. Something she'd picked up from our great-great-not-so-great grandmother Eve.

Don't engage in prolonged conversations with talking snakes.[1]

The Origin of Fear

We've all felt the effects of fear and its sidekicks, worry and anxiety. As a girl who comes from a long line of Swedish worriers, I spent a lot of time in my teenage years being anxious and fearful. Because I operated under the false assumption that if I worried, bad things wouldn't happen, I often worried that I wasn't worrying enough.

Given that history, I had to smile when I read that people with higher IQs tend to worry more than others,[2] perhaps because they're more aware of the dangers and pitfalls of life. But smart or not, it's a miserable way to live.

Perhaps that's why David wrote, "Do not fret—it leads only to evil" (Psalm 37:8). Living in an imperfect world means we're going to feel anxious now and then, even terrified at times. But how we manage our fear—that's what makes all the difference.

Though fear starts in our minds, it triggers an almost instantaneous physical reaction in our bodies. A flush of heat prickles through us, and our heart begins to race. Our breathing quickens as blood flows away from the heart to our limbs, readying us to defend ourselves—to lash out, flee, or hide.[3] As fear revs up the amygdala, the most primitive part of our brain,[4] it slows our higher brain functions, making it difficult to make good decisions or think clearly.[5]

The survival instinct to "fight, flight, or freeze" can be a gift when we are facing actual danger—like a house fire or a mugger. The trouble comes when fear takes over our lives. Stuck in primitive brain reactions, we act and react to people and situations (real or imagined) in less than healthy ways. Prolonged or habitual fear keeps our bodies and minds on a level of constant high alert, leading to debilitating worry, simmering rage, compulsive behaviors, or actual physical disease—just to name a few issues.

But fear was never intended to be our main operating system. In fact, I don't think we were intended to experience it at all. Made for the perfection of the Garden and the safety of God's constant care, the original humans had no need to self-protect. But with the first bite of the forbidden, terror came rushing in to take over with its baser instincts. It's here we find the first mention of fear in the Bible.

"I was *afraid* because I was naked; so I hid," Adam said in Genesis 3:10 (emphasis mine).

Just as sin opened the door to fear in Genesis, fear left unchecked opens the door to sin in our lives. When you consider your sin-prone areas, I think you'll find they're often motivated by fear. Just ask the troubled CEO, who's embezzling funds to keep up appearances. Just ask the lonely woman looking for love in promiscuous sex. Or the church gossip who spreads rumors so that she can feel connected and significant. So many of our blatant sins and subtle compromises—if not all of them—can be traced back to some sort of fear.

Perhaps that's why God addresses fear so often in the Bible: He knows what unhealthy fear—which we'll focus on in the rest of this chapter—does to our souls. It not only torments our mind and ravages our body, it undermines our faith and makes us feel distant from God. Rather than a life dominated by "fight, flight, or freeze," we're invited to a higher form of thinking. To constantly turn our hearts to God as we choose to "trust, trust, and trust."

Rejecting the Spirit of Fear

If we're going to be victorious over fear, worry, and anxiety, we need to understand a few things.

First of all, unhealthy fear isn't our friend. It's an emotional bully that pretends to protect us while terrifying us with the unknown. It convinces us to shrink back to be safe, yet makes us overstep in an attempt to be significant. It pets and coddles us with self-pity, but then devours us with self-hatred. Fear pushes us to run ahead of God when we shouldn't and holds us back when God says it's time to go. It puffs up our ego with pride one day, only to tear us down with insecurity the next. Fear gets us coming and going, doing all of its dirty work within the confines of our mind.

Second, debilitating fear isn't just a thought, feeling, or reaction. According to the Bible, it can actually be a spirit—an unholy response to life that isn't from God. "For God has not given us a spirit of fear, but of power and of love and of a sound mind" (2 Timothy 1:7 NKJV).

As Christians, we can't afford to entertain the spirit of fear when it comes knocking. For if we don't renounce and reject it, this unholy fear attacks the three things God *has* given us according to verse 7—power, love, and a sound mind.

- The spirit of fear wants to make us feel *powerless*.
- The spirit of fear wants to convince us that we're *unloved*.
- The spirit of fear wants to make us *unsound* in our thinking.

Gratefully, God has given us the Holy Spirit to counteract the spirit of fear and help us gain victory in the very places the enemy has targeted. Listen to what the Bible says about that (emphasis mine):

> I pray that from his glorious, unlimited resources he will *empower* you with inner strength through his Spirit. (Ephesians 3:16 NLT)

> For we know how dearly God loves us, because he has given us the Holy Spirit to fill our hearts with his *love*. (Romans 5:5 NLT)

> So letting your sinful nature control your mind leads to death. But letting the Spirit control your *mind* leads to life and peace. (Romans 8:6 NLT)

If we'll cooperate with the Holy Spirit, He will help us neutralize and dismantle the spirit of fear. I love how Romans 8:15–16 describes the freedom He brings:

> So you have not received a spirit that makes you fearful slaves. Instead, you received God's Spirit when he adopted you as his own children. Now we call him, "Abba, Father." For his Spirit joins with our spirit to affirm that we are God's children. (NLT)

Did you hear that? Fear isn't the boss of you, my friend![6] You are God's beloved child, and as you receive that truth deep in your soul, His "perfect love drives out fear" (1 John 4:18). You've been accepted into God's great family with full access to His storehouse of riches. Which means you have all the power, love, and wisdom you need to live a life that isn't dominated by fear.

As you fully surrender and make Jesus Lord of your life, He will give you a reverent understanding of God that breaks the crippling power of anxiety. For when we have a healthy and holy fear of God, there's no need to fear anything else.

Of course, that doesn't mean you'll never feel afraid. Living in this fallen world pretty much guarantees that the primitive part of your brain will be triggered more often than you'd like.

But just as it isn't a sin to be tempted, neither is it a sin to feel afraid. It's what we do with the temptation and fear that matters.

As someone once said, "I can't keep birds from flying over my head, but I can keep them from nesting in my hair."

We can keep those destructive thoughts from landing by a daily decision:

Will I live by fear? Or will I live by faith?

Triggering Trust

David had to choose between fear and faith countless times as he fled from King Saul in those early years. The decision to trust God became even more important in 1 Samuel 30:1–6, when David and his men returned to Ziklag to find their hometown burned and their families taken captive.

But instead of launching an immediate rescue mission, the grieving soldiers turned their anger on their leader. Not surprisingly, David was afraid. In fact, he "was greatly distressed because the men were talking of stoning him," verse 6 tells us. The verb translated "greatly distressed" suggests that David "was pressed into a tight corner, the way a potter would press clay into a mold."[7]

But rather than allowing the spirit of fear to shape his responses, David turned to God in two specific ways:

1. He "found strength in the Lord his God" (v. 6).
2. "He inquired of the Lord" (v. 8).

As David refused to give in to fear and looked to God instead, he received strength and encouragement from his heavenly Father—and the ability to think clearly enough to ask for wisdom.

"Shall I pursue this raiding party?" David asked God in verse 8. "Will I overtake them?"

With confirmation that the rescue would succeed, David rallied his men and pursued the Amalekite raiders. Though it required a fierce, twenty-four-hour battle (v. 17), with the Lord's help they prevailed. "David recovered everything the Amalekites had taken, including his two wives," verses 18–19 say. "Nothing was missing:

4 WAYS TO OVERCOME FEAR

When something happens that triggers deep emotion, unhealthy fear often tries to take over. But instead of giving in to it, my friend Joyce Douglas suggests that we "Stop, Pause, and Choose." I've expanded on these and added a fourth: "Pray."

1. ***Stop***. Cease all activity, mentally, physically, and emotionally. Literally stop yourself in your tracks and get off the roller coaster of emotion. Unclench your hands, relax your jaw, and still your mind.

2. ***Pause***. Back up a bit to put some distance between you and the emotion. In many ways, fear and strong emotions are just vibrations in your body. Release it to God.

3. ***Choose***. Refuse to nurse your fear or rehearse it. Consider where the emotion is trying to take you and, with the Lord's help, choose a different response. Then choose a different response with the help of the Holy Spirit.

4. ***Pray***. Ask God to help you identify what you're feeling and the fear that might lie behind it. Rather than resisting the emotion, allow the Lord to help you process it as you give it to Him.

Memorizing and quoting Scripture out loud has been powerful in overcoming fear. Here's a verse that's really helped me:

> Do not be anxious about anything, but in every situation, by prayer and petition, with thanksgiving, present your requests to God. And the peace of God, which transcends all understanding, will guard your hearts and your minds in Christ Jesus. (Philippians 4:6–7)

"Let not your *hearts* be troubled. *Believe* in God; believe also in me."

John 14:1 ESV

young or old, boy or girl, plunder or anything else they had taken. David brought everything back."

Nothing was lost. Everything was recovered. And the spirit of fear that had oppressed David so cruelly was gone.

I believe the Lord wants to do the same thing for us. Though some of our losses won't be restored this side of heaven—a broken marriage, a deceased loved one, a failed business—God wants to help us resist and renounce the spirit of fear so that, by faith, we invade the enemy's territory and take back everything God wants us to have.

Psalm 56:3 offers a simple prescription from David that's helping me choose faith over fear: "When I am afraid, I put my trust in you."

So when fear comes knocking—and it will, my friend—don't let it trigger panic. Let it trigger trust instead.

Fear may be the enemy of faith.

But faith is the antidote to fear.

Equipped for Perilous Times

In case you don't remember, the year 2020 was crazy. Fear was rampant, even in the hearts of believers. With so many competing opinions and so much "fake news" flying around, it was hard to know what was true and what was false. Some people were terrified of the COVID-19 virus, while others called it a hoax. Some people refused to wear masks because they insisted God would protect them, yet lost sleep at night over deep-state conspiracies and fear of losing their rights. Two years later, as I finish this book, a lot of the chaos continues.

In times like these it can be hard to know where to land as believers, but here's a good place to start. As Christians, we aren't called to live *politically*, and we're definitely not called to live *fearfully*. Instead, we're called to live *biblically* which means we've got to find out what God wants us to do—we've got to exalt God's truth above every other opinion.

In Isaiah 8:11, God warns the prophet not to "follow the way of this people." But He goes on to give instructions that seem especially pertinent today:

> Do not call conspiracy
> everything this people calls a conspiracy;
> do not fear what they fear,
> and do not dread it.
> The LORD Almighty is the one you are to regard as holy,
> he is the one you are to fear. (vv. 12–13)

God isn't shocked by current world events. For human history has experienced much more tumultuous periods than this. Our sovereign Lord was in control then—and He's in control now. The promise Jesus made to believers in Matthew 28:20 is still the same today: "Surely I am with you always, to the very end of the age."

As you and I navigate these troubled times, we can't afford to give the spirit of fear room to operate. We must refuse the discord and hatred that make us love our opinions more than we love people. The worry and skepticism that cause us to talk more about fake news than the good news of the gospel.

Paul and Timothy certainly lived in "perilous times" (2 Timothy 3:1 NKJV). In fact, that's the whole context of Paul's second letter. The Roman emperor Nero was persecuting the church with unimaginable brutality. To be a Christian meant you were literally in danger for your life.

But rather than encouraging the young pastor to self-protect or to demand his religious rights, Paul pointed Timothy to the equipment God had given him to counteract fear—the Holy Spirit of God available to you and me as well. The NIV translation of 2 Timothy 1:7 focuses on this empowering gift: "For the Spirit God gave us does not make us *timid*, but gives us power, love and self-discipline" (emphasis mine).

The spirit of fear wants to intimidate us. It wants to shut us down and shut us up. At the same time, it wants to stir us up and make us angry, living in constant conflict and lacking peace. But as God's people you and I are meant to live above the confusion.

Filled with the Spirit's *power*, the Father's *love*, and the *self-discipline* of our Savior, even in the most perilous of times.

No More Fear

When something stirs up strong emotions in me, I'm learning to pause and ask, "*Is this faith or is this fear?*" Because in situations both big and small, it's vital to discern what operating system I'm using—the Spirit of God or the spirit of fear.

That's what I had to do in Minneapolis that long-ago night. As the spirit of fear tried to overwhelm me with accusations, I turned to God instead.

"Lord, if there's something John and I need to see or a sin we need to confess, I trust that You'll show us," I prayed as I walked to my gate. "We want to be right before You as well as before our people."

With the surrender came a boldness to stand up to the enemy: "Satan, I will not entertain your accusations. John and I belong to God. If you've got an issue with us, you'll need to take it up with Him."

As I took authority over the spirit of fear, the peace of God once again settled around my soul. Though I didn't know what the next day would mean to our future, I felt an unexpected calm. For God was already in our tomorrow.

Just before my flight, however, John called with news that one of the church leadership would read a letter the next day asking for his resignation. Ironically, it would happen on a significant anniversary. Five years earlier, the church had sent our family to Hawaii to celebrate ten years of ministry. On John's fifteenth anniversary as pastor, they would ask us to leave.

In my spirit, I knew the timing wasn't intentional. These men loved Jesus and were trying to do what they thought was best for the church. But of course it hurt, especially when I allowed my mind to wander into the what-ifs, if-onlys, and what-might-have-beens.

Earlier that week a supportive friend had prayed over our ministry. "Lord, show Pastor John and Joanna the handwriting on the wall." I could tell she was unaware of the negative connotation, but her words had immediately brought to mind the mysterious message scrawled on King Belshazzar's wall in Daniel 5:27: "You have been weighed in the balances, and found wanting" (NKJV).

Though John and I had certainly made mistakes over the years, I knew that wasn't what God was saying, for we'd sincerely tried to do everything He asked. Though the Sunday service would be difficult, I felt a supernatural peace inside.

Before boarding the airplane, I decided to take one last bathroom stop. The terminal was new, so the bathroom was spotless—except for one little patch in the second-to-last stall. Next to the toilet paper dispenser, someone had written three little words in black Sharpie. A message that still ministers to me today.

Don't be afraid.

I don't know what you're walking through right now, my friend, but I believe those words were written for you as well. When we've placed our lives in the hands of Jesus, we aren't measured by the "handwriting on the wall."

Instead, He gives us the "handwriting on the stall."

A loving and tender reminder: don't be afraid.

Jesus over Everything

Faith over fear. It's one of the most important elements of trusting God. Exalting what we know above what we feel. Refusing to let anyone's lofty opinion—even our own—exalt itself against our knowledge of God.

Several months ago I had the privilege of interviewing author and Bible teacher Lisa Whittle for *The Living Room with Joanna Weaver* podcast. Lisa had so many great things to say about her book *Jesus Over Everything*.[8] But after our talk, the Holy Spirit took me on a side trip that I want to share with you.

I imagined her title like a fraction:

$$\frac{\text{Jesus}}{\text{Everything}}$$

Now, I'm not much of a mathematician, but I do know that when the number on the top of a fraction is greater than the number on the bottom, it results in at least one whole number and often more. For instance, six over two equals three. But when you put the lesser number on top, you end up with only a fraction of the whole. Two over six will never be anything more than one-third. No matter how you try to manipulate the numbers, unless the top number is greater than the bottom, you'll never come up with anything whole.

Which raises some important questions:

- *Why do we put lesser things over Jesus?*
- *Why is fear allowed to trample our faith?*
- *Why do we allow "our truth" to be truer than the truth of God's Word?*
- *And why does the devil get more airtime in our thoughts than the One who made us?*

When we minimize God by maximizing everything else, we end up with a fraction of the life we were meant to enjoy. Rather than being whole and wholly His, we live a halfway life. Halfway holy. Halfway trusting. All of which results in a halfway peace.

But when we consistently put Jesus over everything—including our fears—that's when we access the full measure of trust and peace the Bible promises:

> You will keep in perfect peace
> those whose minds are steadfast,
> because they trust in you. (Isaiah 26:3)

God was gracious to help us navigate that difficult season in Whitefish. I wish I could say the conflict was easily settled and our ministry at the church resumed with fresh vision. Instead, God chose to lead us on a different path.

As John and I sought the Lord in the weeks after that fateful Sunday, He spoke to us individually in our separate quiet times, telling us that our time in Whitefish was over. Though we'd felt willing and ready to navigate the trouble, God made it clear that He'd prepared someone else to lead the church.

Saying goodbye to a church we dearly loved—and still love—was heartbreaking. Many years later, tears still come to my eyes when I think of it. Yet there was a sweet release as John and I placed the church in God's hands and trusted Him with our future.

But even with a tangible sense of His grace, I still had to battle fear. Fear of what people would think, of what people might say. Fear that we'd be considered failures. Fear that despite our best intentions, we'd done it all wrong. Most concerning of all was the fear that God's work would be hindered in the hearts of our people and the community.

But the Holy Spirit kept reminding me: *This is God's church, Joanna. Not yours.* As Jesus says in Matthew 16:18, "I will build my church, and the gates of hell shall not prevail against it" (ESV).

Though I still don't understand why it all happened the way it did, I've learned that I don't need to understand in order to have peace. It's a lesson that still serves me today whenever a challenge arises and I have to choose faith over fear.

For when we put our hope in Jesus and trust in His power to redeem, He'll make certain the "gates of hell" don't prevail against us.

Rolling Away Our Fears

God has been so faithful to do deep work in my heart in the area of fear. But if I'm not careful I can still catastrophize the most benign of situations—especially when I don't see an easy answer or the conflict remains unresolved.

But instead of fretting, which "leads only to evil," according to Psalm 37:8, I'm learning to follow David's suggestions:

> Trust in the Lord and do good . . .
> Take delight in the Lord . . .
> Commit your way to the Lord. (37:3–5)

The Hebrew word for "commit" in verse 5 is *gālal*. It means to "roll" or "roll away."[9] The word was used to describe how a camel kneels down and rolls to the left to unload its burden. I love what Sheila Walsh writes about that:

> The picture for us is a beautiful one. We are invited to kneel before God but encouraged not to stop there. We are called to roll over and let the burden fall off our backs. . . . Are you anxious about anything? Kneel down in worship of the God who is in control of every detail of your life, and let your burdens roll away.[10]

That simple picture of faith has helped me a lot. But what do you do when the fear just won't leave? When, after rolling your care on the Lord, the anxiety still seems attached to your back? That was my experience back in our early years of ministry, when worry seemed to be my daily companion.

As mentioned before, my need for success nearly destroyed my marriage. But it was my fear of failure that kept me up at night thinking of all the things John and I hadn't done. The things we'd accomplished, but not very well. All the ways we weren't measuring up to my preconceived idea of successful ministry. All the ways John and I needed to change.

What if we flunk out of ministry? I worried. *What will happen to us then?*

The Lord listened to my oh-dears and oh-mys for a season, but then He interjected this important thought: *So . . . what if you did have to leave the ministry, Joanna? What would be your biggest fear then?*

Well, several worst-case scenarios immediately came to mind, but the Lord had me choose the very worst one. Then He asked me to go to the end of my greatest fear and see Him standing there.

If the thing you fear most actually happened, what would still be true of Me?

Though my Flesh Woman didn't want to admit it, the answer was clear. God would still be good, and He'd love me. I would still belong to Him, and He'd take care of my needs.

If you're battling fear right now, I want to encourage you to ask these important questions:

- *What is the worst thing that could happen?*
- *If it happened, what would still be true of God?*

As someone who has had her worst fear become a reality several times—that is, perceived failure in ministry—I can tell you from personal experience that God will be with you. He will "never leave you nor forsake you" (Hebrews 13:5 NKJV). And even though you find yourself walking in the "valley of the shadow of death"—whether literally or figuratively—you will "fear no evil" (Psalm 23:4 NKJV). For God Himself will surround and protect you.

I don't know what the enemy is using to haunt and taunt you, but I can promise you this. If you'll allow God to take you to the end of your fear and trust that He'll be with you no matter what you face, the spirit of fear will lose its grip on your life. As faith dismantles fear, you'll experience the truth of David's words:

> I sought the LORD, and he answered me;
> he delivered me from all my fears.
> Those who look to him are radiant;
> their faces are never covered with shame.
> (Psalm 34:4–5)

As you trust in the Lord with all your heart and commit your cares to Him—including your fear and anxiety—He will turn your worst-case scenario into a display case for His glory.

For when we exalt faith over fear, Jesus is given His rightful place in our life. King over our doubts. Lord over our fears. Master over our circumstances.

Jesus over everything.

And we are made whole.

Fourteen

God-Sized Prayers

Whatever you ask in My name, that I will do.
John 14:13 NKJV

It was a dark time in England as well as the world. Hitler and his Nazi regime had stormed through Europe, taking entire countries captive with barely a fight.

In 1940, Britain was in the crosshairs. It seemed impossible that the small island nation would survive. In aircraft alone, the Royal Air Force was outnumbered four to one.[1] Night after night, Hitler's Luftwaffe hammered London with air raids, raining death and destruction on homes, businesses, churches—even hitting Buckingham Palace several times.[2]

But some 190 miles to the west, at a small Bible college in Wales, a counterwar was being waged by a group of ordinary people. Had Hitler understood their impact, he would have done his best to shut them down. Day after day, this heavenly battalion of one hundred men and women engaged in a campaign of intense intercession.

"Pray as though you were the soldier on the front line," their leader, Rees Howell, had told them.[3] They'd done just that and God had used the group mightily—giving them supernatural insight into the plans of the enemy. As they prayed, battles that seemed hopeless had suddenly turned around.

At Dunkirk, for instance, Hitler's army had mysteriously stopped fighting, allowing the evacuation of 338,226 men. Dubbed a "miracle of deliverance" by Winston Churchill, it had been the largest and most successful evacuation in military history.[4]

The so-called Battle of Britain was raging, and British airmen struggled to fend off wave after wave of large-scale German air attacks on southern England. During one night of especially fierce fighting, it appeared that England's air force would be overcome. But then the Germans unexpectedly broke off attack and retreated. The Royal Air Force gave chase, downing several aircraft and capturing the pilots.

During interrogation, British intelligence asked three of the captured Germans, "Why did your formation retreat when only two planes were fighting you?"

"Two airplanes?" the German pilots answered, looking bewildered. "There were hundreds! Where did you get all the planes?"[5]

Invited to Partner with God

It's truly inspiring to hear stories like that of Rees Howell and his army of intercessors. I can't help but wonder how many miracles we've missed and how many God-sized interventions *didn't* happen because God's people didn't pray—or because our prayers just weren't ambitious enough.

Some people argue that because God is all-knowing and sovereign over human affairs, our prayers don't really matter in the grand scheme of things. But that's not what the Bible teaches. Instead, God seems to link His work on earth to the willingness of His people to pray.

"I looked for someone among them," God says in Ezekiel 22:30, "who would build up the wall and stand before me in the gap on behalf of the land so I would not have to destroy it, but I found no one." Though this passage refers to Old Testament Israel, I believe God is still looking for intercessors who will "stand in the gap" and agree with other believers in prayer.

For Jesus promises in Matthew 18:19, "If two of you agree here on earth concerning anything you ask, my Father in heaven will do it for you" (NLT). The Lord is looking for believers who will dare to pray God-sized prayers—and persist in praying them—so that God's will can be accomplished on earth as it is in heaven.

Sadly, I must confess that I'm not very good at intercessory prayer. While I enjoy a daily, ongoing conversation with my heavenly Father, most of my prayers center around my little world and my little needs. I can get so distracted by personal concerns and burdens that I neglect to "pray big" on behalf of others, faithfully lifting their needs to the Lord in fervent, persistent prayer.

I don't think I'm alone in this. Even those of us who have been Christians all our lives can opt out of ambitious prayer and intercession because we prefer to focus on aspects of our faith that come more easily to us. But think of the miracles that could happen if ordinary-sized Christians dared to pray God-sized prayers and trusted Him to bring about God-sized answers.

The great churchman John Wesley is widely quoted as saying, "God does nothing except in response to believing prayer." If that's true, perhaps we need to reconsider how we spend the bulk of our time.

Prayer was certainly important to Jesus. He often prayed alone in the morning (Mark 1:35) and on at least one occasion He spent an entire night in prayer (Luke 6:12). Though fully God, Jesus emptied Himself of His power and privilege (Philippians 2:6–7). Which means that, like us, Jesus had to tap into the divine power of God to do what He'd been assigned to do.

Jesus prayed in the Jordan River before being anointed by the Holy Spirit for public ministry (Luke 3:21). He prayed before choosing the disciples (Luke 6:12–13). He prayed before raising Lazarus from the dead (John 11:41–42).

Jesus not only prayed *before* active ministry, He also prayed *after*. For He understood that people's applause can be more dangerous than their cruelest rejection. When the crowd wanted to make Jesus king after He fed the five thousand, Matthew 14:23 tells us that Jesus sent away the multitudes and "went up on the mountain by Himself to pray" (NKJV).

If Jesus needed prayer to navigate the challenges of life and ministry, without doubt, we need prayer even more. As pastor Ray Stedman once said, "It is significant to note that, though Jesus never taught his disciples how to preach, he did teach them how to pray."[6]

Prayer moves the hand of God—not only in the world around us, but in our souls as well. As we seek His face, God's will is established *in* us and then *through* us.

The kingdom of God overcoming the kingdoms of this world.

Wielding the Weapon of Prayer

As Israel's king and military leader, David had multiple resources at his disposal—chariots and horses, well-stocked arsenals, and entire regiments of soldiers. When other kings and nations came against Israel, David would check in with God and ride out to war (see 2 Sam. 5:19).

But when the attack was personal, David rarely resorted to the strong "arm of flesh" (2 Chronicles 32:8 NKJV). Even as king, he didn't leverage his power to shut down his critics. He didn't demand their respect or force their allegiance. Instead, David turned to God.

Many of David's prayers are captured in the Psalms. In fact, more than half of the Bible's one hundred fifty Psalms are believed to have been written by David,[7] and many of these are worded as prayers. Psalm 86:1–2 is just one powerful example:

> Hear me, Lord, and answer me,
>   for I am poor and needy.
> Guard my life, for I am faithful to you;
>   save your servant who trusts in you.

Though David certainly wasn't perfect, for the most part, this man after God's own heart was fully dependent on Him. As David looked to the Lord throughout his eventful life, God showed Himself faithful and worthy of absolute trust.

When you consider the intimate friendship David enjoyed with the Lord, it's stunning to realize that you and I have been given even greater access than David. Because of Jesus, we can approach "God's throne of grace with confidence, so that we may receive mercy and find grace to help us in our time of need" (Hebrews 4:16). And His grace for others as well.

So why don't we go to the throne room more often? And why don't we *feel* that confidence when we do? Often it's because we don't know what to ask for or how we should pray in certain situations. That's where the Holy Spirit becomes so precious. For as Paul writes in Romans 8:26–27, though "we do not know what we ought to pray for, . . . the Spirit himself intercedes for us . . . in accordance with the will of God."

Just think of that! You and I have a direct line to heaven. The Spirit of God—the same powerful Spirit who brought order out of chaos at creation and raised Christ from the dead—lives *in* us and wants to pray *through* us. Stirring our hearts. Enlivening our prayers so that the "effective, fervent prayer of a righteous man [or woman] avails much" (James 5:16 NKJV).

Unfortunately, I think we often underestimate the importance of the Holy Spirit when it comes to living out our faith. After all, it's the Spirit who first drew us to Christ by convicting us of sin (John 16:8). It's the "law of the Spirit who gives life" that "set [us] free from the law of sin and death" (Romans 8:2). It's the "Spirit of wisdom and revelation" who helps us know Jesus better (Ephesians 1:17), for without the Holy Spirit, we cannot "understand what God has freely given us" (1 Corinthians 2:12). As we welcome His work, the Spirit who calls out, "*Abba*, Father" within us (Galatians 4:6) confirms that we truly belong to God.

The Third Person of the Trinity also helps us "pray in the power of the Holy Spirit" (Jude 20 NLT). Rather than giving voice to the whims and wants of Flesh Woman, the Spirit helps us pray confidently "according to [God's] will," according to 1 John 5:14. But to access the power of the Holy Spirit, we must give Him full control of our lives, trusting Him to lead and guide us even as we pray.

For Spirit-inspired prayer is part of the "full armor of God" described in Ephesians 6:13–18. While Paul doesn't assign it a specific piece of "armor" (like the "belt of truth" and "breastplate of righteousness" in v. 14), we see how it should be used in verses 17–18: "Take the . . . sword of the Spirit, which is the word of God. And pray in the Spirit on all occasions, with all kinds of prayers and requests."

Do you see how it comes together? When used in combination with God's Word, Spirit-led prayer becomes a superweapon designed to take out the enemy. Helping us bring down "the prince of the power of the air" (Ephesians 2:2 NKJV).

Accessing God's Power in Prayer

I've been blessed to experience moments in prayer when heaven touches earth. Times when, because of the Holy Spirit's quickening power, I pray with a clarity and authority that are definitely not my own. Times when intercession seems effortless and my entire being is engaged—body, soul, and spirit.

Unfortunately, it doesn't happen as often as it should.

Perhaps that's why I've been so blessed by a small book I ran across recently—*How to Pray* by R. A. Torrey. Dwight L. Moody asked his friend Torrey to write the book as a resource to help Christians develop a prayer life.[8] And oh, my goodness, it's helping me! First published in 1900, the updated version I read still feels relevant today.

Rather than making me feel guilty about the weakness of my prayer life, Torrey emphasizes how much God wants to help me pray. He not only acknowledges the blockage many of us feel when praying, he also offers practical tips to help us break through:

> When we feel least like praying is the time when we most need to pray. We should wait quietly before God and tell Him how cold and

> prayerless our hearts are. We should look up to Him, trust Him, and expect Him to send the Holy Spirit to warm our heart and draw us out in prayer. It will not be long before the glow of the Spirit's presence will fill our heart. We will begin to pray with freedom, directness, earnestness, and power. Many of the most blessed seasons of prayer I have ever known have begun with a feeling of utter deadness and prayerlessness. But, in my helplessness and coldness, I have cast myself upon God and looked to Him to send His Holy Spirit to teach me to pray. And, He has always done it.[9]

Allowing the Holy Spirit to "warm our heart and draw us out in prayer" is far better than trying to work up a counterfeit. As Torrey notes, "Many people lose faith altogether by trying to create faith by an effort of their will. When the thing they made themselves believe they would receive is not given, the very foundation of faith is often undermined."[10]

That's why surrender is so important. For until we let go of our agendas, we'll tend to treat prayer as a type of currency to get what we want. God will be demoted to a vending machine rather than honored as our supreme Ruler. When we *don't* get what we want, many of us start avoiding prayer altogether.

But when we press close to Jesus and begin to hear His heartbeat, our resistance to prayer will begin to weaken. For we'll see prayer as a divine conversation that doesn't pull God to our will but prepares us to know and cooperate with His. As we partner with the Holy Spirit, He will help us pray effectively so that heaven can impact earth.

Piercing holes in the darkness so that the light of God's love can invade our lost planet. Reaching and then saving one soul at a time.

Pray Big—and Keep On Praying

The world is looking for something real. Something genuine. Something so powerful and supernatural, it can't be explained apart from God. But in order for that to happen, we've got to let God out of the box we sometimes place Him in. We've got to be willing

HOW TO PRAY EFFECTIVELY

We all know we should pray, but we don't always know how to do it. These tips from R. A. Torrey have definitely helped me:

1. ***We must come into God's presence.*** "There must be a definite and conscious approach to God when we pray." A deliberate coming into His presence and a "vivid realization that God is bending over us and listening as we pray."[11]

2. ***We must earnestly reach out to God.*** "The prayer which prevails with God is the prayer into which we put our whole soul, stretching out toward God in intense and agonizing desire. Much of our . . . prayer lacks power because it lacks heart."[12]

3. ***We must be obedient to God's Word.*** "If we want power in prayer, we must be earnest students of His Word to find out what His will concerning us is. Then having found it, we must do it."[13]

4. ***We must pray according to God's will.*** One of the greatest secrets of prevailing prayer is to "study the Word to find what God's will is as revealed there in the promises. Then [prayerfully claim the promises] with the absolutely unwavering expectation that He will do what He has promised."[14]

5. ***We must look to the Holy Spirit to help us.*** When we come into God's presence, "we should be silent before Him. We should look up to Him to send His Holy Spirit to teach us how to pray. We must wait for the Holy Spirit and surrender ourselves to the Spirit. Then, we will pray correctly."[15]

6. ***We must pray with faith and believe that God will answer.*** Jesus says, "Whatever you ask for in prayer, believe that you have received it, and it will be yours" (Mark 11:24). When our prayer request is based on God's promises and our obedience lines up with His Word, we can have "confident, unwavering expectation" that God will answer our prayer.[16]

7. ***We must thank God in advance.*** "In approaching God to ask for new blessings, we must never forget to thank Him for blessings already granted."[17] As we meditate on what God has done in the past, our "faith grows bolder and bolder. We come to feel, in the very depths of our soul, that there is nothing too hard for the Lord."[18]

These are just a few of Torrey's suggestions, but there's another one that has brought fresh breath to my prayer life and helped me focus on the most important outcome: "The true purpose of prayer is that God may be glorified in the answer."[19]

May it be so, Lord. May it be so.

Devote yourselves to prayer
with an alert mind and a thankful heart.

Colossians 4:2 NLT

to pray God-sized prayers so that He can be revealed in God-sized answers. No longer *praying* small. No longer playing small. Even when it comes to our personal requests.

This is where I tend to hesitate, however. Because I'm aware of my Flesh Woman's demanding spirit, I'm often reluctant to ask God for anything more than my general needs. "If it's your will, Lord," I often pray at the end of my requests—for I want to continually acknowledge God's right to rule and reign in my life.

But I've recently become aware that below my submission there sometimes lies an undercurrent of unbelief. "If it's your will" can be an unconscious attempt to head off disappointment, a preemptive acknowledgment that my prayers might not be answered the way I'd like. And let's be honest—that's the risky part of prayer.

But you and I have been issued a clear invitation:

> Don't worry about anything; instead, pray about everything. Tell God what you need, and thank him for all he has done. (Philippians 4:6 NLT)

Listen to that promise! We don't need to censor our prayers or tone down our requests. We can bring anything and everything to the Lord and trust that He'll answer in the way that is best.

I've heard people say that prayers are often answered in one of three ways: *Yes. No.* Or *wait awhile.* But sometimes, in His wisdom, I suspect God offers a fourth response: *You've got to be kidding!* Because He's a wise Father, God doesn't always give us what we want. And when He does, it's rarely as fast as we'd like.

Which is why effective prayer often involves perseverance. As R. A. Torrey writes,

> God does not always give us things at our first effort. He wants to train us and make us strong by compelling us to work hard for the best things. Likewise, He does not always give us what we ask in answer to the first prayer. He wants to train us and make us strong people of prayer by compelling us to pray hard for the best things. He makes us *pray through.*[20]

My friend Barb prayed for her unsaved husband for years. Though he gave no sign of softening, she kept loving and serving him even as his health declined. A year before his death, God opened a door for Barb to lead Jim to Jesus. I'll never forget the peace that marked his countenance and the smile that lit up hers as they attended church for the first time together. It was an answer to prayer that was long in coming. But now that Jim is in heaven with Jesus, I think Barb would agree—the answer was precisely on time.

My friend Kelly hasn't experienced the physical healing she's needed for over a decade. But despite the continued suffering, she keeps on praying—asking and believing that the God who promised to heal her will be faithful to His Word.

To be honest, I don't understand why God seems to answer one person's prayer quickly and another's slowly—or sometimes not at all. But a lack of understanding shouldn't keep us from continuing to pray.

You're probably familiar with Matthew 7:7. It contains Jesus's warm invitation to bring our needs to God in prayer. "Ask and it will be given to you; seek and you will find; knock and the door will be opened to you." But what we may not understand from most translations is the *persistence* the original language implies. The Amplified Bible puts it like this:

> Ask *and* keep on asking and it will be given to you; seek *and* keep on seeking and you will find; knock *and* keep on knocking and the door will be opened to you. For everyone who keeps on asking receives, and he who keeps on seeking finds, and to him who keeps on knocking, it will be opened. (vv. 7–8)

Jesus told two stories in Luke to illustrate this kind of tenacious prayer. The first, found in Luke 11:5–10, is about a man who goes to a friend's house "at midnight" (v. 5) and requests loaves of bread for another friend. Comfy in bed, the first friend refuses. But the man keeps on asking. Because of his bold persistence—the NIV calls it "shameless audacity" (v. 8)—his friend eventually gets out of bed to "give him as many [loaves] as he needs" (v. 8 NKJV).

The second story, found in Luke 18:1–8, features a persistent widow who continually pleads for justice from an ungodly judge. Finally the judge, who by his own description didn't "fear God or care what people think" (v. 4), decides to help the widow just to keep her from "bothering" (v. 5) him.

While both of these stories are kind of humorous, they speak to the serious importance of persistent, prevailing prayer.

It's significant that Jesus told the first story directly after teaching the disciples to pray the Lord's Prayer. After praying, "Give us each day our daily bread" (Luke 11:3), Jesus encourages them to also pray *for a friend* by telling the story about persistent prayer. Because He wants us to pray for others with just as much intensity as we pray for ourselves.

Luke's introduction to the second story only reinforces the importance of tenacious prayer: "Then Jesus told his disciples a parable to show them that they should always pray and not give up" (Luke 18:1). But at the end of the story Jesus reminds them of God's good intentions toward all of us: "Will not God bring about justice for his chosen ones, who cry out to him day and night?" Jesus says in verses 7–8. "I tell you, he will see that they get justice, and quickly."

God isn't a reluctant friend or a grumpy judge giving in to our wishes just to get us off His back. He's a good and loving Father who longs to give "good and perfect" gifts to His children (James 1:17). God *wants* to move on our behalf—but He also wants us to be involved in the process. As we actively pray (and keep on praying), we learn patience, persistence, and trust. Practicing the art of going to Him regularly rather than giving up or depending on ourselves.

One day during my quiet time, I asked the Lord why I hadn't experienced many miracles in my life. Both my parents and John's have wonderful stories of God's provision. As I thought through the many miracles, I felt the Spirit whisper these words to my heart, calling to mind Philippians 4:19.

When you insist on providing for your needs according to your "riches in glory," Joanna, you never experience the joy of tapping into Mine.

Trusting the Father's Heart

When our youngest son was about six or seven, Walt Disney World put out a big ad campaign. Josh would sit smiling in front of the TV as he watched families enjoy the theme park. I waited for him to ask if we could go someday, but instead he'd just comment, "Sure looks like they're having fun."

Always the diplomat, Josh rarely comes out and asks for things. In fact, even today when I offer dessert he usually says, "If it's all right with you, Mom."

I've always admired my son's nondemanding nature. But recently the Holy Spirit convicted me of a similar tendency in my own life—one that's not so admirable. I can be so afraid of impure motives that I push down my honest desires and hesitate to ask God for anything big. But what if, in holding back my requests, I'm missing out on the things God wants to do *for* me? The work He longs to do *through* me? Not to mention the rich relationship that grows when I bring my whole heart to God in anticipation and trust.

When the Disney World ads played, Josh's desire was obvious. But because we didn't have the money to make it happen, I left his dream unrecognized. Now, all these years later, I find myself wondering . . . what if I had handled things differently? Without making promises or setting up false hopes and expectations, I could have acknowledged Josh's longing and together shared his dream.

"Wouldn't it be fun to go to Disney World?" I could have said. "If you had a chance to go, what would you want to do first?"

We could have enjoyed talking together about the experience—the rides we'd want to ride, the delicious treats we'd like to eat. And I could have used the opportunity to teach my son that there's nothing too big or outrageous, too small or inconsequential, that we can't take to God in prayer. For our heavenly Father loves to hear our hopes and dreams. He even welcomes our wishes.

And sometimes—sometimes!—He makes those dreams come true.

Several years later, God opened a door for us to take Josh to Disney World. A few years after that, we were given passes to Disneyland while in California. Just think . . . had I been willing to dream with my son and had we taken that dream to God in prayer, Josh would have seen an undeniable link between our prayer request and God's answer. What a time of rejoicing that would have been!

After that insight, I've tried to practice a more balanced approach to prayer. I do want to monitor my motives so I don't "ask amiss" (James 4:3 NKJV). But rather than prejudging God as unwilling and my desires as self-serving, I'm trying to come like a child going to her Father.

I want to have the childlike faith Jesus recommends in Matthew 18:3–4, but I don't want it to be childish or immature. The difference is subtle but important.

Childish faith makes demands, but childlike faith makes requests.

Childish faith pouts and moans when a request is delayed or denied. It gets stuck in resentment and questions the Father's love.

Childlike faith, on the other hand, may weep when tested, but it chooses to press close and not turn away. It allows the Lord's love to dry its eyes so it can move forward—free of resentment and willing to believe God for more.

Whatever We Ask

You and I have been invited to pray God-sized prayers. To dream along with God about ways to bring His redemptive solution to earth. Refusing to worry, we present our requests with thanksgiving. For we know that our loving Father can and will sort through them all and determine what is best.

Several summers ago, we celebrated Nathaniel's first birthday along with the second birthday of the twins, Jaxson and Quinley. As I watched them open their presents, I couldn't help but think back to those years of desperate prayer. Though our requests weren't answered right away, these babies were right on time. For God has a specific plan and purpose for each of these children—as Psalm 139:16 declares:

> The days ordained for me were written in your book
> before one of them came to be.

Had the Lord answered our prayers when we first started praying them, would these unique and precious little people even exist? I have no way of knowing, but I'm certain of one thing: God is wiser than we know and kinder than we think.

If our hearts are focused on the Lord and how to please Him, if we allow the Holy Spirit to purify our motives and shape our prayers, if our requests line up with Scripture and bring God glory, and if we will trust Him with the substance and timing of the answers, then you and I can take God at His word when it comes to our prayers:

> Now this is the confidence that we have in Him, that if we ask anything according to His will, He hears us. And if we know that He hears us, whatever we ask, we know that we have the petitions that we have asked of Him. (1 John 5:14–15 NKJV)

So, keep on praying, my friend. Keep on asking and seeking and knocking.

And whatever you do, don't diminish God's greatness by the smallness of your request.

PART FOUR

Living Faith

Lord, today I accept my calling
not to perfection or performance.
My calling is to faith.
I have been chosen for this generation.
I have a place in the heritage of faith.
I'm going to stop wishing and whining
and start believing and receiving.
What Your Word says is mine.
I won't let others steal my hope. . . .
For You, my God, are huge.
Nothing is too hard for You.
Our world needs your wonders.
Rise up, oh Lord!
Please renew Your works in our day.
I confess the unbelief of my generation
and ask You to bring Your revival of faith
in my own heart.
For You are who You say You are.
You can do what You say You can do.
I am who You say I am.
I can do all things through Christ.
Your Word is alive and active in me . . .
I'm believing God!

Beth Moore[1]

Fifteen

Resting in God's Sovereignty

For you have been my hope, Sovereign Lord,
my confidence since my youth.
Psalm 71:5

It had been a terrible, no-good day.

My husband had said something that embarrassed me, and I was mad. We'd tried to talk about it, but John couldn't see the problem. I, on the other hand, couldn't see anything else.

On his way to an appointment, John dropped me off to look at some small shops in the town we were visiting. As I wandered through a store decorated for Christmas, I fell in love with a set of brown wooden blocks that spelled out "Peace." Festooned with pine cones and holly, the blocks could be displayed all year long. Best of all, the whole set was only eight bucks.

Later, at the coffee shop where John had agreed to pick me up, I ordered a mocha and started rehearsing a short but powerful speech that would help my husband understand the depth of my hurt. But when he arrived and I started to climb into the truck, another set of words came out of my mouth.

"Stop!" I exclaimed. "I've lost my peace!" I ran back into the coffee shop and searched the area where I'd been sitting. I asked at the counter and even dug through the trash. But alas, there was no sign of the small paper bag that held the set of blocks.

Back at the truck, I slammed the door in frustration. "Someone stole my peace!" I told my bewildered husband, swiping away a tear. I really loved those blocks.

The next morning I called the shop to see if they had any more in the back. The woman on the phone offered to check as I whispered a prayer.

"Good news! I found another set," she said when she got back on the line. We rejoiced at the discovery. But then she said, "Hey . . . I just noticed a bag under the counter. It has a set of blocks in it. Do you think they're yours?"

Suddenly the Lord put everything together. *No one stole your peace, Joanna. And you didn't lose it.*

You left it, my dear, He whispered to my chastened heart.

Resting in God's Peace

Peace is hard to come by in our restless and unsettled world. Even those of us who love Jesus can get so consumed by the cares of life that we miss the inner calm Jesus came to give. "Peace I leave with you; my peace I give you," Jesus says in John 14:27. "I do not give to you as the world gives. Do not let your hearts be troubled and do not be afraid."

The peace Jesus offers is truly remarkable. It's meant to infiltrate every part of our being, giving us peace *within* and peace *without*. A deep-rooted stability that isn't easily ruffled, stolen, or misplaced. For it's not just peace *with* God. It's the peace of God Himself.

Remember the dream I described in chapter 3? The large gaping holes in a building's foundation that needed to be filled? I had to smile when I heard the Bible Project's[1] description of *shalom*, the Hebrew word used in the Old Testament to describe God's peace:

> The most basic meaning of *shalom* is complete or whole. The word can refer to a stone that has . . . no cracks. It can also refer to a completed stone wall that has no gaps and no missing bricks. *Shalom* refers to something that's complex with lots of pieces that's in a state of completeness, wholeness.[2]

Oh how I want to be whole and complete in the *shalom* peace of God! I want the gaps in my soul to be filled with His love and any holes in my faith to be shored up by His grace. Don't you want that for your life too?

It's available, my friend, but it starts by trusting the Lord with all of our hearts—letting go in surrender so we can hold on in faith. Allowing the Holy Spirit to rewire our souls so that "the peace of God, which transcends all understanding" guards our hearts and minds (Philippians 4:7).

It's the kind of life Jesus lived when He came to earth. Fully dependent on God, Jesus never seemed to rush from one place to another. He was purposeful rather than driven, available rather than busy, touchable rather than distant. Because He was led by the Holy Spirit, Jesus saw everything and everyone as part of God's will for His life. And because He trusted that the Father had everything under control, His life was marked by a beautiful peace.

Imagine what our lives would be like if we did the same.

Resting in God's Goodness

In a familiar passage found in Matthew 6:25–34, Jesus lists the things we shouldn't worry about. What to eat or drink. What clothes to wear. But before He recites the list, Jesus instructs His listeners, "Take no thought for your life" (v. 25 KJV).

"Take no thought . . ."

I don't know about you, but I take a *lot* of thought about my life. When something happens or someone does something that affects me—well, I have thoughts about that. Lots and lots of thoughts. So many thoughts that they keep me up at night and spill over into my days.

But Jesus modeled a different kind of life. He moved through the world unhurried and unworried. Instead of plotting to get ahead and trying to micromanage the people around Him, Jesus simply trusted the Father and did everything He asked. His life provides a master class in resting:

- *Jesus rested in God's provision.* Though "the Son of Man has no place to lay His head," Jesus said in Luke 9:58, He never seemed to suffer lack. Because of His reliance on God, Jesus was able to miraculously supply wine for weddings and enough Happy Meals to feed the massive crowds who came to hear Him preach.
- *Jesus rested in God's protection.* Because His life was in God's hands, Jesus was able to sleep during storms and stand up to critics. Though there were attempts on His life (Luke 4:28–30; John 8:59; 10:31–32), God protected Him. When Pilate warned that he could have Him killed, Jesus said, "You would have no power over me if it were not given to you from above" (John 19:11).
- *Jesus rested in God's direction.* Rising early, Jesus received His marching orders through prayer (Mark 1:35). But He also remained open to the leading of the Spirit throughout the day. He took time to play with children and never turned a needy person away. Rather than being irritated by interruptions, Jesus welcomed them as divine appointments arranged by His Father.

God offers each of us the same kind of provision, protection, and direction that Jesus enjoyed. If we'll trust in His sovereign goodness and allow our hearts to settle deep into His love, we'll experience the *shalom* peace that Jesus offers. But there's a supernatural "rest" the Lord wants to give us as well.

"Come to me, all you who are weary and burdened, and I will give you rest," Jesus says in Matthew 11:28–29, "Take my yoke upon you and learn from me, for I am gentle and humble in heart, and you will find rest for your souls."

Though most English translations use the word *rest* in both verses, in Greek they are two different but related words. The first one is a verb meaning "to give rest, quiet, recreate, refresh."[3] But the second one is a noun and suggests the idea of "inward tranquility while one performs necessary labor."[4]

Isn't that beautiful? Jesus wants to offer us a quiet place to rest our souls but He also wants to give us an inner tranquility—a sense of peace and calm even in the middle of our many responsibilities.

When we trust in the Lord and learn to experience both types of "rest," we won't be so concerned with our lives. For we'll understand that God's thoughts toward us are so vast and numerous that, as David writes in Psalm 139:18,

> Were I to count them,
> they would outnumber the grains of sand.

With God always thinking about us and taking care of our needs, you and I can experience the inner tranquility and *shalom* peace Jesus offers, no matter what we're going through or the challenges we face.

For we've tapped into the strength and wisdom of Jesus as we rest in the sovereignty of God.

Letting God Be God

We touched on the topic of God's sovereignty back in chapter 3—the reality that nothing is outside God's control and that He can do as He wishes. Unfortunately, many of us struggle with that idea, finding it hard to understand why God still allows evil and suffering—though it was human free will that unleashed it on earth. Because we don't understand God's power to redeem, we question His goodness when He doesn't interrupt or intervene.

But I think our biggest resistance to the idea of God's sovereignty is that it doesn't sit well with our own control issues. To accept that God is free to do whatever He wants simply because He is God causes our Flesh Woman to freak out and our inner label maker to go wild.

It's something that Hudson Taylor had to come to terms with as well. Though he'd experienced a revelation of God's faithfulness that changed his life (see chap. 3), he went through a dark period at age fifty-two. Confined to bed by chronic illness and feeling forgotten, the missionary wrestled with many of the fears and doubts that tend to plague us in hard times. But then Hudson wrote these powerful words to himself:

> Make up your mind that God is an infinite Sovereign, and has the right to do as He pleases with His own, and He may not explain to you a thousand things which may puzzle your reason in His dealings with you.[5]

While I don't understand how it all works, for me it comes down to this: either God is in control, or He is not. One option brings hope, the other despair. One may raise questions, but the other offers no answers at all. It's important to keep in mind, however, that God's sovereignty is always weighted in our favor. For God is good, and He loves us. We belong to Him, and He is working on our behalf.

I recently spent time with a dear friend, JoAnn Roberts, who shared some of the things the Lord has been teaching her, especially in the area of trusting God's sovereignty. JoAnn has faced a lot of challenges over the past few years. As a result she's spent a lot of time in prayer, pouring out her questions to God: "What are You doing, Lord? How can this be happening?"

But recently, she told me, the Holy Spirit has led her to ask a different set of questions—not of God, but of herself. Questions like,

- *What would it be like if I really believed my circumstances don't dictate God's goodness or faithfulness?*

- *How would I pray and how would I worship if I really believed that God is in control?*

I've been asking myself similar questions. It's crazy how I can trust God with all my heart one day, only to wake up the next day plagued by fear and doubt. Rather than experiencing inner tranquility, I often allow the troubles of life to steal my peace and swallow my joy. But the Lord's been using a snippet from an old Orthodox prayer to recalibrate my heart as I declare my trust in His sovereign rule:

> Teach me to treat all that comes to me with peace of soul and with firm conviction that Your will governs all.[6]

When my plans get interrupted and my heart feels overwhelmed, I bring myself back to center with these simple words: *Lord, teach me to treat all that comes to me with peace of soul and with firm conviction that Your will governs all.*

When fear rises and panic tries to grip my heart, I pray: *God, please give me peace of soul and firm conviction.*

When something happens that upends my plans, I declare over the situation, *This isn't a mistake—Your will governs all.*

Trusting God's sovereignty isn't easy, for it requires that we lay down our label maker and eat from the Tree of Life rather than the Tree of Knowledge. But there's incredible joy when we do. For rather than leaning on our own understanding, we allow God to be God in our lives. The God who declares,

> I am God, and there is no other;
> I am God, and there is none like me.
> I make known the end from the beginning,
> from ancient times, what is still to come.
> I say, "My purpose will stand,
> and I will do all that I please." . . .
> What I have said, that will I bring about;
> what I have planned, that I will do. (Isaiah 46:9–11)

Even in the worst of circumstances, you and I can rest in the knowledge that nothing touches us without God's permission, and nothing has the power to ruin His purposes for our lives. But to get to that place of rest we must accept two important truths:

1. God doesn't exist to serve us; we were made to serve Him.
2. Until we submit to His rule, we'll live in conflict with His purposes.

Despite popular belief, this life isn't about us. God's story is being written across eternity. He's the main character in an epic saga involving an ongoing battle between evil and good, darkness and light, destruction and creation. We're just supporting actors—but we can't underestimate the role that we play. For how we live matters. We either glorify God or disregard Him by the way we choose to trust or distrust His work in our lives.

Resting in the Testing

Though David is considered the greatest king in Israel's history, sadly, his success stopped at the door of his home. For whatever reason, David seemed to prefer his kingly duties over the hard work involved in being a good dad.

Eventually David's lack of parental leadership caused his family to unravel—and I do mean unravel. Second Samuel 13–14 is a long, sordid tale filled with betrayal and revenge. When David's son, Amnon, raped his half sister, Tamar, the passive king did nothing about it. So Tamar's brother Absalom killed Amnon and fled the country.

Though the young man was finally allowed to return, David refused to be reconciled to Absalom. As a result, the son's resentment against his father eventually turned into open rebellion. He initiated a four-year campaign to win the heart of Israel (2 Samuel 15:1–7), and in a well-orchestrated coup, he sent out messengers to boldly declare that "Absalom is king in Hebron" (v. 10).

With his renegade kingdom established just twenty miles south of Jerusalem, David finally woke up to the threat posed by his son. Packing up a huge entourage, the king left Jerusalem (vv. 14–24), taking the ark of the covenant with him. Some commentaries see this response as fear-filled and, once again, passive. But when David instructs Zadok the priest to return to the city in the passage that follows, I see a beautiful submission to God's sovereign right to do whatever He wished.

> Take the ark of God back into the city. If I find favor in the LORD's eyes, he will bring me back and let me see it and his dwelling place again. But if he says, "I am not pleased with you," then I am ready; let him do to me whatever seems good to him. (vv. 25–26)

Like David, we've all experienced consequences linked to our passivity or sin as well as cruel injustices that fill us with fear. Even on our best days, none of us deserves God's favor. But you and I, like David, can fling ourselves on God's mercy. For ultimately,

> it is God alone who judges;
> he decides who will rise and who will fall.
> (Psalm 75:7 NLT)

Absalom's pride-filled coup eventually failed, and God returned David to the throne of Israel. For the Lord was deeply moved—as He is today—by people who choose to humble themselves and submit to Him.

Trusting His sovereignty by saying, "My life is in God's hands. Let Him do to me whatever seems good to Him."

The Hard Choice to Trust

I find it interesting that some chronological reading plans place the story of Job near the story of Adam and Eve's temptation—that is, somewhere between Genesis 11 and 12.[7] For there's an interesting contrast between the choices made in those two cautionary tales.

THE SERENITY OF GOD'S SOVEREIGNTY

The "Serenity Prayer" has been quoted millions of times. Most of us are familiar with the first four lines, but many recovery groups use the prayer in its entirety. Written by the great theologian Reinhold Niebuhr more than eighty years ago, it's a prayer worth repeating today.

> God, grant me the serenity
> to accept the things I cannot change,
> the courage to change the things I can,
> and the wisdom to know the difference.
> Living one day at a time,
> enjoying one moment at a time;
> accepting hardship as a pathway to peace;
> taking, as Jesus did,
> this sinful world as it is,
> not as I would have it;
> trusting that You will make all things right
> if I surrender to Your will;
> so that I may be reasonably happy in this life
> and supremely happy with You forever in the next.
> Amen.[8]

Which part of this prayer do you need to focus on today? If there's a phrase that causes a pushback, take time to discuss it with the Lord. If there's something He wants you to do—remember, you don't have to do it alone. The Holy Spirit—your Helper—walks beside you as you bring your life under submission to God's sovereign rule.

But as for me, I trust in You, O Lord . . .
My *times* are in Your hand.

Psalm 31:14–15 NKJV

Despite enjoying perfect blessings in the Garden, Adam and Eve's hearts were lured away from their Maker. But Job, stripped bare of every blessing and afflicted, chose to trust in God's sovereign rule.

Though we don't have time to cover all of Job's story, suffice it to say God allowed the man to go through extreme testing. Struck by Satan with one tragedy after another, Job lost his children, his wealth, and finally his health. He ended up in the ashes of his once-prosperous life while his friends debated arcane points of philosophy and his wife urged him to "curse God and die" (Job 2:9).

Yet in the middle of all his pain and confusion, Job kept turning his heart to God. And that's where we see the beautiful contrast between Job's submission and the rebellion of Adam and Eve.

The first couple vilified God, but Job vindicated Him.

Though Satan may have triumphed in the Garden, God prevailed on the ash heap. And a crucial battle in the epic saga was won.

While none of us want to go through the kind of suffering Job experienced, I believe his story can help us navigate the struggle to trust when something terrible happens in our lives or the life of someone we love. Job makes four powerful statements about God's sovereignty that, if embraced, can help us find peace when our world is turned upside down.

The first statement was in response to his wife's insistence that he give up on God because of all that had happened. But despite his sorrow, Job reasoned,

> Shall we indeed accept good from God, and shall we not accept adversity? (Job 2:10 NKJV)

The second came in response to the arguments and lofty opinions of his so-called friends. Tired of their self-important prattle, Job countered it with this powerful statement:

> Though [God] slay me, yet will I trust Him. (13:15 NKJV)

Later, though he still had no real answers from God, the weary man affirmed,

> I know that my Redeemer lives,
> And He shall stand at last on the earth. (19:25 NKJV)

All three of these statements are built on Job's initial declaration of trust found in Job 1:21. As his world crumbled around him, Job chose to bow his knee and worship:

> The LORD gave, and the LORD has taken away;
> Blessed be the name of the LORD. (1:21 NKJV)

Perhaps you're going through a difficult time right now that's causing a lot of questions and fear. I hope you'll follow Job's example and keep your heart tender to the Spirit's leading. For He wants to provide grace to help you

- receive what God allows in your life, the painful as well as the pleasant,
- trust in God's character and goodness no matter how difficult things may seem,
- remember that God's redemptive purposes will prevail in the end, and
- continue to bless God even in the midst of your pain.

As you choose to keep your heart centered on the Lord—taking your questions to Him rather than running away—He will meet you on the ash heap. Though the revelation of His presence may not come as quickly as you'd like, as you continue to seek and trust Him, I believe you'll come to see God in a brand-new way. Just as Job did when, at the end of his extended trial, he had a chance to talk to God:

> I had only heard about you before,
> but now I have seen you with my own eyes. (42:5 NLT)

Bowing to God's Will

When God asked us to resign the pastorate in Whitefish, John and I weren't certain what God might have in mind next. Because of

His blessing on my book *Having a Mary Heart in a Martha World*, we had time to seek His face rather than scramble for another job. But we had once again found our version of nirvana—the state of perfect nothingness. Though we'd learned a lot about resting in God's sovereignty, we still had to resist the temptation to just *do* something rather than wait on the Lord to show us what came next.

John sent out a few résumés when he felt prompted, but for the most part we just trusted God and did our best not to fret or fear. (Something new for me!) We were confident that God had led us to Whitefish. So it only made sense that, when it was time for our next assignment, God would lead us to that place as well.

As our wait stretched from a month into over a year, we discovered something powerful: we didn't need a ministry or a title to confirm our identity. For as the blind poet John Milton wrote four hundred years ago, "They also serve who only stand and wait."[9]

Perhaps you, too, are in between assignments. Perhaps you're struggling with resentment and fear over how your life has turned out. In times like these, I've found that we can either *rest* in God's sovereignty or we can *wrestle*. We can bow our knee, or we can raise our fist. But only one choice brings peace. The other brings turmoil.

Though our unplanned sabbatical lasted far longer than we expected, God finally gave us a church filled with beautiful believers to serve in Hamilton, Montana—just forty-five minutes away from my parents' home. The very day we moved to the valley, my father was admitted to the hospital with a serious brain bleed. Living nearby, I was able to be by my parents' side almost immediately.

"God was so good to bring you closer," my mother cried as we waited in the emergency room. The truth of her words has come back to me many times since, as both of my parents have experienced serious health problems.

Last June we celebrated our twelfth anniversary at our current church. Looking over the congregation, I found myself weeping at God's faithful kindness. Even when we were uncertain about our future, He was already in our tomorrow—causing all the things we'd walked through to work together for our good.

Allowing God to Be God

From the beginning of this project, I've had one prayer—that this book might help readers (and myself) build an unshakeable trust in God that goes beyond mere head knowledge and embeds itself deep in our hearts. Helping us to be "steadfast [and] immovable" (1 Corinthians 15:58 NKJV) as we anchor our lives to these rock-solid truths: God is good. He loves me. I belong to Him. And He takes care of His own.

Remember the story I opened with? When John's parents came for Thanksgiving, I asked them to pick up the bag of blocks on their way. I couldn't wait to display them as a constant reminder not to give away or leave my peace. But God had another lesson to teach me from those five wooden blocks.

When my father-in-law handed me the bag, I noticed that the saleswoman had clearly marked it with my name. But above that she'd written three large letters in wide marker: PIF.

What in the world could that mean? I wondered.

Then it hit me: "paid in full."

The peace that you and I need has already been purchased by Jesus. As we accept all that God is and all that Christ offers, we experience *rest* for our souls along with an inner tranquility in the midst of necessary labor.

Even in the midst of trouble, the Holy Spirit helps us to treat all that comes to us with "peace of soul and firm conviction that God's will governs all."[10] And in our choice to trust Him, the Prince of Peace helps us experience the life described by the prophet Isaiah:

> The fruit of . . . righteousness will be peace;
> its effect will be quietness and confidence forever.
> (Isaiah 32:17)

The *shalom* peace of God guards our hearts and our minds. Filling the holes in our spiritual foundations so we're no longer shaken by trouble or influenced by the enemy's lies. Instead, we are quiet and confident. Steadfast and immovable. For we've learned how to rest our hearts in the sovereignty of God.

Sixteen

Leaving a Legacy of Trust

> Let me proclaim your power to this new generation,
> your mighty miracles to all who come after me.
>
> Psalm 71:18 NLT

Of all the beauty I've witnessed in the world, my favorite place is Glacier National Park. Nestled in the northwest corner of Montana, it's known by many as the crown jewel of our national park system. More than two million people visit Glacier each year. And one of the most popular drives in the park is the Going-to-the-Sun Road.

Created in the early decades of the twentieth century to make the glories of the mountain landscape more accessible, the fifty-one-mile highway winds around pristine lakes and along streams. It meanders through ancient forests before making its way up and along the mountainside to a rocky ridge called Logan's Pass, then down the other side.

It's hard to imagine Congress agreeing to build a highway that leads to nowhere but beauty, but that's exactly what they did. After two decades of periodic building and a cost of more than two million dollars, the Going-to-the-Sun Road opened on July 15, 1933.[1] With much of it carved out of sheer rock, it's still considered an engineering marvel today.

And all of it was made possible by men who, by careful planning and sheer determination, dared to build a highway to the top of the world—preparing the way for ordinary people like you and me to access previously unseen treasures of the natural world.*

Prepare the Way

When Isaiah prophesied about the coming Messiah, he told the people in Isaiah 40:3,

> In the wilderness prepare
> the way for the LORD;
> make straight in the desert
> a highway for our God.

Quoted in all four Gospels (Matthew 3:1–3; Mark 1:2–3; Luke 3:4–6; John 1:23), Isaiah's words still echo today. For each of us must ready our heart for God's coming. We all need to prepare a "way for the Lord" and "make straight paths for him," so that "all people will see God's salvation" (Luke 3:4, 6).

But highways in the wilderness aren't built overnight, as the hardy men who built Glacier's Going-to-the-Sun Road learned firsthand. Even planning the route was tricky, for a "straight path" up the mountain was obviously not an option.

At first a series of fifteen switchbacks—a kind of zigzag path up the mountain face—was proposed to tackle the steep climb to the pass. But Thomas Vint, a lowly assistant to the National Park Service landscape architect, disagreed. Such a direct approach would scar the mountain and give a very limited view of Glacier's beauty.

*Some of the companion video study for this book was filmed in Glacier! Learn more at JoannaWeaverBooks.com.

Instead, Vint suggested a longer road with a single switchback that would cut along the face of the Continental Divide.[2]

Though more costly and time-consuming, Vint's proposal was accepted, and the work began. But the task was daunting.

Because the construction season at that altitude was very short, it didn't make sense for workers to commute to the work site, so they lived in camps established along the mountain route. Massive amounts of rock had to be blasted away to form a bench to hold the road, with the stone rubble carried elsewhere to build retaining walls, arched bridges, and guardrails along much of the route. Danger loomed constantly from falling rocks, explosives, human error, even wild animals.

Remarkably, only three men lost their lives in building Glacier's "highway to the sky."[3] But each April, snow removal crews still put their lives at risk to clear as much as ninety feet of snow[4] so visitors can experience the beautiful drive by the end of June or early July.[5]

Clearing the way for God's coming in our lives is a time-consuming process for us as well. But as we allow the Lord to blast through obstacles to our faith and break through any hardness of heart, He takes the rubble and builds something lasting. Helping us leave a legacy of trust for those who come behind.

Following Trailblazers

Before real construction could start on the Going-to-the-Sun Road, surveyors had to mark out the route to Logan's Pass. Each day a team of thirty men climbed more than seventeen hundred vertical feet to reach the proposed path, hacking through thick underbrush and traversing narrow ledges as they staked out the route. The work of these trailblazers was challenging, but without them, building the road would have been impossible.

I'm so grateful for trailblazers of faith in my life, godly men and women who have paved the way for my own journey. Some I have known well, while others I've met only in books or videos. But each one has left a legacy that's made my life richer.

Oswald Chambers is one of those trailblazers. Though he died in 1936, the sermons that his wife, Biddy, compiled into a devotional, *My Utmost for His Highest*, have mentored my faith for nearly forty years. Other writers from the past like Andrew Murray, Charles Spurgeon, Mrs. Charles E. Cowman, Amy Carmichael, and Catherine Marshall—as well as current authors like Philip Yancey, Beth Moore, Priscilla Shirer, and others—have opened my understanding of Scripture and also mentored my work as a speaker and a writer.

But I have been blessed with other flesh-and-blood trailblazers as well. My parents, of course—I'll get to them later in the chapter—but also leaders in my childhood church who taught the Word of God and honored His presence. My faith grew by rubbing up against the faith of godly people who regularly came together to worship at our church.

When John and I married and entered ministry, we were fortunate to serve under several wonderful pastors who faithfully preached and lived God's Word—including John's dad. But when we moved to Oregon for an associate position, we found mentors in Pastor Gordon and Terry Myers. They poured into our lives in so many ways.

I'll never forget listening to Terry teach at women's Bible study and praying beside her after Sunday night services. I had never met a woman so on fire for Jesus. Her love for God's Word ignited a hunger of my own, but it was her personal walk with Jesus that showed me what it looked like to have a friendship with God. So much of my faith and love for ministry were shaped during that time—I'm not sure who I'd be today without Terry's beautiful example.

But of all the people who've influenced my life over the years, no one has changed me so elementally as my husband, John. I've been blessed by his love and challenged by his sermons, but it's his Christlike nature that constantly convicts me. I often joke that it's hard "living with Jesus" because John's gentle, servant-hearted leadership at church and in our home often points out my lack. But I know I'm a better person because of John's example, and I'm definitely a better woman because of his love.

A Pattern to Follow

I've heard people say, "You shouldn't look at people. You've got to keep your eyes on Jesus." And in a way they're right, for even well-meaning Christians will let us down. Perhaps you've had some negative models in your life, people who failed you or failed God to the point that you've questioned your own faith. But if you'll look back, I think you'll find positive examples as well.

God puts role models into our lives for a reason. Positive or negative, they help shape us into the people God wants us to be by showing us what works and what doesn't work. Ideally we'll have access to trailblazers who live out their faith with a purity and passion that doesn't cause us to stumble. And ideally we'll become inspiring role models too. But because we're all flawed people—even the most dedicated of Christ-followers—it won't always work that way.

Take me, for instance. I'd never deliberately hurt you. But if you hang around me long enough, I'll inevitably fail and disappoint you. Though I'm striving to be more like Jesus, I'm still not the accurate reflection of God that I long to be. I'm sure that's true of your life as well, for we "all have sinned and fall short of the glory of God" (Romans 3:23).

Yet despite our human imperfections and the gravitational pull of sin, God has called each of us to leave a legacy of faith. As 1 Timothy 4:12 puts it, we are to "set an example for the believers in speech, in conduct, in love, in faith and in purity."

The Greek word for "example" in this verse is *túpos*. It refers to a "mark, print or impression" but also a "prototype, pattern."[6] Our lives are meant to be working prototypes that people can refer to when building their faith. But for that to happen, we need to be willing to be perfected by the Holy Spirit into patterns worth replicating.

Becoming an "example for the believers" isn't an easy process, as the original Greek points out. *Túpos* comes from a root word that means "to strike, smite with repeated strokes," and refers to "something caused by strokes or blows."[7]

As we humble ourselves on God's anvil and allow the hammer of His love to leave its mark, we become prototypes worth imitating. Patterns worth repeating. For blow by blow, strike by strike, we're being transformed into the image of Christ (2 Corinthians 3:18).

"Only let us live up to what we have already attained," Paul writes in Philippians 3:16. I find those words comforting—for it isn't how far we have to go that matters as much as how far we have come. If we sincerely desire to honor God in our faith and conduct and allow the Holy Spirit to change us from the inside out, we can echo the words of Paul in 1 Corinthians 11:1: "Follow my example, as I follow the example of Christ."

Role models to emulate. Trailblazers to follow. Templates of godliness who are building a legacy for those who come behind.

Building for the Next Generation

When David became king in 2 Samuel 5, God's favor was so clearly upon his life that the king of Tyre volunteered to build him a palace (v. 11). But once David was settled in this "house of cedar," he began thinking about the ark of God sitting in a tent, and it just didn't seem right (7:2).

Determined to build God a sanctuary worthy of His name, David consulted with the prophet Nathan (v. 3), who initially thought it was a great idea. But God made it clear that He had a different plan. It wouldn't be David who completed the temple, but his son Solomon (1 Chronicles 22:7–10).

Nevertheless, King David's passion for the project compelled him to start the process—securing a building site (1 Chronicles 21:18–26) and gathering building materials (22:1–4). "My son Solomon is young and inexperienced," he reasoned, "and the house to be built for the LORD should be of great magnificence and fame and splendor in the sight of all the nations." So he made "extensive preparations before his death" (v. 5).

Extensive is an understatement! First Chronicles 22–29 outlines David's plans, including detailed lists of supplies needed and the

Levites who would serve as priests, singers, gatekeepers, treasurers, and temple officials. He also arranged for the workers needed to build the temple: "Stonecutters, masons and carpenters, as well as those skilled in every kind of work in gold and silver, bronze and iron—craftsmen beyond number" (22:15–16).

But David did much more than plan. He also collected material and funds for the project, telling Solomon in 1 Chronicles 22:14, "I have taken great pains to provide for the temple of the Lord a hundred thousand talents of gold, a million talents of silver, quantities of bronze and iron too great to be weighed, and wood and stone." With 7.5 million pounds of gold and 75 million pounds of silver at his disposal, Solomon had everything he needed to finish the glorious temple.

David was committed to building a house for God, and the fact that his son would get the credit didn't matter in the least. He only wanted to honor God and make His name famous. "Now devote your heart and soul to seeking the Lord your God," David told Solomon in 1 Chronicles 22:19. "Begin to build the sanctuary . . . for the Name of the Lord."

In the rich and unselfish legacy David left behind, I see clues for compiling our own:

1. Be willing to work toward something that requires more than one lifetime.
2. Be willing to equip the next generation and pass the torch well.
3. Be willing to serve God's call on someone else's life.

I've had the privilege of visiting many churches in my travels and seeing amazing ministry teams at work. I love what God does when His people serve Him together, both mentoring and encouraging each other as they do God's work. But I have to confess that I haven't always done a good job at building those kind of teams. Often it seemed easier to do the work by myself.

I'm trying to change my tactics, however, because I'm convinced that if God's kingdom is to continue and flourish, we must raise up younger men and women by including them in the work. Equipping and encouraging them as they pursue God's call on their lives. For as ministry and business leaders, teachers, and mentors, part of our job is making sure the next generation has everything they need to construct the spiritual temple in their lives.

So that they, too, blaze a trail of faith others can follow.

Trust-Fund Babies

Several years ago my parents set up a trust fund to help simplify legal matters on their passing. The trust puts all their assets under one umbrella, with clear directions as to how to distribute them after death.

But my brother and sister and I have already received our inheritance. It isn't measured by dollar signs, but by the love of our parents and their godly example.

As I look over their beautiful legacy, I realize it's my mom and dad's absolute faith in God that I want to replicate most. Religion wasn't something my parents practiced on Sundays. They lived it out every moment of the week.

I saw it in their hospitality as they opened their homes to strangers (1 Peter 4:9). I saw it in their generosity as they faithfully tithed and gave beyond what the Bible requires (1 Corinthians 16:2). I saw it in their commitment to church attendance as they ended camping trips on Saturday so we could be in church on Sunday (Hebrews 10:25). I saw it in the faithful love they had for each other and the clear boundaries they set for their kids (Proverbs 22:6). But it shone brightest in their passionate love for Jesus and the way they shared Him with those around them.

"I've had a wonderful life," Dad told me many years ago as we waited for him to undergo a complicated surgery. "If the Lord takes me, I'm ready. My life is in His hands."

We knew it was a possibility. Kidney cancer and prescribed blood thinners had contributed to a massive blood clot in the major artery leading up to his heart, and he might not survive the risky surgery. Yet we all felt God's amazing peace.

"We *have* had a wonderful life, Daddy," I said, kissing his cheek and sharing my tears. "Thank you for loving Jesus and your family so well."

Though the complicated surgery was successful, the anesthesia caused his "early dementia" to progress. In recent years it's worsened to the point that Dad can't do many of the things he loves, which really frustrates him. Recently, a severe decline in Dad's health made it necessary for my parents to leave their home to get the care he needs. The process has been excruciating, especially for my mother. But once again she has showed me the "shape of godliness" as she's chosen to trust God, laying down her personal preferences in order to love and cherish my father.

My parents are still teaching me so much about living out my faith. But one day I know that the phone will ring, and everything will change. One or both of my parents will have gone to their reward. Though I don't look forward to that moment, I know all will be well. For in the way that they've lived and loved, my parents have been preparing me for years.

I'm a trust-fund baby, you see. Cliff and Annette Gustafson have left a rich heritage of faith that will continue for generations. For they've followed David's advice in 1 Chronicles 22:19—devoting their "heart and soul to seeking the Lord."

The Power of Your Testimony

I'm aware that many of you didn't grow up with the kind of godly heritage I've been privileged to enjoy. But no matter your background, if you've surrendered your life to Jesus, you've been adopted into God's family and are now a "joint [heir] with Christ" (Romans 8:17 NKJV).

Because of that, you have a new "family of origin." According to 2 Peter 1:4, you and I are "partakers of the divine nature" (NKJV). Which means a new DNA flows through your spiritual veins, my friend! The Divine Nature of the Almighty.

Each and every one of us has a powerful story to tell. As we allow the Lord to transform us inwardly, our outer lives become

WRITING YOUR TESTIMONY

One of the most powerful ways we point people to Jesus is by sharing our testimony in a simple and concise way. Set aside fifteen minutes and use the following prompts from The Navigators to help identify key milestones in your faith walk.

If you accepted Christ as a child and can't remember your B.C. days (that is, before Christ!) the following questions may help tell your story.

BEFORE

1. Before you met Christ [or fully dedicated your life to Him], what were some of your needs, what was lacking, or what was missing in your life?
2. What methods for improving your life did you try that didn't work?

HOW

1. What were the circumstances that caused you to consider following Jesus [or go further to make Him your Lord]?
2. What has become your favorite Bible verse and why?
3. Share about how you trusted Christ [or fully surrendered] and give a brief explanation of the gospel. John 3:16 is a great verse to use.

AFTER

1. Give an example of how God has met your needs—either physical or emotional—since you accepted Jesus.
2. Share about what part of your relationship with God you're most grateful for today.[8]

Fine-tune your testimony by writing and rewriting it until it is under three hundred words (about three minutes when read aloud). Delete any unnecessary details and shape it for your listener—simply share what Jesus means to you. You can find more resources for witnessing at Navigators.org.

Always be prepared to give an *answer* to everyone who asks you to give the reason for the *hope* that you have.

1 Peter 3:15

testimonies of God's life-changing power. Holy prototypes that blaze a trail for someone else.

Given what I've just written about my family, you might think that I come from a long history of believers, but that isn't true. My father's father didn't come to know Jesus until his forties. Before that he led a pretty wild lifestyle marked by drinking and carousing. My mother was a teenager when her parents met Jesus. Before that, her dad often drank and gambled their money away.

But both my grandfathers had such radical encounters with Jesus that the trajectories of their lives were completely changed—along with the lives of their children and grandchildren and great-grandchildren. And now their great-great-grandchildren as well.

Their testimonies are part of my testimony, just as your story will be part of generations to come. So I encourage you to take a moment and consider God's work in your life. For your testimony isn't just about the moment you were saved. It involves every decision you've made to trust God despite your circumstance. Every time you've given the Holy Spirit room to work in your life.

The disciplines you've embraced.

The fig leaves you've discarded.

The idols you've laid down.

New opportunities for transformation are all around you! Every time you let God get His hands on you, you have a fresh testimony of God's faithfulness to share with others who need to know the One who saves.

Accessing God's Riches

As I've sought to understand what trusting God should look like, I've been drawn to Christian biographies of great men and women of the past. One of my favorites is about a man named George Müller, a German native who spent most of his long life in nineteenth-century Bristol, England.

A scoundrel in his youth, Müller was an unlikely candidate for God's work. At ten years of age, he started stealing money from his wealthy father.[9] By his teens he was cheating and stealing from his own friends. Even twenty-four days in jail wasn't enough to make him change his ways.[10]

Until God's love apprehended Müller, that is, and his life was entirely changed. After moving to England, he got married and began to preach the gospel. Greed had so lost its power that George and his first wife, Mary, decided to depend completely on God for their resources.

When Müller saw the desperate needs of orphaned street kids in England at the time, he was convinced that God wanted him to build an orphanage. But there were to be no appeals or fundraisers. If this was of God, Müller believed that God would provide.

Miraculously, money and workers poured in, and the first orphanage was established in 1836. But as the ministry grew, Müller's faith was often tested. At times they had nothing to feed the children. But as George led the staff and children in prayer, a knock would come at the door, and food would be miraculously supplied. Though there were plenty of close calls, not once did the children miss a meal, and by God's grace they lacked nothing.[11]

Over the course of his ninety-plus years, George Müller went on to build a compound of five houses that held more than two thousand children at a time. Müller's daily dependence upon God not only provided for over ten thousand orphans during his lifetime,[12] it also crafted an intimate trust that moved the hand of God time and time again.

During a voyage to Quebec to share about God's faithfulness, Müller's ship was delayed by intense fog. The ship's captain told Müller there was no way they'd make it in time for his speaking appointment. To which Müller responded, "Let us go down to the chart room and pray."

The captain, also a believer, later described Müller's prayer as very simple, something along the lines of, "O Lord, if it is consistent with Thy will, please remove this fog in five minutes. You know the engagement You made for me in Quebec for Saturday. I believe it is Your will."

Though the captain didn't have faith for such a miracle, he started to add a prayer of his own. But Müller stopped him, saying:

> Captain, I have known my Lord for fifty-seven years and there has never been a single day that I have failed to gain an audience with the King. Get up, Captain and open the door, and you will find the fog is gone.

And it was! Unimpeded by fog, the ship arrived in Quebec that Saturday afternoon.[13]

Müller's daily "audience with the King" shaped an extraordinary friendship with God. Near the end of his life, Müller wrote,

> I am a happy old man; yes, indeed, I am a happy old man! . . . Lord Jesus, I am not alone, for You are with me. I have buried my wives and my children, but You are left. I am never lonely or desolate with You and with Your smile, which is better than life itself!![14]

What a beautiful legacy. What an incredible life. And what an inspiring pattern to follow. For trusting God is the only way to access the rich inheritance that is ours in Jesus Christ. A mighty, living faith that literally has the power to change the world.

The Long Route Upward

While writing the final chapters of this book, I felt prompted to drive the Going-to-the-Sun Road two different times.

The first drive was picture-perfect. Golden aspen trees shimmered in the early October sunlight as I wound my way to the top of Logan's Pass. Taking advantage of well-placed turnouts, I took several pictures of the amazing views. And I found myself thanking God for the long, winding journey He'd taken me on during the writing of this book. For so many perceived "detours" had proved to be scenic turnouts as Jesus revealed Himself to me in intimate ways.

My second trip later in the week was far from perfect, however—the sky dark and heavy with rain clouds. It reminded me of the previous year, when I'd tried to take my Texas friend, Jana Kennedy-Spicer, to the top in similar weather. Though I'd hoped the clouds would break when we got to the top of Logan's Pass, we'd been disappointed to find the view obliterated by thick and dense fog.

"There's an amazing mountain over there," I'd told Jana as we stood in the visitor center. Pointing to pictures in a brochure, then pointing in the general direction, I'd informed her, "That's Mount Reynolds, and over there is Clements Mountain . . ."

Jana had shrugged and laughed. "I guess I'll have to take your word for it!"

God reminded me of that moment as I drove through the rain a year later. *No matter how dark your situation or how many clouds block My face, I'm always there, Joanna. Whether you feel Me or see Me doesn't diminish My reality. I'm as real in the clouds as I am in the sunshine. Trust Me, My child.*

I was pondering His words that day as I drove through the rain when the clouds in front of me suddenly parted, and I caught a view of Mount Oberlin—my favorite peak. Rising up from the valley floor, it seemed even more glorious as a light dusting of snow accentuated each crevice and crack. As the road climbed, the fresh powder brought new definition and beauty to the familiar mountains around me.

That stormy day I saw Glacier Park in a way I'd never seen it before, and I couldn't help but thank God for the brave people who had risked their lives to build the road I traveled.

"Prepare the way of the Lord." That's the mission we've been given as believers—to live our faith in such a way that it creates a pathway that points people to Jesus and gives them a glimpse of the glory of God.

> We will not hide them from their descendants;
>   we will tell the next generation
> the praiseworthy deeds of the LORD,
>   his power, and the wonders he has done. . . .
> So the next generation would know them,
>   even the children yet to be born. (Psalm 78:4, 6)

I want to be part of that great highway of faith God's been building through the ages. I want to be one of those faith-filled believers who've forged their part of the path by trusting the Lord. Blasting out unbelief and laying a solid foundation on which others can travel.

True believe-ers who have let go in surrender so they can hold on in faith—clinging to a forever-faithful God who is always with them and working on their behalf. Ambassadors of the upside-down kingdom of God who bring His presence wherever they go.

It's our turn to leave a legacy, my friend. It's time to trust God with all our hearts and cooperate with the Spirit so that we, too, construct a life worth following.

Blazing a trail that truly leads to the Son.

Acknowledgments

After carrying this book in my heart for so long, it's almost hard to believe that it's here. I'm so grateful to all the people who came beside me and made it possible.

To all my friends at church and online who lifted this book in prayer—my beautiful church family, the women of our Tuesday morning Bible study, and "The Living Room with Joanna Weaver" private Facebook group—thank you for your intercession and support. I'm grateful for my parents, Cliff and Annette Gustafson, and for dear friends such as Jodi Detrick, Kelly Balarie, JoAnn Roberts, and Beth Epley, who prayed powerful prayers that pushed back the darkness and brought strength to my soul. Special thanks to my incredible assistant, Rachel Krahn: I couldn't have written this book without the many ways you came beside me and did what I couldn't do.

As always, my family's loving and tangible support means so much to me. Thank you, Jessica, for being a fabulous sounding board and for praying me out of tight spots. John Michael, I am still overwhelmed by the video Bible study you helped me create. Josh, this book is richer because you allowed me to tell your story. And John, my husband and dear gift from God, thank you for believing in me—but even more, for believing in the message

God wanted to write through me. So much of what I've written, I learned from you.

To those who allowed me to use their cabins for extended times of writing, special thanks to my brother and sister-in-law Steve and Polly Gustafson, Ron and Corky Pigman, Randy and Kay Creech, and Glacier Bible Camp.

I've loved working with the incredible publishing team at Revell. Andrea Doering, acquisitions editor and dear friend, thank you for championing this message and cheering me on, even when it took so long to write the book. To Eileen Hanson, Holly Maxwell, and everyone at Revell, who work hard to get books into people's hands: thanks for doing what you do with such excellence. Also, a special thanks to Anne Christian Buchanan, my longtime editor, who helped me hone my thoughts and finalize my words.

Looking back over twenty-plus years of writing, I'm so grateful for Janet Grant, my literary agent extraordinaire! I can't imagine doing this writing thing without you by my side. You are one of God's sweetest gifts.

But my deepest gratitude goes to my Lord Jesus, the Author and Perfecter of my faith. Thank You for writing this message of trust deep in my heart and helping me put it on the page. May this book change others as You've used it to change me. Teaching us how to speak God's love language as we let go in surrender and cling only to Him.

May You be glorified in it all, Lord.

Soli Deo gloria. Amen.

For from him and through him
and for him are *all things*.
To him be the glory forever! Amen.

Romans 11:36

Appendix A

Study Guide

Introduction

I'm so honored you're reading this book, but I want to point you to the most important book of all—the Bible! Embracing a deep trust in God doesn't come naturally to any of us. It's a mindset and a heart response that must be cultivated each and every day. And one of the best ways to do that is by spending time in God's Word and allowing the Holy Spirit to speak to us. For "faith comes by hearing, and hearing by the word of God" (Romans 10:17 NKJV).

Each week, you'll be assigned chapter(s) to read in this book. As you do so, make it your own by underlining key phrases and recording things God speaks to your heart in the margins. Then open your Bible and complete that week's study. Each lesson starts with two questions for discussion or reflection that lead to going deeper in your study of biblical principles. You'll also be asked what spoke most to you that week.

If you'd like to do more Bible study, look up the verses mentioned in the chapter(s).

As you read the book and do the Bible study, I hope you'll invite God into your trust journey. Ask Him questions and be alert to the different ways He might answer, for the Lord wants to have an intimate friendship with you. He wants to help you increase your faith so that you become fluent in His love language of trust.

You can access a downloadable workbook of this study that features space to record your answers at JoannaWeaverBooks.com/ETstudy. Teaching videos are available for purchase, along with a detailed leader's guide for using the study as a group.

You're in my thoughts and prayers, my friend. I'd love to hear what God teaches you as you learn to embrace trust—letting go and holding on to your forever-faithful God!

Blessings,
Joanna

Connect with me online:
Instagram & Facebook: @JoannaWeaverBooks
Email: Joanna@JoannaWeaverBooks.com

Week One

Read chapter 1, "The Journey to Trust," and chapter 2, "Total Surrender."

Questions for Discussion or Reflection

1. When it comes to trusting God, why do you think many of us struggle—even as Christians?

2. In chapter 2, I talk about going skydiving. What's the most daring thing you've done or would like to do if you could push past the fear?

Going Deeper

3. Read "10 Signs You Might Have Trust Issues" on page 22–23. Which signs do you tend to struggle with most? How could you trust God more in those areas?

4. Living in a fallen world means we will face trouble. Read the verses below and draw a line from the reference to what it promises.

Psalm 34:19	God comforts us so we can comfort others.
John 16:33	Nothing can separate us from God's love.
Romans 8:38–39	God will deliver us.
2 Corinthians 1:3–4	Jesus has overcome the world.

5. Write out Proverbs 3:5–6 in your favorite Bible translation and consider memorizing it. Which phrase means the most to you, and why?

6. Why is it important to surrender our entire life to Jesus according to these verses?

   Matthew 6:24 ______________________________

   ____

   Mark 8:35–36 ______________________________

   ____

   Luke 14:33 ______________________________

   ____

7. On page 45, I talk about three areas of freedom that come when we trust God with all of our hearts. How could trusting God change your life in the following areas?

    - Fear

    - Regret

    - Resentment

8. What spoke most to you in these chapters?

Week Two

Read chapter 3, "Unshakeable Faith."

Questions for Discussion or Reflection

1. This chapter opens with the story of an unusual dream I had. What's the craziest or most memorable dream you've had?

2. Unshakeable faith is often formed by being shaken. Read Hebrews 12:26–29 and describe how God used a time of shaking to purify your faith and build deeper trust in Him.

Going Deeper

3. If you were able to see your spiritual foundation, what would it look like? Draw or describe it below. Identify visible holes or invisible trouble spots that weaken your faith and need attention. Include any situations in which you are struggling to trust.

4. Read the story of the wise and foolish builders in Luke 6:46–49. Then read 1 Corinthians 3:10–15. What advice do these two passages of Scripture give for building a successful life?

5. I've listed "10 Faith-Building Exercises" on pages 50–51. Along with daily "asking God to increase your faith," choose one other exercise to practice this week. Come back and record what you experienced. Note any growth—no matter how small.

   Exercise: ______________________________

   Growth: ______________________________

6. We'd all prefer an easy life, but God has harnessed difficulties to do a deep work in us. Read the following verses, and list the process and benefits you discover.

   Luke 22:31–32

   Process: ______________________________

   Benefits: ______________________________

   2 Corinthians 12:7–9

   Process: ______________________________

   Benefits: ______________________________

   1 Peter 1:6–7

   Process: ______________________________

   Benefits: ______________________________

7. As you look back at the weak places you identified in question 3, how could truly believing the following truths fill in holes in your spiritual foundation? Look up the corresponding verses, then label any holes with the truth(s) each one needs using G, L, B or C.

   G: God is good. (Psalm 119:68)
   L: God loves you. (Psalm 86:15)
   B: You belong to Him. (Romans 8:15)
   C: God takes care of His own. (2 Corinthians 9:8)

   Invite the Lord to fill each and every hole with truth about His love and grace.

8. What spoke most to you in this chapter?

Week Three

Read chapter 4, "Laying Down Fig Leaves," and chapter 5, "Not-So-Great Expectations."

Questions for Discussion or Reflection

1. In the opening of chapter 4, I talk about the pom-poms I used to cover my inability to do the splits. What do you tend to use to cover your inadequacies?

2. Imagine you're standing at a Victory Circle fire like the one described on pages 79–80. What would you write on your slip of paper? Would you struggle to release it to the flame or let go of it willingly? Explain why.

Going Deeper

3. Read the story of David and Goliath found in 1 Samuel 17:1–54. List the ways you see David trust God. What aspect of David's faith would you like to emulate, and why?

4. Using the "Identifying Fig Leaves" sidebar on page 71, choose the fig leaf you tend to use most (or name one that's not listed) and respond to the following prompts.

   Fig leaf: ______________________________

   How it shows up: ______________________________

   ____

   God wants to replace it with: ______________________________

   ____

5. Rather than wearing the fig-leaf armor of the world, we're called to daily put on "the armor of God" described in Ephesians 6:13–18. List the different pieces of armor (don't forget to include prayer!). While it's important to wear all of them, which piece do you need most today, and why?

6. Read the "Letting Go of Expectations" sidebar on page 87, then work through the following prompts to help identify expectations you may need to release.

   My husband (or closest friend) should . . .

   My children need to . . .

   My friends ought to . . .

My life must be . . .

I can't be happy until . . .

Using Psalm 62:5 (NKJV) as a prayer template, release those expectations to God.

7. Read Habakkuk 3:17–18 on page 92 and personalize it below by filling in the blanks with your situation. Read it out loud as a declaration of faith over your current situation. Commit your "thoughs" to the Lord and ask that He be glorified in them all.

   Though . . .

   Though . . .

   Though . . .

   Yet I will rejoice in the LORD,
   I will be joyful in God my Savior.

8. What spoke most to you in these chapters?

Week Four

Read chapter 6, "Upside-Down Kingdom."

Questions for Discussion or Reflection

1. If you had to live in a different country, which one would you choose, and why?

2. Which of the names of God listed on page 109 and in Appendix B do you need most right now, and why?

Going Deeper

3. According to the following verses, what is necessary in order to be a citizen of God's kingdom?

   Luke 18:16–17 ______________________

   John 3:3–6 ______________________

   Acts 14:21–22 ______________________

4. In order to be good ambassadors in God's kingdom, 1 Timothy 4:12 tells us we need to "set an example" in five different areas: (a) speech, (b) conduct, (c) love, (d) faith, and (e) purity. Read the following verses and label them with the quality or qualities they describe.

   ___ Matthew 12:36–37
   ___ John 13:34–35
   ___ Romans 4:20
   ___ 1 Corinthians 16:13–14
   ___ Ephesians 4:1–2
   ___ Ephesians 5:2
   ___ Colossians 1:10
   ___ Colossians 3:8–9
   ___ James 4:8
   ___ 1 Peter 2:12

5. Read Alex Seeley's story about moving in the "opposite spirit" on page 100. Describe a time when choosing an opposite response changed a situation for the good, and what you learned from it.

6. In Luke 6:27–36, Jesus calls us to a counterintuitive way of life. Which part causes resistance in your Flesh Woman? According to 1 Peter 2:12, why is it important that we live differently than the world?

7. Using the "Oath of Allegiance" on page 107 as a template, write your own declaration of devotion to God's kingdom. Don't worry about doing it perfectly, just write it from your heart.

8. What spoke most to you in this chapter?

Week Five

Read chapter 7, "Smashing Idols," and chapter 9, "Living Beyond Your Dreams."

Questions for Discussion or Reflection

1. When you were young, what did you dream of being or doing when you grew up?

2. Though idolatry isn't as outwardly visible in our modern world as it was in Bible times, how does it tend to show up today?

Going Deeper

3. With Timothy Keller's definition of idolatry in mind, are there any people, possessions, positions, or desired power that you might be exalting above God?

> [An idol is] anything more important to you than God, anything that absorbs your heart and imagination more than God, anything you seek to give you what only God can give. . . . Anything so central and essential to your life that, should you lose it, your life would feel hardly worth living.[1]

4. Read 1 Kings 11:1–10. How did King Solomon fall prey to the following "Downward Ds of Idolatry"? How do they tend to show up in your life?

   Divided attention

   Solomon: ________________________________

   My life: ________________________________

   Diluted devotion

   Solomon: ________________________________

   My life: ________________________________

   Detestable idolatry

   Solomon: ________________________________

   My life: ________________________________

5. Ask the Holy Spirit to help you identify any idols in your life. Then, with His help, work through the "6 Idol-Smashing Strategies" sidebar on pages 120–121. What did you discover in this exercise? How can you guard against idolatry in the future?

6. Which lesson from the life of Joseph, gleaned from Genesis 37, 39–50, do you need most right now, and why?

   Lesson #1: Don't parade your dream before people; ponder it before God.

   Lesson #2: God never wastes our pain. He uses it for His purposes.

Lesson #3: You can prosper in difficult times if you work hard and serve well.

Lesson #4: Don't let other people's bad behavior determine your own actions.

Lesson #5: God uses trials to prepare and position us.

Lesson #6: Be willing to serve someone else's dream.

Lesson #7: You can trust God's methods, His timing, and His plans.

7. How do the following verses encourage you when it comes to testing and learning to live beyond your dreams?

Psalm 138:8 ______________________________

____

Philippians 1:6 ___________________________

____

James 1:2–4 ______________________________

____

1 Peter 1:6–7 _____________________________

____

8. What spoke most to you in these chapters?

Read chapter 8, "The Unoffendable Heart."

Questions for Discussion or Reflection

1. When it comes to your propensity toward offense, rank yourself honestly:

1	2	3	4	5
easily offended	often offended	occasionally offended	rarely offended	never offended

2. Described on page 130, have any of the following affected your ability to forgive: personality, family of origin, past trauma, mismanaged hurt? Explain.

Going Deeper

3. Read Cain's story in Genesis 4:1–16. What lessons can we learn from Cain's unwillingness to let go of offense? In verses 6–7, what does God say we should do instead? (Also see 2 Corinthians 2:10–11.)

4. What do the following verses teach us about forgiveness?

   Proverbs 19:11 ______________________________

   ____

   Matthew 6:14–15 ______________________________

   ____

   Ephesians 4:32 ______________________________

   ____

5. Consider the following qualities of love from 1 Corinthians 13:5 (TLB). Explain how your life would be different if you allowed God to help you love like this.

   Not being irritable or touchy:

   Not holding grudges:

   Hardly noticing when others do it wrong:

6. Read the story of the prodigal son and his father's forgiveness on pages 136, 139–141 (see Luke 15:11–32). Which of the father's qualities would you most like to emulate and why?

7. Forgiveness isn't an event—it's a choice we have to continually make. With the Holy Spirit's help, work through the "Nine Ways to Cultivate an Unoffendable Heart" sidebar on pages 137–38, then answer the following questions.

   Which step causes the most pushback?

   Which step could bring the most freedom?

   Write a prayer asking for the unoffendable heart of Jesus.

8. What spoke most to you in this chapter?

Week Seven

Read chapter 10, "Believing God."

Questions for Discussion or Reflection

1. In the opening, I talk about jumping into my dad's arms at the swimming pool. What's the biggest leap of faith you've ever taken? What would you attempt if you really believed God would help you?

2. Remembering what God has done in the past helps us believe Him in the present. Looking back, describe an instance when God had intervened on your behalf or someone elses's behalf in a miraculous way.

Going Deeper

3. In Matthew 13:58, we're told that Jesus didn't do many miracles in His hometown "because of their unbelief" (NLT). Read the stories of the following people who had extraordinary faith. Note how they interacted with Jesus and expressed their belief. What can you learn from their examples?

   Centurion (Matthew 8:5–13)

   Gentile woman (Matthew 15:21–28)

   Suffering woman (Mark 5:25–34)

4. What challenge to faith are you currently facing? Read 2 Corinthians 10:4–5 and, with that challenge in mind, work through the following prompts.

What argument (or lie) is exalting itself against the knowledge of God in this situation?

What lofty opinion have I believed more than the opinion of God?

Where did this thought come from? Where does it want to take me?

Ask the Holy Spirit to help you replace any arguments, lofty opinions, and wayward thoughts with the truth of God's Word. Write down verses or scriptural principles He brings to mind.

5. Believing God isn't a passive activity. But with the Lord's help, like the desperate father in Mark 9:24, we can "overcome [our] unbelief." What instructions do we find in the following verses? Choose one and describe how you will put it into practice today.

John 6:28–29 ______________________________

____

1 Corinthians 16:13 ______________________________

____

1 Timothy 6:12 ______________________________

____

Today I will . . . ______________________________

____

6. Read the following verses about believing God, then draw a line to match the reference to the benefit it describes.

Matthew 21:22	Be filled with inexpressible joy.
John 11:40	Receive answers to prayer.
John 20:31	Have life in His name.
1 Peter 1:8	See God's glory.

7. Using the challenge to faith you identified in question 4, read through the following aspects of Abraham's faith, outlined in Romans 4:18–22. With the Holy Spirit's help, write a prayer of faith declaring your belief in God's sovereign power over your situation.

   Against all hope, Abraham in hope believed.

   Without weakening in his faith, Abraham faced the facts.

   Abraham did not waver through unbelief regarding the promises of God.

   Abraham was strengthened in his faith and gave glory to God.

   Abraham was fully persuaded that God had the power to do what He had promised.

8. What spoke most to you in this chapter?

Week Eight

Read chapter 11, "Content in His Love," and chapter 12, "The Gift of Discipline."

Questions for Discussion or Reflection

1. Do you have a "happy place," a physical location or memory (real or imagined) where you feel most content and at peace? Describe it.

2. Read the story of baby Josh and his strengthening exercises on pages 195–97. Now read Hebrews 12:5–6 in the Message translation at the opening of chapter 12. How do these two things change how you view God's discipline in your life?

Going Deeper

3. Paul talks a lot about the importance of contentment though he wrote many of his epistles in prison. Read the following passages and rewrite the one that speaks most to you in your own words.

   Philippians 4:11–13

   1 Timothy 6:6–10

4. To become a "Psalm 131 Woman," we need to pursue the attributes listed on pages 189–190. What do the corresponding verses teach you about each quality?

   Her "heart is not proud." (Philippians 2:3–4)

   Her "eyes are not haughty." (Psalm 101:5)

She isn't obsessed by "great matters or things too wonderful." (Matthew 20:25–26)

She has "calmed and quieted" her soul like a weaned child. (Isaiah 32:17)

5. From the sidebar on page 188, which of the "Secrets of a Settled Soul" do you need right now and why?

6. Hebrews 12:10–13 describes the reasons for God's discipline, its results, and the part you and I play. Categorize what you learn below.

   Reasons: ______________________________

   ____

   Results: ______________________________

   ____

   Our part: ______________________________

   ____

7. Read through the descriptions of the "training schedule" outlined on pages 203–204 and in 2 Peter 1:5–8. Which element comes easy to you? Which element needs work? What could you do this week to "make every effort to add" at least one of these skills to your routine?

8. What spoke most to you in these chapters?

Week Nine

Read chapter 13, "Faith over Fear," and chapter 14, "God-Sized Prayers."

Questions for Discussion or Reflection

1. Which survival instinct do you usually default to: fight, flight, or freeze? Do you have a funny story about that?

2. Read Psalm 145:4. Share the greatest miracle you've ever experienced or heard about. Our faith grows when we tell stories of God's mighty power.

Going Deeper

3. When David was afraid because his men spoke of stoning him, 1 Samuel 30:6 tells us that he "strengthened himself in the LORD his God" (NKJV). What do the following verses say we should do when we're afraid? Circle the one that speaks most to you.

   Joshua 1:9 ____

   ____

   Psalm 42:5–6 ______________________________________

   ____

   John 14:1 ____

   ____

4. Read 2 Timothy 1:7 (NKJV). In which of the following areas does the spirit of fear tend to attack you most? How do the corresponding verses encourage you?

   Power (Colossians 1:11)

   Love (Romans 5:5)

   Sound mind (Romans 8:5–6)

   Consider memorizing 2 Timothy 1:7 as part of your arsenal against fear.

5. Going to the end of your worst fear and finding God there is a powerful exercise. Respond to the following questions, then read Psalm 34:4–5 out loud and commit that fear to the Lord.

   What is your worst fear?

   If it happened, what would still be true of God?

6. Bring together what you've learned in chapters 13 and 14 by doing the following:

   a) Read Philippians 4:6–7, then list all your current worries and fears.
   b) Draw a line over your list and write the name of JESUS on top of the line.
   c) Using the prayer template in Philippians, take your concerns to the Lord.
   d) After committing them to Him, allow "the peace of God" to rule your heart and mind.

7. Read the "How to Pray Effectively" sidebar on pages 230–231. Which suggestions from R. A. Torrey resonate in your spirit? Implement one of the tips in your prayer time this week, then come back and share the results.

   Tip: ____

   ____

   Result: ____

   ____

8. What spoke most to you in these chapters?

Week Ten

Read chapter 15, "Resting in God's Sovereignty," and chapter 16, "Leaving a Legacy of Trust."

Questions for Discussion or Reflection

1. Read my story about losing my "peace" on pages 241–242. What sort of things tend to steal your peace? How would life be different if you lived by the following prayer?

   > Teach me to treat all that comes to me with peace of soul and with firm conviction that Your will governs all.[2]

2. Do you have any treasured keepsakes that have been passed down through generations? What kind of spiritual legacy would you like to pass on to your descendants?

Going Deeper

3. Go back to week 2 and look at the "holes" you identified in your spiritual foundation.

    a) Describe progress you have made during this study in filling those holes.
    b) Read the description of *shalom* on page 243 and John 14:27.
    c) How would fully accepting Christ's offer—peace *with* God and peace *from* God—fill your remaining gaps? Take a moment and do that.

4. Though he was severely tested, Job made some incredible statements of faith in God's sovereignty. Rewrite the following verses and make your own declarations of faith.

    Job 1:21 ________________________________

    ____

    Job 2:10 ________________________________

    ____

    Job 13:15 _______________________________

    ____

    Job 19:25 _______________________________

    ____

5. We explored 1 Timothy 4:12 in a previous lesson, but let's take it a step further. What kind of legacy would you like to leave behind in the following areas?

   Speech: ______________________________

   Conduct: ______________________________

   Love: ______________________________

   Faith: ______________________________

   Purity: ______________________________

6. Think of the spiritual "trailblazers" in your life who have brought you closer to Jesus. What qualities in their life impacted you? If possible, tell them what they've meant to you.

7. As we close this study, I'd like us to start creating a legacy of trust. Write a letter to your descendants (both physical and spiritual) that includes the following:

   What Jesus means to you

   Two or three important truths about following God

   A prayer of blessing over their lives

   The letter doesn't need to be long, but rewrite it until it clearly expresses your heart. Pray over the letter, then seal it in an envelope and place it with your important documents.

8. What spoke most to you in these chapters?

Appendix B

Knowing the God You Can Trust

"Christianity . . . is strong or weak depending upon her concept of God," A. W. Tozer writes in his classic book, *The Attributes of God*.[1] So, how do we strengthen our concept, that is, our understanding of who God is and how He works?

Studying God's attributes and the names given to His Son has expanded my heart—at times blown my mind!—and helped me forge a deeper faith. Because, Jesus is "the radiance of God's glory and the exact representation of his being" (Hebrews 1:3), we can learn a lot about God from the names given to Jesus in the Bible. But I've also included a list of God's attributes that have really blessed me, and I trust they will do the same for you.

Though there are many other names and attributes found in the Bible, I've compiled these two lists to help you begin to "think magnificently" of God. Work through both lists slowly, reflecting on one name or attribute at a time as you read the related verses.

As you gaze on the Lord's beauty, allow your mind to expand and your heart to respond in worship. For in doing so, you'll come to know the God you can trust.

Names of Jesus

In the Gospel of John, Jesus defines our great "I AM" God (Exodus 3:14) with the following statements about Himself:

- I am the Bread of Life (6:35)
- I am the Light of the World (8:12)
- I am the Gate (10:9)
- I am the Good Shepherd (10:11–14)
- I am the Resurrection and the Life (11:25)
- I am the Way and the Truth and the Life (14:6)
- I am the Vine (15:1–5)

More names of Jesus to study and pray through:

- Advocate (1 John 2:1)
- Alpha and Omega (Revelation 1:8)
- Author of Life (Acts 3:15)
- Creator (John 1:3)
- Chief Cornerstone (Ephesians 2:20)
- Faithful and True (Revelation 3:14)
- Great High Priest (Hebrews 4:14)
- Hope of Glory (Colossians 1:27)
- Immanuel "God with us" (Matthew 1:23)
- Indescribable Gift (2 Corinthians 9:15)
- Lamb of God (John 1:29)
- Lord of All (Acts 10:36)
- Peace (Ephesians 2:14)
- Pioneer and Perfecter of Faith (Hebrews 12:2)

- Power and Wisdom of God (1 Corinthians 1:24)
- Savior (Luke 2:11)
- Spiritual Rock (1 Corinthians 10:4)
- True God and Eternal Life (1 John 5:20)
- Wonderful Counselor (Isaiah 9:6)
- Word (John 1:1)

Attributes of God

God is infinite

Our God is self-existing. Our uncreated Creator made everything and "in him, all things hold together" (Colossians 1:17). Just as He has no beginning and no end, neither do His attributes. They extend in every direction without limit. God is infinitely good, infinitely wise, infinitely everything He's promised to be (Psalm 102:25–27; Romans 11:33–36; Revelation 22:13).

God is unchanging

God is "the same yesterday and today and forever" (Hebrews 13:8). His attributes aren't determined by His mood or our behavior. He is dependable. His promises remain as they have always been. His love is unfailing and His power is unchanging (Numbers 23:19; Psalm 33:11; James 1:17).

God is holy

God is infinite and unchanging in His holiness—He is perfect in every way. Though He is all-powerful, God never acts in a way that contradicts His holiness. He cannot lie, He does not tempt, and He will not tolerate sin. He sent His Son so that we can be made holy as He is holy (1 Samuel 2:2; Isaiah 6:3–5; James 1:13; 1 Peter 1:15–16).

God is good

Good seems like such a tame word, but it encompasses God's perfection, His absolute morality, and His unfailing love toward us. His perfect goodness has no shadow side marred by bad days or wrong motives. Instead, He is altogether good—both His works as well as His ways (Psalm 100:5; 119:68; Romans 2:4; 1 John 1:5).

God is loving

Everything God does is motivated by His love. And His love is perfect. Unlike human love, it isn't tainted by self-interest or a desire to control. Instead, His intentions toward us are always for our good. And He longs to have a personal, intimate friendship with us (Jeremiah 31:3; Romans 5:8; Ephesians 3:17–19; 1 John 4:16–18).

God is wise

God is infinitely and perfectly wise. He knows the end from the beginning. Because He understands all the facts and sees the big picture, He knows what is best for us. If we'll trust Him, He'll give us the wisdom we need and show us the way we should go (Isaiah 46:9–11; Psalm 139:1–6; 1 Corinthians 1:25; James 1:5).

God is all-powerful

God has unlimited power—there is nothing He can't do. Yet His power is always consistent with His character. Nothing thwarts God's purposes and plans. Though He may not act according to our timing, we can trust Him to cause all things to work together for our good and His glory (Genesis 18:14; Psalm 33:6; Jeremiah 32:17; Ephesians 3:20).

God is just

God's justice should bring us comfort just as it produces holy fear. Because He is just, God will avenge and repay every wrong done to us. But that same justice requires a penalty for sin. Unless we accept Christ's atoning death, we can't stand in His presence or expect that He will help us (Deuteronomy 32:4; Ecclesiastes 12:14; Micah 7:18–19; 2 Corinthians 5:10).

God is merciful

Because God loves us, He has satisfied justice by sending His Son to die for our sins. His loving compassion and mercy continually seek to heal our brokenness. While our sin is great, His grace is greater. His mercy comforts and heals us. It mends and restores us. It makes us new (Psalm 51:1–2; Daniel 9:9; Hebrews 4:16; 2 Peter 3:9).

God is faithful

God isn't forgetful, nor does He fail to do what He's promised. No matter how long it takes, God will remain faithful. Though we might let Him down, God will never let us down. He will be faithful to help us overcome temptation and finish the work He has started in us (Deuteronomy 7:9; Psalm 119:90; 1 Corinthians 10:13; Philippians 1:6).

God is unfathomable

While we are made in His image, God is entirely above us and beyond us. We can't begin to comprehend His thoughts or His ways (Isaiah 56:8–9), which means we must make peace with mystery. Rather than demanding that He explain Himself, we can rest in the knowledge that He is altogether good (Psalm 139:5–6; Psalm 145:3; Isaiah 40:28; Romans 11:33–34).

God is knowable

Though we can't fully comprehend Him, God wants us to know Him through His Word and by His Holy Spirit. As we allow Jesus to live within us, we become intimately acquainted with our Father: a God who's working for our good and worthy of our trust (Jeremiah 9:23–24; Romans 1:20; 1 Corinthians 2:10–12; Ephesians 3:10–12).

God's Personal Biography

If you long to know God better and "think magnificently" of Him, I can't think of a better place to start than Exodus 34:6–7.

For in the self-description God gave to Moses, we find revelations of His nature as well as His heart:

> The Lord, the Lord, the compassionate and gracious God, slow to anger, abounding in love and faithfulness, maintaining love to thousands, and forgiving wickedness, rebellion and sin. Yet he does not leave the guilty unpunished.

Perhaps you struggle with that last sentence. How can a God of compassion also be a God of wrath? It's important to understand that God's attributes never contradict each other; instead, they work together in beautiful harmony. Because He is holy, He cannot tolerate sin. But because He is love, He provided the needed sacrifice.

When we accept His Son and embrace God *as He is* rather than trying to shape Him into our image—we not only discover a Father who loves us but a forever-faithful God we can trust.

Those who know your *name*
trust in you, for you, Lord,
have never forsaken
those who *seek* you.

Psalm 9:10

Notes

Part 1 Trusting God

1. Paraphrased from Amy Carmichael, *If: What Do I Know of Calvary Love?* (Fort Washington, PA: Christian Literature Crusade, 1938), 93, in Leslie Ludy, *Authentic Beauty: The Shaping of a Set-Apart Young Woman* (Colorado Springs: Multnomah, 2007), 248.

Chapter 1 The Journey to Trust

1. Lysa TerKeurst, *Uninvited: Living Loved When You Feel Less Than, Left Out, and Lonely* (Nashville: Thomas Nelson, 2016), 53–54.
2. Source unknown.
3. Brennan Manning, *Ruthless Trust: The Ragamuffin's Path to God* (San Francisco: HarperOne, 2000), 180–81.
4. Adapted from Alan Watts, "The Story of the Chinese Farmer," *Wellsbaum.blog: Writing about Life and Arts*, January 27, 2018, https://wellsbaum.blog/alan-watts-story-of-the-chinese-farmer.
5. Charles R. Swindoll, *David: A Man of Passion and Destiny*, Great Lives from God's Word (Dallas: Word, 1997), 7.
6. I picked up this memorable line from Martha Tennison, in a sermon given September 25, 1999.
7. Swindoll, *David*, 21.
8. As quoted by the great Scottish preacher Alexander Whyte (1836–1921) in a sermon called "The Magnificence of Prayer," *Lord Teach Us to Pray: Sermons on Prayer* (London: Hodder and Stoughton, 1922), accessed at Christian Classics Ethereal Library, September 18, 2021, www.ccel.org/ccel/whyte/pray.ii.html.
9. A. W. Tozer, *A Journey into the Father's Heart*, vol. 1 of *The Attributes of God* (Chicago: WingSpread, 2007), 195.
10. C. Michael Hawn, "History of Hymns: 'Tis So Sweet to Trust in Jesus,'" Discipleship Ministries: The United Methodist Church, September 18, 2014, www.umcdiscipleship.org/resources/history-of-hymns-tis-so-sweet-to-trust-in-jesus.

Chapter 2 Total Surrender

1. Julie Sprankles, "55+ Gilmore Girls Quotes That'll Make You Crave Coffee & Witty Banter," *Scary Mommy* (blog), January 13, 2021, www.scarymommy.com/gilmore-girls-quotes.

2. Joel Schmidgall, quoted in Mark Batterson, *All In: You Are One Decision Away from a Totally Different Life* (Grand Rapids: Zondervan, 2013), 132.

3. References about losing life to find it are found in Matthew 10:39; 16:25; Mark 8:35; Luke 9:24; and John 12:25.

4. Batterson, *All In*, 20.

5. Elisabeth Elliot used this term to describe her hero of faith, Amy Carmichael. See Ian Hamilton, "Lessons from the Life of Amy Carmichael (Part II)," blog post, *Radius International*, February 9, 2021, www.radiusinternational.org/lessons-from-the-life-of-amy-carmichael-part-ii.

6. Greg Laurie, "How to Know God," Harvest.org, accessed September 16, 2021, https://harvest.org/know-god/how-to-know-god, emphasis mine.

7. Joanna Weaver, *Having a Mary Spirit: Allowing God to Change Us from the Inside Out* (Colorado Springs: Waterbrook, 2006). Though Flesh Woman is discussed throughout that book, chapter 3 describes in detail the battle we experience inside.

8. Bethel is the name of the spot where Jacob encountered God in a dream, received a blessing, and set up an altar to God (Genesis 28:10–22; 35:1–3).

9. Henri Nouwen, *Henri Nouwen*, ed. Robert A. Jonas, Modern Spiritual Masters (Maryknoll, MD: Orbis, 1998), 55.

10. Warren Baker and Eugene Carpenter, *The Complete Word Study Dictionary: Old Testament* (Chattanooga: AMG, 2003), s.v. 7503 (Strong's H7503).

11. Larry Pierce, ed., "Outline of Biblical Usage," s.v. "*ḥāzaq*" (Strong's H2388), Blue Letter Bible, accessed October 25, 2021, www.blueletterbible.org/lexicon/h2388/kjv/wlc/0-1.

Chapter 3 Unshakeable Faith

1. *Pistis* (Strong's G4102) and usage on Bible Hub: https://biblehub.com/greek/4102.htm

2. I'm aware that *trust* can be a noun too, but making this distinction helps me grasp the active nature of faith lived out by trust, which I believe is fully biblical. And there is some basis for the noun/verb designations in the Greek. *Pistis* is a noun related to the verb *peithó*, which means to trust or have confidence. For more information see *pistis* (Strong's G4102) and *peithó* (Strong's G3982) on Bible Hub: https://biblehub.com/greek/4102.htm and https://biblehub.com/greek/3982.htm.

3. Used by permission. You can learn more about Jodi and her books at JodiDetrick.com.

4. Kenneth L. Barker, ed., *NIV Study Bible*, 10th Anniversary Edition, New International Version (Grand Rapids: Zondervan, 1995), text note on Revelation 12:10.

5. John Piper, "Are God's Providence and God's Sovereignty the Same?," transcript of episode 1383 of *Ask Pastor John*, podcast, Desiring God, October 18, 2019, www.desiringgod.org/interviews/are-gods-providence-and-gods-sovereignty-the-same?

6. Barker, *NIV Study Bible*, text note on 1 Samuel 18:4.

7. Dr. & Mrs. Howard Taylor, *Hudson Taylor's Spiritual Secret* (Chicago: Moody Publishers, 2009), 163.

8. Dr. & Mrs. Howard Taylor, *Hudson Taylor and the China Inland Mission: The Growth of a Work of God* (London: Morgan & Scott LD, 1920), 278.

9. Dr. & Mrs. Howard Taylor, *Hudson Taylor and the China Inland Mission*, 493.

10. "Coronavirus World Map: Tracking the Global Outbreak," *New York Times*, October 7, 2021, www.nytimes.com/interactive/2021/world/covid-cases.html.

Part 2 Letting Go

1. A. W. Tozer, *The Pursuit of God: The Human Thirst for the Divine* (Harrisburg, PA: Christian Publications, 2015), 30.

Chapter 4 Laying Down Fig Leaves

1. Paul Lee Tan, *Encyclopedia of 7700 Illustrations: Signs of the Times* (Rockville, MD: Assurance, 1990), 1566, s.v. "7124: Epigram."

2. Jackie Carroll, "Fig Types: Different Types of Fig Trees for the Garden," Gardening Know How, updated June 23, 2021, www.gardeningknowhow.com/edible/fruits/figs/different-types-of-fig-trees.htm.

3. "Fig Leaves Information and Facts" Specialty Produce, https://www.specialtyproduce.com/produce/Fig_Leaves_7136.php.

4. "Is Fig Tree Sap an Irritant?," EverythingWhat.com, July 23, 2021, https://everythingwhat.com/is-fig-tree-sap-an-irritant.

5. Dorothy Hildebrand Irvin, "Sew," in *The International Standard Bible Encyclopedia*, ed. Geoffrey W. Bromiley, rev. ed. (Grand Rapids: Eerdmans, 1988), 4:428–29.

6. Lauren Migliore, "I Can't Decide! Why an Increase in Choices Decreases Our Happiness," *BrainWorld*, December 7, 2019, https://brainworldmagazine.com/cant-decide-increase-choices-decreases-happiness.

7. Josh Fiallo, "U.S. Falls in World Happiness Report, Finland Named Happiest Country," *Tampa Bay Times*, March 20, 2019, www.tampabay.com/data/2019/03/20/us-falls-in-world-happiness-report-finland-named-happiest-country.

8. Barry Schwartz, *The Paradox of Choice: Why More Is Less* (New York: Ecco/Harper-Collins, 2004), 221.

9. Hans Christian Andersen, "The Emperor's New Clothes" ("Kaiserens Nye Klaeder"), trans. Jean Hersholt, University of Southern Denmark Hans Christian Andersen Centre, last modified September 19, 2019, https://andersen.sdu.dk/vaerk/hersholt/TheEmperorsNewClothes_e.html.

10. Andersen, "Emperor's New Clothes."

11. Colin J. Hemer, *The Letters to the Seven Churches of Asia in Their Local Setting* (Grand Rapids: Eerdmans, 2000), 191, quoted in Tony Garland, "A Testimony of Jesus Christ: A Commentary on the Book of Revelation," Spirit and Truth, accessed September 20, 2021, www.spiritandtruth.org/teaching/Book_of_Revelation/commentary/htm/chapters/03.htl#27394.

12. Monty S. Mills, *Revelations: An Exegetical Study of the Revelation to John* (Dallas: 3E Ministries, 1987), Revelation 3:14, quoted in Garland, "A Testimony of Jesus Christ."

13. Robert L. Thomas, *Revelation 1–7* (Chicago: Moody, 1992), Revelation 3:4, quoted in Garland, "A Testimony of Jesus Christ."

14. Hemer, *Letters to the Seven Churches*, 193, quoted in Garland, "A Testimony of Jesus Christ."

15. Warren Wiersbe, *Be Victorious (Revelation)*, (Colorado Springs, CO: David C. Cook, 1985), 56.

16. Hemer, *Letters to the Seven Churches*, 193.

Chapter 5 Not-So-Great Expectations

1. Melissa Camara Wilkins, "7 Expectations to Let Go of Right Now," *No Sidebar* (blog), February 26, 2017, https://nosidebar.com/expectations.

2. Wilkins, "7 Expectations to Let Go of Right Now."

3. Brennan Manning, *The Ragamuffin Gospel: Embracing the Unconditional Love of God* (Colorado Springs: Multnomah, 1990), 22.

4. Adapted from Wilkins, "7 Expectations to Let Go of Right Now."

5. *Strong's Exhaustive Concordance*, s.v. "*tiqvah*" (Strong's H8615), Bible Hub, accessed September 20, 2021, https://biblehub.com/hebrew/8615.htm.

6. Cindy and Steve Wright, "Finishing Well—Ruth and Billy Graham—MM 309," Marriage Missions International, accessed September 21, 2021, https://marriagemissions.com/finishing-well-ruth-billy-graham-finishing-well-mm-309.

7. Oswald Chambers, *My Utmost for His Highest: Selections for the Year: The Golden Book of Oswald Chambers*, The Christian Library (Westwood, NJ: Barbour, 1963), entry for May 3, 90.

8. John Newton, "Amazing Grace! (How Sweet the Sound)," *Ancient and Modern: Hymns and Songs for Refreshing Worship*, accessed at Hymnary.org, September 15, 2021, https://hymnary.org/text/amazing_grace_how_sweet_the_sound.

9. Wikipedia, s.v. "Miss Havisham," last modified September 20, 2021, 18:38, https://en.wikipedia.org/wiki/Miss_Havisham.

Chapter 6 Upside-Down Kingdom

1. This number is from my personal count of references in the NIV using Biblegateway.com. (I counted 104.) Here are the references found in just the Gospel of Mark: 1:15; 4:11, 26, 30; 9:1, 47; 10:14, 15, 23–25; 12:34; 14:25; and 15:43.

2. Jeremy R. Treat, *Seek First: How the Kingdom of God Changes Everything* (Grand Rapids: Zondervan, 2019), 24–25.

3. Treat, *Seek First*, 183.

4. Treat, *Seek First*, 184–85.

5. Alex Seeley, *The Opposite Life: Unlocking the Mysteries of God's Upside-Down Kingdom* (Nashville: W Publishing Group, 2019), 3.

6. Seeley, *Opposite Life*, 4.

7. Arthur Bennett, ed., *The Valley of Vision: A Collection of Puritan Prayers and Devotions* (Carlisle, PA: Banner of Truth, 2009), xxiv–xxv.

8. Seeley, *Opposite Life*, 6.

9. Footnote to Matthew 5:3 in The Passion Translation (Minneapolis: Passion & Fire Ministries, 2020), Bible Gateway, accessed September 21, 2021, www.biblegateway.com/passage/?search=Matthew+5%3A3&version=TPT.

10. "Naturalization Oath of Allegiance to the United States of America," U.S. Citizenship and Immigration Services, accessed September 23, 2021, www.uscis.gov/citizenship/learn-about-citizenship/the-naturalization-interview-and-test/naturalization-oath-of-allegiance-to-the-united-states-of-america.

11. John Avery, "Father," Names for God, accessed September 23, 2021, https://namesforgod.net/father.

12. *Merriam-Webster.com*, s.v. "holy," accessed September 26, 2021, https://www.merriam-webster.com/dictionary/holy.

13. Lloyd John Ogilvie, *Silent Strength for My Life* (Eugene, OR: Harvest House, 1990), 316.

Chapter 7 Smashing Idols

1. Hope Bolinger, "What Is an Asherah Pole?," Christianity.com, December 30, 2019, www.christianity.com/wiki/bible/what-is-an-asherah-pole.html.

2. Timothy Keller, *Counterfeit Gods: The Empty Promises of Money, Sex, and Power, and the Only Hope That Matters* (New York: Riverhead, 2009), xix-xx.

3. Kyle Idleman, *Gods at War: Defeating the Idols That Battle for Your Heart*, rev. ed. (Grand Rapids: Zondervan, 2018), 48.

4. John Calvin, *Institutes of the Christian Religion*, ed. John T. McNeill, 2 vols., Library of Christian Classics (Philadelphia: Westminster, 1960), 1:108, quoted in Elyse M. Fitzpatrick, *Idols of the Heart: Learning to Long for God Alone*, rev. ed. (Phillipsburg, NJ: P&R, 2016), 25.

5. Spiros Zodhiates, gen. ed., *The Complete Word Study Dictionary: New Testament*, rev. ed. (Chattanooga: AMG International, 1992), "*pleonéktēs*" (Strong's G4123).

6. Kurt Richardson, *James*, vol. 36 of *The New American Commentary: An Exegetical and Theological Exposition of Holy Scripture* (Nashville: Broadman & Holman, 1997), 80–81.

7. Jeffery Curtis Poor, "6 Surprising Idols Worshiped Today (What Is Idolatry?)," Rethink, April 6, 2020, www.rethinknow.org/2020/04/06/idol-worship-today.

8. "Vlogs a Job: Children Turn Backs on Traditional Careers," accessed February 5, 2022, https://www.thesun.co.uk/news/3617062/children-turn-backs-on-traditional-careers-in-favour-of-internet-fame-study-finds/.

9. "My Gaze | Worship Yourself | Nair," YouTube video, 0:15, posted by "Nair," April 7, 2021, https://www.youtube.com/watch?v=IWesPpwokf8.

10. Ray Vander Laan, "Fertility Cults of Canaan," That the World May Know, accessed September 24, 2021, www.thattheworldmayknow.com/fertility-cults-of-canaan.

11. Vander Laan, "Fertility Cults of Canaan."

12. Bolinger, "What Is an Asherah Pole?"

Chapter 8 The Unoffendable Heart

1. *Strong's Exhaustive Concordance*, s.v. "*skandalon*" (Strong's G4625), Bible Hub, accessed September 30, 2021, https://biblehub.com/greek/4625.htm.

2. John Bevere, *The Bait of Satan: Living Free from the Deadly Trap of Offense*, 20th anniversary ed. (Lake Mary, FL: Charisma House, 2014), 6.

3. Francis Frangipane, "Unoffendable, Part 1," The Frangipane Chronicles, March 2010, www.francisfrangipane.info/2010/03/unoffendable-part-1.html.

4. Max Lucado, *You'll Get Through This: Hope and Help for Your Turbulent Times* (Nashville: Thomas Nelson, 2013), 117.

Chapter 9 Living Beyond Your Dreams

1. John Duckworth, *Just for a Moment, I Saw the Light: Fresh Glimpses of Heaven from a Down-to-Earth Life* (Wheaton: Victor, 1994), 217–18.

2. Duckworth, *Just for a Moment, I Saw the Light*, 217–18.

3. Mrs. Charles E. Cowman, *Springs in the Valley*, in *Springs in the Desert and Springs in the Valley*, Zondervan Treasures (Grand Rapids: Zondervan, 1996), entry for July 25, 210.

4. Sadly, the conference happened so many years ago, I can't remember the speaker's name nor the specific date and time of the event, but I am forever grateful for her advice.

5. Holley Gerth, *Opening the Door to Your God-Sized Dream: 40 Days of Encouragement for Your Heart* (Grand Rapids: Revell, 2013), 23–24.

6. Henry Blackaby and Claude V. King, *Experiencing God: How to Live the Full Adventure of Knowing and Doing the Will of God*, rev. ed. (Nashville: Broadman & Holman, 1994), 69.

7. Warren W. Wiersbe, *50 People Every Christian Should Know: Learning from Spiritual Giants of the Faith* (Grand Rapids: Baker Books, 2009), 160.

8. Wiersbe, *50 People Every Christian Should Know*, 160–61.

9. Wiersbe, *50 People Every Christian Should Know*, 160.

10. Wiersbe, *50 People Every Christian Should Know*, 161.

11. Olgivie, *Silent Strength for My Life*, 15.

12. Olgivie, *Silent Strength for My Life*, 15.

13. Joseph was seventeen when he had his dreams (Genesis 37:2–11). He was thirty when he entered Pharaoh's service (41:46). After seven years of plenty, the famine started. Joseph's brothers came to Egypt to buy grain and bowed before Joseph (42:6). A total of at least twenty years.

14. Charles R. Swindoll, *Joseph: A Man of Integrity and Forgiveness*, Great Lives from God's Word (Nashville: W Publishing Group, 1998), 11.

15. David Santistevan, "How Serving Another's Vision Prepares You for Your Own," *Ron Edmonson* (blog), June 7, 2011, https://ronedmondson.com/2011/06/how-serving-anothers-vision-prepares-you-for-your-own.html.

16. Jodi Detrick, *The Jesus-Hearted Woman* (Springfield, MO: Salubris Resources, 2013), title of chapter 8: First-Clappers.

17. Philip Yancey, *Disappointment with God: Three Questions No One Asks Aloud* (Grand Rapids: Zondervan, 1988), 224.

18. Kosuke Koyama, *Three Mile an Hour God* (London, UK: SCM, 1979), quoted in Craig Thompson, "God's Speed: Slowing Down, Listening, and Learning," Clearing Customs, July 18, 2021, https://clearingcustoms.net/2021/07/18/godspeed-slowing-down-listening-and-learning.

Part 3 Holding On

1. Lysa TerKeurst, *Uninvited*, 65.

Chapter 10 Believing God

1. Barnabas Piper, "Four Differences between Believing and Unbelieving Doubt," *Barnabas Piper* (blog), May 12, 2020, https://barnabaspiper.com/2020/05/4-differences-between-believing-and-unbelieving-doubt.html. For a more in-depth exploration of this topic, see Barnabas Piper, *Help My Unbelief: Why Doubt Is Not the Enemy of Faith*, rev. ed. (Epsom, UK: Good Book Co., 2021).

2. Got Questions Ministries, "What Does It Mean That All Things Are Possible to Him Who Believes (Mark 9:23)?," GotQuestions.org, updated September 16, 2021, www.gotquestions.org/all-things-possible-him-who-believes.html.

3. Notes from "God-Sized Prayer" sermon by Randy Ruiz, May 3, 2017 in Billings, MT.

4. Living Proof Ministries with Beth Moore, "Beth Moore Bible Studies: Believing God," YouTube video, 0:56, posted by Living Proof Ministries, August 1, 2019, www.youtube.com/watch?v=XXQFUDcfCgs.

5. Beth Moore, *Believing God* (Nashville: Broadman & Holman, 2015), 30.

6. Moore, *Believing God*, 31.

7. *Strong's Exhaustive Concordance*, s.v. "*amen*" (Strong's H543), Bible Hub, accessed October 4, 2021, https://biblehub.com/hebrew/543.htm.

8. *Strong's Exhaustive Concordance*, s.v. "*aman*" (Strong's H539), Bible Hub, accessed October 4, 2021, https://biblehub.com/hebrew/539.htm.

9. Abraham and Sarah started life as Abram and Sarai and went by those names for many years. God changed their names in Genesis 17 as a sign of His covenant with Abraham. For ease of explanation, I refer to them as Abraham and Sarah throughout.

10. This beautifully concise statement is widely attributed to the great Victorian preacher Charles Haddon Spurgeon but is actually a paraphrase that gained traction in the late twentieth century. The original quotation is from Spurgeon's sermon "A Happy Christian," sermon no. 736, delivered at the Metropolitan Tabernacle, Newington, England, 1867, from *Metropolitan Tabernacle Pulpit, Volume 13*, The Spurgeon Center for Biblical Preaching, https://www.spurgeon.org/resource-library/sermons/a-happy-christian/#flipbook. For more information about the paraphrase, see "6 Quotes Spurgeon Didn't Say," blog post, *The Spurgeon Center*, accessed October 4, 2021, https://www.spurgeon.org/resource-library/blog-entries/6-quotes-spurgeon-didnt-say.

11. Quoted by Emily P. Freeman, "Never Believe Anything Bad about God," EmilyPFreeman.com, accessed October 4, 2021, https://emilypfreeman.com/never-believe-anything-bad-god.

12. IVF, or in vitro fertilization, is a medical procedure whereby an egg is fertilized by a sperm outside the body to create an embryo that is implanted in a woman's uterus. People have different views on this procedure, and our story isn't meant to be a recommendation. Each couple should carefully and prayerfully determine what the Lord would have them do.

Chapter 11 Content in His Love

1. Joni Eareckson Tada and Steven Estes, *When God Weeps: Why Our Sufferings Matter to the Almighty* (Grand Rapids: Zondervan, 2000), 171.

2. *Cambridge Dictionary*, s.v. "contentment," accessed October 5, 2021, https://dictionary.cambridge.org/dictionary/english/contentment.

3. *Macmillan Dictionary* (American English), s.v. "contentment," accessed October 5, 2021, www.macmillandictionary.com/us/dictionary/american/contentment.

4. Dick Meyer, "Meyer: 'Prosperity Paradox' at Center of American Discontent," Online Athens, *Athens Banner-Herald*, November 28, 2016, www.onlineathens.com/opinion/2016-11-28/meyer-prosperity-paradox-center-american-discontent.

5. Meyer, "Meyer: 'Prosperity Paradox' at Center of American Discontent."

6. Used by permission. Learn more about Joy and her wonderful resources at https://www.toolsformentoring.com/.

7. Greg Allen, "From Christ to Contentment: Philippians 4:10–14," transcript of sermon delivered November 2, 2008, Bethany Bible Church (Portland, Oregon), https://bethanybible.org/new/sermon/2008/2008-11-02/from-christ-to-contentment-philippians-410-14.

8. Jack L. Arnold, "Lesson 19: Contentment: Philippians 4:10–13," Equipping Pastors International, accessed October 5, 2021, http://www.cleartheology.com/expo/40Philippians/Philippians%2019.html.

9. Ray C. Stedman, "To Be Content," transcript of sermon delivered September 29, 1963, Ray Stedman: Authentic Christianity, accessed October 5, 2021, www.raystedman.org/new-testament/philippians/to-be-content.

10. Erik Raymond, *Chasing Contentment: Trusting God in a Discontented Age* (Wheaton: Crossway, 2017), 22.

11. This line is widely quoted and attributed to Socrates but generally unsourced. See "Talk:Socrates," Wikiquote.org, last edited July 30, 2021, https://en.wikiquote.org/wiki/Talk:Socrates#Unsourced.

12. Allen, "From Christ to Contentment."

13. Allen, "From Christ to Contentment."

14. Alan Carr, "The Secret Society of the Satisfied," sermon, The Sermon Notebook: Biblical Resources for Preachers and Teachers of the Word of God, accessed October 5, 2021, https://sermonnotebook.org/new%20testament/Philippians%204_10-13.htm.

15. John Piper, *Desiring God*, rev. ed. (Colorado Springs: Multnomah Books, 2011), 10, emphasis mine.

Chapter 12 The Gift of Discipline

1. *Strong's Definitions*, s.v. "*ma'as*" (Strong's H3988), Blue Letter Bible, accessed October 6, 2021, https://www.blueletterbible.org/lexicon/h3988/niv/wlc/0-1.
2. *Strong's Definitions*, s.v. "*qus*" (Strong's H6973), Bible Hub, accessed October 6, 2021, https://biblehub.com/hebrew/6973.htm.
3. *Strong's Exhaustive Concordance*, s.v. "*paideia*" (Strong's G3809), Bible Hub, accessed October 5, 2021, https://biblehub.com/greek/3809.htm.
4. "Simone Biles," Olympics.com, accessed October 6, 2021, https://olympics.com/en/athletes/simone-biles.
5. Liz Roscher, "Simone Biles Reflects on Olympics Ordeal: I Should Have Quit Way Before Tokyo," Yahoo! Sports, September 28, 2021, https://sports.yahoo.com/simone-biles-reflects-on-olympics-ordeal-i-should-have-quit-way-before-tokyo-163022915.html.
6. "Simone Biles," Olympics.com, accessed October 6, 2021, https://olympics.com/en/athletes/simone-biles.
7. Camonghe Felix, "Simone Biles Chose Herself," *The Cut*, September 27, 2021, https://www.thecut.com/article/simone-biles-olympics-2021.html.
8. Alice Park, "These Are All the Gymnastics Moves Named after Simone Biles," *Time*, July 26, 2021, https://time.com/6083539/gymnastics-moves-named-after-simone-biles.
9. *Strong's Exhaustive Concordance*, s.v. "*epichorégeó*" (Strong's G2023), Bible Hub, accessed October 6, 2021, https://biblehub.com/greek/2023.htm and "*chorégeó*" (Strong's G5524), accessed October 6, 2021, https://biblehub.com/greek/5524.htm.
10. Kenneth O. Gangel, "2 Peter," *The Bible Knowledge Commentary/New Testament*, ed. J. F. Walvoord and R. B. Zuck (Colorado Springs: Cook Communications, 2000), 2 Peter 1:5–7, accessed in PC Study Bible v5.
11. Gangel, "2 Peter."
12. Rick Renner, *Sparkling Gems from the Greek 2: 365 New Gems to Equip and Empower You for Victory Every Day of the Year* (Tulsa: Harrison House, 2017), entry for October 19, 950.
13. Barker, *NIV Study Bible*, text note on 1 Chronicles 22:9.

Chapter 13 Faith over Fear

1. From a personal conversation with Alicia Britt Chole.
2. Alice Jones, "Restless Intelligence: Why Smart People Are So Anxious," RtoR.org, January 6, 2021, www.rtor.org/2021/01/06/restless-intelligence-why-smart-people-are-so-anxious.
3. "5 Things You Never Knew About Fear," Northwestern Medicine, October 2020, www.nm.org/healthbeat/healthy-tips/emotional-health/5-things-you-never-knew-about-fear.
4. Namita Gujral, "Anxiety and the Amygdala," Unlearning Anxiety, accessed October 25, 2021, https://www.unlearninganxiety.com/amygdala.
5. "5 Things You Never Knew About Fear."

6. Check out Jennifer Allwood's book *Fear Is Not the Boss of You: How to Get Out of Your Head and Live the Life You Were Made For* (Grand Rapids: Zondervan, 2020).

7. Warren Wiersbe, *The Bible Exposition Commentary: Old Testament* (Colorado Springs: Cook Communications, 2003), 1 Samuel 30, accessed in PC Study Bible v5.

8. Joanna Weaver, "#043: Jesus Over Everything with Lisa Whittle," in *The Living Room with Joanna Weaver*, podcast, September 23, 2020, https://joannaweaverbooks.com/2020/09/23/043-jesus-over-everything-with-lisa-whittle-tlr. Lisa's book is *Jesus Over Everything: Uncomplicating the Daily Struggle to Put Jesus First* (Nashville: Thomas Nelson, 2020).

9. Pierce, "Outline of Biblical Usage," s.v. "*gālal*" (Strong's H1566), Blue Letter Bible, accessed October 25, 2021, https://www.blueletterbible.org/lexicon/h1556/kjv/wlc/0-1.

10. Sheila Walsh, *The Heartache No One Sees: Christ's Promise of Healing for a Woman's Wounded Heart* (Nashville: Thomas Nelson, 2004), 92.

Chapter 14 God-Sized Prayers

1. "Rees Howell—Intercessor—The Bible College of Wales," YouTube video, 58:00, posted by "Revelation TV," July 10, 2017, www.youtube.com/watch?v=WkbKeTXT__s.

2. "Rees Howell—Intercessor." Buckingham Palace would be "struck on sixteen separate occasions" between September 1940 and June 1944, nine of them "direct hits." On September 13, a single pilot dropped five bombs, which did extensive damage. See "Buckingham Palace and the Blitz, 1940," The Guards Depot, March 31, 2019, https://theguardsdepot.co.uk/buckingham-palace-and-the-blitz-1940.

3. "Rees Howell—Intercessor."

4. "Rees Howell—Intercessor."

5. "Rees Howell—Intercessor."

6. Ray Stedman, "The Holy Spirit and Prayer," transcript of sermon delivered April 19, 1964, Ray Stedman: Authentic Christianity, accessed October 11, 2021, www.raystedman.org/thematic-studies/prayer/the-holy-spirit-and-prayer.

7. "How Many Psalms Did David Write?," Got Questions: Your Questions, Biblical Answers, accessed October 12, 2021, www.gotquestions.org/Psalms-David.html.

8. Beverlee J. Chadwick, ed., *Torrey on Prayer: The Power of Prayer & the Prayer of Power* (Alachua, FL: Bridge-Logos, 2009), xii.

9. R. A. Torrey, *How to Pray* (New Kensington, PA: Whitaker House, 1983), 44.

10. Torrey, *How to Pray*, 46.

11. Torrey, *How to Pray*, 23–24.

12. Torrey, *How to Pray*, 26.

13. Torrey, *How to Pray*, 31.

14. Torrey, *How to Pray*, 40.

15. Torrey, *How to Pray*, 44.

16. Torrey, *How to Pray*, 45.

17. Torrey, *How to Pray*, 59.
18. Torrey, *How to Pray*, 60.
19. Torrey, *How to Pray*, 63.
20. Torrey, *How to Pray*, 50–51.

Part 4 Living Faith

1. "The Commission to Faith" by Beth Moore, *Believing God Bible Study* (Nashville, TN: LifeWay Press, 2004), 223.

Chapter 15 Resting in God's Sovereignty

1. If you haven't discovered Bible Project, you really need to check it out. Tim Mackie, Jonathan Collins, and their crew have spent years studying biblical truths and distilling them into digestible videos that make theology come alive to the average Christian. Access their material at www.BibleProject.com.
2. Bible Project, "Shalom/Peace," Advent Series video, 3:49, accessed November 4, 2021, https://bibleproject.com/explore/video/shalom-peace. The script for the video can be found in PDF format at https://d1bsmz3sdihplr.cloudfront.net/media/Script%20References/Advent_Peace_Script-References.pdf.
3. Zodhiates, *Complete Word Study Dictionary: New Testament*, *"anapa'u-o"* s.v. 373.
4. Zodhiates, *Complete Word Study Dictionary: New Testament*, *"ana'pausis"* s.v. 372.
5. Jim Cromarty, *It Is Not Death to Die: A New Biography of Hudson Taylor* (Fearn, Tain, Ross-shire, UK: Christian Focus, 2001), 8, quoted in John Piper, "The Ministry of Hudson Taylor as Life in Christ," transcript of message delivered at Desiring God 2014 Conference for Pastors, February 5, 2014, Desiring God, www.desiringgod.org/messages/the-ministry-of-hudson-taylor-as-life-in-christ#fn36.
6. Quoted in Elisabeth Elliot, *A Path Through Suffering* (Grand Rapids: Revell, 2014), 58.
7. "Blue Letter Bible Daily Bible Reading Program Chronological Reading Plan," Blue Letter Bible, accessed November 8, 2021, www.blueletterbible.org/assets/pdf/dbrp/1Yr_ChronologicalPlan.pdf.
8. "The Serenity Prayer by Reinhold Niebuhr," Common Prayers, December 1, 2019, www.commonprayers.org/the-serenity-prayer.
9. John Milton quoted by Richard Foster and Emilie Griffin, *Spiritual Classics: Selected Readings for Individuals and Groups on the Twelve Spiritual Disciplines* (New York: HarperCollins 2000), 171.
10. Elliot, *A Path Through Suffering*, 58.

Chapter 16 Leaving a Legacy of Trust

1. National Park Service, U.S. Department of the Interior, "Going-to-the-Sun Road: An Engineering Feat," PDF, excerpted from a brochure of the same name produced by Historic American Engineering Record, 1990, www.nps.gov/glac/learn/news/upload/Going-to-the-Sun-Road-An-Engineering-Feat.pdf.

2. C. W. Guthrie, *Going-to-the-Sun-Road: Glacier National Park's Highway to the Sky* (Helena, MT: Farcountry Press, 2006), 22.

3. Guthrie, *Going-to-the-Sun Road*, title page (subtitle).

4. Tia Troy, "Plowing Glacier National Park's Going-to-the-Sun Road," blog post, *Glacier Country Montana*, May 30, 2014, https://blog.glaciermt.com/plowing-glacier-national-parks-going-to-the-sun-road-2.

5. Troy, "Plowing Glacier National Park's Going-to-the-Sun Road."

6. Zodhiates, *Complete Word Study Dictionary: New Testament*, *"túpos"* s.v. 5179.

7. Zodhiates, *Complete Word Study Dictionary: New Testament*.

8. "How to Prepare Your Personal Testimony," Navigators, accessed on February 7, 2022, https://www.navigators.org/resource/how-to-prepare-your-personal-testimony.

9. Arthur T. Pierson, *George Müller of Bristol: 1805–1898*, Hendrickson Classic Biography (Peabody, MA: Hendrickson, 2008), 6.

10. Pierson, *George Müller of Bristol*, 9.

11. Pierson, *George Müller of Bristol*, 180.

12. Pierson, *George Müller of Bristol*, 312.

13. This story was told by the ship's captain to the evangelist Charles Inglis. It is retold in "My Eye Is Not on the Fog," devotional, GeorgeMuller.org, June 10, 2016, https://www.georgemuller.org/devotional/my-eye-is-not-on-the-fog2874126.

14. Roger Steer, *George Müller: 1805–1898: Delighted in God* (Fearn, Tain, Ross-shire, Scotland, UK: Christian Focus Publications, 1997), 228.

Appendix A Study Guide

1. Tim Keller, *Counterfeit Gods: The Empty Promises of Money, Sex, and Power, and the Only Hope That Matters* (New York: Riverhead, 2009), xix–xx.

2. Elliot, *A Path through Suffering*, 58.

Appendix B Knowing the God You Can Trust

1. A. W. Tozer, *A Journey into the Father's Heart*, 195.

Joanna Weaver is the bestselling and award-winning author of *Having a Mary Heart in a Martha World*, as well as *Having a Mary Spirit*, *Lazarus Awakening*, and a devotional *At the Feet of Jesus*. A pastor's wife, mother of three, and avid Bible teacher, Joanna loves speaking to women about the powerful freedom that is found in making Jesus Lord and trusting Him for things bigger than themselves. She lives with her family in Hamilton, Montana. Learn more about Joanna's books and video studies at JoannaWeaverBooks.com.

Connect with Joanna

Joanna Weaver is the bestselling and award-winning author of *Having a Mary Heart in a Martha World*, as well as *Having a Mary Spirit*, *Lazarus Awakening*, and *At the Feet of Jesus* devotional. A pastor's wife, mother of three, and avid Bible teacher, Joanna loves speaking to women about the powerful freedom found in trusting Jesus for things bigger than themselves.

JoannaWeaverBooks.com

@JoannaWeaverBooks @JoannaWeaverBooks

The Living Room with Joanna Weaver

PODCAST

Join bestselling author (and fellow struggler) Joanna Weaver as she interviews Christian leaders on topics shaped to a woman's heart. This podcast is designed to give you practical tools for living, loving, and leading like Jesus.

Available everywhere you listen to podcasts.

ONLINE COMMUNITY

Looking for a community of like-hearted women who love Jesus and want to grow? Joanna's private Facebook group is a great place to link hearts and encourage one another in the Lord.

Request to join: Facebook.com/groups/JoannaWeaverLivingRoom